José, Can You See?

José, Can You See?

Latinos On and Off Broadway

Alberto Sandoval-Sánchez

THE UNIVERSITY OF WISCONSIN PRESS

The University of Wisconsin Press
2537 Daniels Street
Madison, Wisconsin 53718

3 Henrietta Street
London WC2E 8LU, England

Library of Congress Cataloging-in-Publication Data

Sandoval-Sánchez, Alberto.
    José, can you see?: Latinos on and off Broadway / Alberto Sandoval-Sánchez.
    pp.   cm.
    Includes bibliographical references and index.
    ISBN 0-299-16200-1 (cloth: alk. paper)
    ISBN 0-299-16204-4 (pbk.: alk. paper)
    1. Hispanic American theater.   2. Hispanic Americans in motion pictures.   3.
Hispanic Americans in literature.   I. Title.
    PN2270.H57S26   1999
    792'.089'68073—dc21   98-47441

Some of this material has appeared before, in slightly different form, in the following
publications; I am grateful for permission to reproduce this copyrighted material:
"A Puerto Rican Reading of the America of *West Side Story.*" *Jump Cut* 39, special issue:
U.S. Latinos and the Media, Part 2, ed. Chon Noriega (1994): 59–66.
"*A Chorus Line:* Not Such a 'One, Singular Sensation' for Puerto Rican Crossovers."
Ollantay Theater Magazine 1, no. 1 (January 1993): 46–60.
"'An Octopus with Many Legs:' U.S. Latino Theater and Its Diversity." *Ollantay Theater
Magazine* 5, no. 1 (Winter–Spring 1997): 66–78.
"Re-Viewing Latino Theater: Issues of Crossing Over, Mainstreaming, and
Canonization." In *New Voices in Latin American Literature/ Nuevas voces en la literatura
latinoamericana*, ed. Miguel Falquez-Certain, 157–72. New York: Ollantay Press, 1993.
"So Far from National Stages, So Close to Home: An Inventory of Latino Theater on
AIDS." *Ollantay Theater Magazine* 2, no. 2 (Summer–Fall 1994): 54–72.
"Staging AIDS: What's Latinos Got To Do With It?" In *Negotiating Performance: Gender,
Sexuality, and Theatricality in Latin/o America*, ed. Diana Taylor and Juan Villegas, 49–66.
Durham: Duke University Press, 1994.

Contents

Illustrations

Acknowledgments

Like all books *José, Can You See?* is the result of long hours of research, writing, and editing. Contrary to what some might think, putting a book together is not a solitary endeavor but rather a constant dialogue. First of all, I must thank former president of Mount Holyoke College, Elizabeth T. Kennan, and former provost and dean of the faculty Peter Berek for their support and interest in my work; I am also grateful to the college itself for the grants that I received to carry on my research.

The list of all my colleagues, students, and friends who have contributed to this book with their interest, enthusiasm, and critical response is a long one. Miles de gracias a Gail Hornstein, Karen Remmler, Nancy Saporta Sternbach, Diana Taylor, Sally Sutherland, Eliana Ortega, David Román, Patricia González, Suzanne Oboler, Carlos Rodríguez, Steve Legler, Beatriz Rizk, Juan Gelpí, Lyndy Pye, Daniel Czitrom, José Esteban Muñoz, Adriana Gómez, Luis Felipe Díaz, Awam Amkpa, Arnaldo Cruz, Jane Crossthwaite, Matthew Corcoran, Frances Aparicio, Ellen McCracken, Mario García, Jean Grossholtz, Eileen Elliott, Rosa Luisa Márquez, Mary Heyer, Grace Dávila López, Thomas Wartenberg, Lillian Manzor-Coats, Roozbeh Tavakoli, Becky and David Fisher, Joyce Devlin, Elizabeth Young, Kim Euell, Carl W. Harder, Donald Weber, Ruth Smith, Roberta Uno, Clara E. Rodríguez, Chon Noriega, Erica Wilson, Elena Martínez, Robert Graber, and so many others.

I am deeply indebted to all the librarians at Mount Holyoke College, especially those in the interlibrary loans and reference departments, for their help.

I want to express my gratitude to Silvia Spitta and Efraín Barradas for their careful reading of the manuscript, their suggestions, thoughtful remarks, and support.

Without the energy and commitment of my student assistants as well as their interest in the subject matter, I would not have been able to imagine the student readership to whom this book is addressed. I thank them for their enthusiasm, intellectual curiosity, and insightful comments. Muchas gracias a Neeta Bhasin, Meredith Field, Ellie Walsh, and Vanessa Sequeira. Also crucial to the book were all the U.S. Latinas I taught and advised in my thirteen years of teaching at Mount Holyoke College. This book was also informed by my role as advisor to La Unidad, the U.S. Latina organization at the College. Las quiero mucho.

I am indebted to all the playwrights and performers who contributed their manuscripts, stories of the history of U.S. Latino/a theater, and detailed information. Thanks to their *lucha* and *sobrevivencia*, U.S. Latino theater is alive and necessary.

I do not mean to sound melodramatic or tragic, but this book has given meaning to my life after an AIDS diagnosis in 1990. It has been written during hours and days of health complications, recoveries, side effects, and hospitalizations. It has given me life and hope. I would not have been able to finish this book without the care of all of my doctors, who have had faith in my ability to negotiate with my body. Without them, I never would have survived. Gracias al Dr. Robert K. Gale, Dr. Thomas Lincoln, Dr. Jeff Scavron, and Dr. Dennis Passer, the guardian angel who saved me and then left suddenly. (I miss you. Doctors are not supposed to die.) Since my CMV diagnosis in 1991, my ophthalmologists have been both encouraging and indispensable with their concern and prevention of what will be my inevitable and total loss of vision. Thanks to Dr. A. Joseph Ruddick, Jr. and Dr. David D. Agahigian, I still believe in miracles. I express my deep gratitude to all the nurses who kept me animated with their daily and weekly visits and celebrated my health recoveries and optimism.

I am indebted to my editor Raphael Kadushin at the University of Wisconsin Press. Thank you for believing in my book, for your support, and for your generous advice and friendship. It was indeed a pleasure to work with the staff at the Press; I would like to acknowledge the hospitality that they showed me when I visited Madison. I would also like to thank my copy editor, Brian Bendlin, for his meticulous reading and for making this an enjoyable experience.

To my companion John R. Schwartz, thank you for your patience, and for worrying about my long hours and weekends full of work. Thank you also for your generosity, which allowed me to spend many hours on this book that would otherwise have been our time together.

I dedicate this book in memory of my close friend and confidant Otto Thieme. I hope you like it. By the way, how lumpen is heaven?

OVERTURE

AN INTRODUCTION TO CULTURAL AND CRITICAL ANALYSIS

"José, Can You See?"
An Introduction

All titles have a history. The title of this book, *José, Can You See? Latinos On and Off Broadway*, materializes a long journey of assimilation, decolonization, and critical thinking. After I migrated to the United States from Puerto Rico in 1973 to attend college, I had the opportunity to use the private primary and secondary Anglo-American education that I had received in San Juan. Coming to the U.S. meant performing the Anglo-American ways of seeing, doing, and being that I had memorized and internalized for years in a Catholic school under the tutelage of Irish Josephine sisters from New England. Undoubtedly, my "Americanization" was my father's dream for my future economic and professional success: if not in Puerto Rico, then definitely on the mainland. I was already completely assimilated, since my education entailed all reading and writing in English and included no courses in Puerto Rican history, politics, literature, or cultural reality. I had been trained to move to the U.S. and to leave my past behind.

Ironically, the opposite happened. Seen as an outsider, as a minority, I was forced to distance myself from my assimilative educational preparation. Many times I found myself at odds with the dominant socio-ideological construction of reality. The more I immersed myself in Anglo-American culture, the more I faced dislocation, deterritorialization, estrangement, alienation. I had to redefine my position in the U.S.

3

as a contradictory subject, coming from a colonial system of education, who had assimilated Anglo-American cultural models and Eurocentric literary canons. I had to articulate a new identity in order to situate myself in relation to Puerto Ricans on the island itself, U.S. Puerto Ricans, Latin Americans, U.S. Latinos/as, other peoples of color, and Anglo-Americans. I started to question, scrutinize, and come to terms with my colonial identity. In short, as African writer Ngugi wa Thiong'o has stated, I entered the process of "decolonizing the mind."[1]

As I questioned what I had learned in a colonial educational system, I had to recover what was left out. I had to stand at the periphery, at the border, in order to reeducate myself and to "re-vision" my history. I understand "re-vision" in Adrienne Rich's terms:

Re-vision—the act of looking back, of seeing with fresh eyes, of entering an old text from a new critical direction—is for women more than a chapter in cultural history: it is an act of survival. . . . A radical critique of literature, feminist in its impulse, would take the work first of all as a clue to how we live, how we have been living, how we have been led to imagine ourselves, how our language has trapped as well as liberated us, how the very act of naming has been till now a male prerogative, and how we can begin to see and name— and therefore live—afresh.[2]

Indeed, feminism provided me with the tools to reread, to re-vision, and to reimagine myself and others. First of all, I learned that the personal and the cultural are political. Second, I learned to be a "resisting reader" and to see my scholarship as an act of intervention, as Judith Fetterley has formulated it, saying that "feminist criticism is a political act whose aim is not simply to interpret the world but to change it by changing the consciousness of those who read and their relation to what they read."[3] Thus I see the self as the site of constant negotiation between discursive junctures and geopolitical intersections. My critical cultural readings stand in dialogic relationship with my immediate reality. This correspondence produces a particular kind of reading, one that is alternative, ex-centric, and interrogative.

In addition to feminism, two other theoretical approaches offered me the methodological apparatus to do cultural analysis: semiotics and reception theory. I will never forget reading Roland Barthes's *Mythologies* and John Berger's *Ways of Seeing* for the first time.[4] Barthes and Berger materialized the kind of scholarship that I was ready to undertake. By questioning ideologies, by decentering hegemonic worldviews and subject positionings, by demythifying the cultural imaginary, I was able to undertake what can be called "radical readings" that question traditional ways of knowing, seeing, doing, and being. As opposed to a conservative criticism that aims to fix meanings and identities, a radical criticism stops, interrupts, and destabilizes the "flow of things as they are" and "suggests[s] a plurality of ways in which texts might be read in the interests of extending the reach of what is thinkable, imaginable or possible."[5] Both my feminist agenda and my constant practice of decolonization have located me in a singular position on the margin from which to question and to decenter dominant ideologies, cultural imaginaries, and daily images and representations that interpellate social subjects in specific ideological and discursive formations.[6] From that queer margin (being, both an ethnic minority and gay), I was at a crossroads where the margin, as bell hooks has brilliantly theorized, is "to be a part of the whole but outside the main body," to look "both from the outside in and from the inside out."[7]

It is precisely my location at the margin that made me question the dominant discourses and the ideological constructs that sustain the "American dream." I found myself deconstructing a universe of ideals, values, icons, symbols, images, narratives, and discourses that have been taken for granted and magnificently hold together the U.S. "imagined national community" and its imperial presence in Puerto Rico.[8] As I invented myself as a cultural critic, I was eager to question and examine what ideologemes—such as "the American way of life," "the land of the free," "American pie," "We're number one," "the sky's the limit," and "the bigger the better"—really mean.[9] Most important, how does ideology interpellate individuals in given social formations and power relations?

While mapping the Anglo-American hegemonic ideological apparatus, I encountered two popular cultural idiomatic phrases in which the emitter addresses a fictitious guy named José: "José, can you see?" and "No way, José!" After situating myself in José's place, I realized that both statements attempted to force someone to understand a given situation, or to contradict someone's point of view or opinion by renaming that person José. Although my name is Alberto, I had to come to terms with these idio(ma)tic constructs when I was called José, even though I never responded to it. Inside of me, a little voice challenged this label that marked and stereotyped my ethnicity and otherness. As a Puerto Rican, a Latino, I could not see the joke; if there was one, it was not funny. Moreover, the use of the Spanish name José only served as an index of colonial relations between North America north of the Río Grande and North America south of the Río Grande.

At times when colleagues used the phrases, naming me José was an embarrassing act of reprehension and a mode of silencing me. I could not identify with this José, because for me it was a negative stereotype, a misperception, and a misconception that demonstrated one more way in which Anglo-Americans visualize their Latin American neighbors, and U.S. Latinos/as, in their own imagined community. I always had the feeling that this stereotyped José had its referent "south of the border," and that it encapsulated primarily the Mexican immigrant male in order to browbeat him into total assimilation and control his difference. Of course, what difference does it make if one is from Argentina, Brazil, Puerto Rico, or Mexico once the Anglo-American imagined community configures, enunciates, labels, and positions you?

As far as I know, in the Anglo-American mainstream cultural landscape, there have been only a handful of well known Josés: Joe (José) Carioca; Donald Duck's Brazilian tour guide in *The Three Caballeros*, and Bill Dana's comical characterization of a "Hispanic" in the sixties, whose famous line "My name José Jimenez" became a popular joke about Latin American ethnicity and otherness. And, how can we forget the well-publicized violations, in 1989, of baseball player José Canseco, a series of court citations for speeding, not carrying his driver's license, and for having tinted his car windows? Three other Josés should not be left out: José Feliciano—who *cannot* see and who is perhaps one of the first Latinos to cross over in the Anglo-American music world; José Ferrer, who was the first Latino to win an Oscar as best actor, in *Cyrano de Bergerac* in 1950; and finally, José Carreras, the Spanish tenor. However, these are not the same Josés that the cultural constructs "José, can you see?" and "No way, José!" represent, especially when they are used to rectify José's actions, behavior, point of view, and alternative ways of seeing.

The act of seeing in "José, can you see?" installs, a priori, a paternalizing and patronizing attitude toward José—toward Latin Americans in general, be it the inhabitants "south of the border," or Latinos/as in the U.S. As a goal-directed speech act, this phrase can address anybody who does not fulfill the dominant expectations and "models of/for social action and interaction.[10] José can be anybody. Yet, when using it as a cultural shorthand, the user—who has never questioned, decoded, or analyzed it—has an engraved stereotype in mind whose origins have been erased. Once uttered, it does not matter anymore if the phrase has ethnocentric, xenophobic, or even racist implications. Still, José is a revealing presence of difference and a powerful ethnic marker. This phrase constitutes a well-condensed and frozen construction that has retained only José as a sign eclipsing its referent, its history, and its social utilization.

Being addressed as José forces a passing and an ethnic impersonation. For a moment you become an other, a Latino, and as a Latino you are taught how to see things and how to act. The goal of "can you see?" is to influence or change the addressee. It looks like a question, but it contains an implied command. Once a person is addressed as José, a series of associations and connotations emerge and merge. As José, one is forced to look up at an imagined flagpole and to look at El Norte as it is symbolically embodied in the flag. The flag of the U.S., which is what José is to look at while singing the national anthem, reflects and refracts onto José himself. "Oh, say, can you see?" becomes "José, can you see?" to define and articulate a new identity for José and, perhaps, to remind him of his illegal-alien status or second-class citizenship. In this transubstantiation, José must imitate, ventriloquize, and assimilate the ways of doing in El Norte. In this manner, the stereotype is constantly activated and reproduced for him. Inferiorized, José must submit to the status of a generic subjected being. He is the focus of attention, its own referent, and at the same time his attention is called to directly see how things are done the "American way." In this authoritative positioning and power relation, José must succumb to the flag, the nation, the patriotic country, the powerful empire, the omnipotent El Norte, and the "all-American" way of doing and ordering things. Indeed, José is positioned—or rather, expected to position himself—in the political and social space of the other, as allocated by the dominant culture and its powerbrokers.

What about "No way, José!"? On the surface, it is a speech act expressing a challenge to an assumption, a direct act of interdiction which leaves the renamed José no room for argument or contestation. What has the appearance of a joke is a covert command with definite effects on the addressee's stand. It is used to scold, to overrule, and to contradict a decision, while simultaneously putting down José's attitudes, intentions, and agency. José is not given a chance to speak, to respond, or to act in his own way. Once "No way, José!" is pronounced, and we cannot forget the tone used and the circumstances around using it, the act of communication comes to an abrupt end—on the sender's terms. The command aims to establish a social and power relation between the speakers in which the addressee is expected to do and perform whatever the addresser demands. In short, the utterance is an act of intimidation that dictates that there are no alternatives, possibilities, or considerations for a differing opinion or course of action. Indeed, José is anchored in an inferior position and is expected to do as told. At this point the "No way, José!" becomes "José, can you see?" The act of seeing activates an imposed act of becoming, doing, accepting. José is silenced.

I asked myself over and over again, But, who is José? Why is the
Spanish name used at all? Why is there a need to interdict José? What
is the difference when a Latino is addressed as José versus when he
reverses the role and addresses an Anglo-American as José? *José, Can
You See? Latinos On and Off Broadway* signifies the search for an answer
to these questions. By appropriating such a cultural and ideological construct, I subvert the original signification of the idiomatic
expression and other stereotypical constructions of Latinos/as in
dominant cultural discursive representations. In my own teaching
practice, the ironic mobilization and circulation of the utterance "José,
can you see?" served as a model to equip my students with the necessary critical tools and analytical skills to carry on their own cultural
and literary analyses, their own critical inquiries and practices. By doing so, by having them read "against the grain," I hoped to help them
begin the long process of deconstructing stereotypes of Latinos/as in
their own daily lives. If the utterance "José, can you see?" meant a way
of controlling someone's way of seeing and doing, now it can be used
to undermine the demeaning dominant representations, biases, and
prejudices that have led to such cultural disfigurations and stereotypical representations of the other. Indeed, the readers of this book, like
my students, will be able to respond to "José, can you see?" with "No
way, José!" once they realize that they possess the mechanisms to intervene, challenge, subvert, deconstruct, and demythify dominant cultural representations. Once the idio(ma)tic phrase is seen from a critical vantage point that reverses the gaze, its alternative reading will be
"Can you see what you have made José see?"

Given that theater is a privileged imaginary space, where fictitious
worlds and illusory social actions and transactions are represented, I
have selected Broadway and U.S. Latino theater as discursive locations
where ideas, myths, fictions, ideologies, and social models are produced, displayed, negotiated, and contested. American theater, a cultural site where Latino otherness has been stereotyped for decades,
provides an ideal backdrop and starting point for my cultural analysis.
Latino/a self-representations and challenges to these dominant cultural
representations constitute the second part of my inquiry.

In a hegemonic theatrical domain like Broadway, Latino/a stereotypes are both visual configurations and discursive representations.
It is because of this visibility and objectification—through images,
words, linguistic constructions, gestures, and bodily presence—that
the Great White Way, as it is known, represents the ideal discursive and
cultural formations where liminal, imagined, and sometimes utopian
realities are put to test. It is in the domain of the theater that "make

believe" takes shape as the dramatic action unfolds, and where audiences identify and become participants in their own, and/or collective, horizon of expectations. Once the curtain rises on Broadway, through the suspension of disbelief, audiences follow the "yellow brick road" to the American dream. No other theatrical genre can better celebrate the American way of life than the Broadway musical. Through song and dance, domestic and international audiences fantasize magical worlds that are bigger than reality, like the Big Apple itself. The truth is that Broadway is an entertainment industry, "show business"—that is, a commodity that theatergoers must consume. It is not merely a matter of material consumption; rather, it is the need, the urge, the desire to experience and internalize imaginary and enchanted worlds where dreams come true and happiness is guaranteed forever after.

This book is divided into two parts, "Act One" and "Act Two." In "Act One: A Critical Reading of Latino/a Representations on Broadway," I demonstrate how Carmen Miranda's and Desi Arnaz's respective debuts on Broadway in *The Streets of Paris* and *Too Many Girls,* and the highly acclaimed classical Broadway musicals of *West Side Story* and *A Chorus Line,* objectify, typecast, and stereotype Latinos/as. Chapter 4, "'An Octopus With Many Legs:' U.S. Latino Theater and Its Diversity" functions as an "intermission" and as a transition from "Act One" to "Act Two." In this chapter I map a concise history of U.S. Latino theater nationwide, including the production of the only three U.S. Latino plays on Broadway: *Short Eyes, Zoot Suit,* and *Cuba and His Teddy Bear.* The goal of this chapter is not to provide or make official a canon of U.S. Latino theater, but rather to introduce the reader to its heterogeneity. Despite the difficulties in defining this cultural form, I delineate particular characteristics, topics, models of dramatic action, functions of protagonists, and even modes of reception that pave the way to an understanding and critical reading of U.S. Latino theater in all its diversity.

In the second part of the book, "Act Two: Latino/a Self-Representations in Theatrical Productions," I explore how U.S. Latinos/as construct their own self-representations, theatrical models, and cultural imaginary. This second part bears witness to U.S. Latino/a identity formations through multiple forms of theater that are acts of resistance, challenges, or alternatives to dominant stereotypes. Here I concentrate specifically on three significant thematic and dramatic constituencies in U.S. Latino theater that open a theatrical space for the staging of new cultural manifestations, political agendas, and the creation of new protagonists: (1) AIDS theater and its relation to gay identity framed within a politics of affinity; (2) U.S. Latina playwriting as shaped by feminism and the articulation of lesbian identity; and (3) the construction of hybrid bilingual and bicultural identities as the protagonists from a second generation struggle with the conceptualization of "home." Given that U.S. Latino theater is a privileged cultural site for the production of identity formations, it functions as a contestatory space where identities are dynamic and processual, always performed in all their contradictions in given cultural and historical moments. It is precisely in the theater where identities can re-present and display critical and dramatic dislocations that destabilize assumed and essentialized notions of identity as unitary, stable, and coherent. Indeed, theater is the medium to experiment with identity formations: in those of people of color, the stage puts into action how race and ethnicity, gender, and class are represented and performed. By displaying racial and ethnic identities, theater constitutes a discursive site of political struggle, ideological contestation, and communal survival for U.S. Latinos/as and other people of color.

If, in dominant theater, Latinos/as lack agency and therefore subjectivity, U.S. Latino theater enunciates a politics of representation, identity, and ethnicity where subjectivities in process are hybrid, plural, porous, contradictory, bicultural, and bilingual. The purpose of focusing in this book on both modes of practicing theater—Broadway and U.S. Latino dramaturgy—is to establish a dialogue between hegemonic and marginal theater, between centralized and peripheral theater, between official and alternative theater, between mainstream and regional theater.

José, Can You See? Latinos On and Off Broadway, as a whole enacts my own mobility and displacement from Broadway to minority community-based theater. The book mirrors my own trajectory back and forth, my oscillations between official theater and alternative and marginal theatrical spaces. I feel as comfortable on the Great White Way as I do Off-Broadway, or in El Barrio. As long as there is a performance, I don't think twice about taking the subway to go to the heart of the Bronx, Spanish Harlem, or Loisaida (New York's Lower East Side). Being a theater lover, I have painfully paid seventy dollars to see a Broadway musical megahit. I recognize my own privilege in having the option to do that; I also acknowledge that not everyone has accessibility to Broadway. I, like many other Broadway fans, can only afford it after waiting in line for two hours at Times Square's discount TKTS booth. Even so, for most people, even a half-price ticket costs a huge chunk of money.

On a four-day weekend in New York City I feast on performances at matinee and evening shows. On a Saturday afternoon I have attended *Titanic* and, in the evening, Amparo García's *Under The Western Sky* at INTAR (International Arts, Relations, Inc.). In Chicago, I have comfortably seen Migdalia Cruz's *Lolita de Lares* at the Latino Chicago Theater Company, and Edwin Sánchez's *Unmerciful Good Fortune* at the Victory Garden Theater; in Florida, I have attended the International Hispanic Theater Festival, in Spanish, at Teatro Avante in Coral Gables; and in San Francisco, I have attended the annual AIDS Theater Festival at the National AIDS Update Conference, and theatrical works in progress at BRAVA! I am a fervent consumer of Broadway. I saw *Kiss of the Spider Woman: The Musical* at least six times; *Evita*, five times; and *A Chorus Line*, seven times. I have witnessed a few flops: *Rags, Legs Diamond, Shogun, Raggedy Ann*, and *Smile*. I have followed productions like *Marisol*, which has been staged at Hartford Stage, New York's Joseph Papp Public Theater, and by students at Dartmouth College. I can easily juggle aesthetics and politics, straddle between spectacle as a commodity and agitprop as activism, and negotiate dominant ideology and alternative worldviews.

I love being a spectator as much as I love being a cultural critic. Given that both roles depend on the act of seeing, as a spectator I witness an ephemeral theatrical performance, and as a critic I employ my own alternative, ex-centric, and queer ways of seeing. My desire and pleasure at seeing theater converges with my critical practice. Indeed, it is specifically at this intersection that the title of the book, *José, Can You See? Latinos On and Off Broadway*, incarnates its full signification.

What's in a Name?

> It is not what you call me,
> It is what I answer to.
> —African Proverb

Before embarking on a critical cultural reading of Anglo-American dominant representations of Latinos/as and Latino/a self-representations in the theater, it is necessary to clarify the "mumbo jumbo" caused by the proliferation of multiple ethnic labels and categories. I begin by defining my political position in relation to "Latino" and "Hispanic." I use the term "Latino/a" to signal a conscious political positioning of/for self-affirmation and proclamation of ethnic pride by Latin American immigrants, second-generation children, and, in the case of "Chicanos/as," a succession of generations that were in the Southwest before its annexation to the U.S. in 1848. The term "Latino" not only demands the usage of a Spanish word, but also incorporates present and past migrations of people to El Norte from Latin America and the Caribbean. This term also acknowledges gender differences ("Latina" versus "Latino"). It registers the political undertakings and strivings, the implementation of activist agendas, and the organizational strategies employed by U.S. Latino communities to confront exploitation, disenfranchisement, racism, underrepresentation, and marginalization. The term itself functions as a stratagem of/for political intervention, solidarity, and coalition.[11] I employ the term "Hispanic" only when referring to Spanish/Iberian heritage, cultural roots, and values.

"Hispanic" is a term imposed by the U.S. Census Bureau in 1980 to lump together all immigrants from Latin America and Spain with those born and raised in the United States.[12] The intent of the imposition was the creation of a generic "Hispanic." Institutionalized in the Reagan years as a political denomination, "Hispanic" both creates and perpetuates the misconception that the Americas are not composed of many races and cultures.[13] In the U.S., "Hispanic" alludes primarily to a racial imprint. The usage of "Hispanic" can constitute an act of racism when functioning as a ficticious homogenization of all Latin American countries into one language and one race.

The labeling process is further complicated by the translation of "Hispano" into "Hispanic." The translation comprises a construction of reality that establishes—and confuses—a cultural and ethnic identity without taking into consideration specific historical contexts (such as different reasons for migration) and specific power relations. "Hispano" is an ideological construct that derives from a Spanish imperial and colonial system of power. It is usually employed by recent or first-generation immigrants from Spanish-speaking countries who use the term out of their need to imagine a direct liaison with their native national identities and to convince themselves that they belong to a Pan-American *Liga de las naciones*. In brief, for me, "Hispano," in Spanish, means to claim a Hispanic heritage and the Spanish language as vernacular; whereas in English, "Hispanic" means to be a member of a racial and ethnic minority which, by definition, has been relegated to a lower class.

Latin American migrants who call themselves "Hispanos" had no need to define themselves as "Hispanos" in their native homelands; what "Hispano" meant was taken for granted. After migration, however, their new social situation locates them in relation to the Anglo-American mainstream culture and its dominant language, English. After arrival, they suddenly find out that they are "Hispanic." These immigrants have to face the cultural and political shock that in the U.S. their identities are determined by a minority status. This status is not only minority, but subaltern: it creates the image that all "Hispanics" are poorly skilled, uneducated individuals who belong to a lower socioeconomic status; are grounded on welfare dependency; have a high rate of gang delinquency, drug addiction, criminality, teenage pregnancy, and AIDS; and, as a whole, are defined as a "social problem" or as a "culture of poverty."[14] Once living in the U.S., many feel that they have no alternative to accepting imposed labels of ethnicity and race, while others, by adopting "Latino/a," exercise an act of self-denomination that voices a new ontological definition and a hybrid identity. As a result, the anxiety produced by newly assigned difference problematizes the immigrant's search for identity.

Given that "Hispano" does not translate as "Hispanic," there is much confusion. For example, Univisión, the Spanish-speaking TV network in the U.S., uses the terms "Hispano" and "Latino" interchangeably to address all Spanish-speaking people. Lately, everybody seems to be Latino, including entertainers Julio Iglesias, Azúcar Moreno, Thalía, and Antonio Banderas. This group is defined as "Latino" based on its use of Spanish and its exaltation of Hispanic values and traditions. In this way, "Univisión" tries to create a common denominator, an imagined national, even hemispheric, audience of Spanish descent, with the intention of "Hispanizing" U.S. Latinos/as. Ultimately, this action is a new form of imperial economic enterprise, one which wants to take advantage of the opportunity for expanding its economic markets in the new global economy. Such labeling glosses over the political struggles, class differences, racial discrimination, and vicissitudes of those U.S. Latinos/as, the majority of whom are working class, underrepresented, and have a history of migration. Latin Americans and Spaniards who tend to be Hispanophilic and prejudiced against those with a more hybrid and fluid identity contribute to the marginalization and silencing of those U.S. Latinos/as who are bilingual and whose code-switching and interlingual constructions characterize their usage of Spanish and English. For example, a few years ago, Paul Rodríguez, the Chicano stand-up comedian, served as master of ceremonies for *Premios Lo Nuestro*, the televised entertainment awards show for the Spanish-speaking world. When Julio Iglesias's daughter Chaveli appeared onstage, Rodríguez asked her when she was going to invite him on her show, in which she interviews Spanish and Latin American celebrities. Chaveli responded that the show was in Spanish, as if that were a reason he could not appear on it. Ironically, Paul Rodríguez was speaking Spanish. Chaveli's refusal to acknowledge Rodríguez as a Spanish-speaking person exposes the hierarchy within the domain of Spanish speakers. Who, in the established relations of power, determines what is "authentic" Spanish and/or who is the "real Hispano?"[15]

"Hispanic" also contributes to further confusion in identity formation, because it subsumes previous national and regional identities. Confusion reaches its peak when U.S. Latinos/as who are bilingual and bicultural, and who emblematize a new problematic and hybrid identity, elude any attempt at categorization because the term "Hispanic" categorizes them by means of superficial denominators and commonalties: surname and lineage, Latin American and Spanish origins, "Hispanic" parenthood, birthplace. Where is the place for mestizos and mulattos in this limited and limiting act of identification? How do you constrict identity to a label when there are huge class, ethnic, and racial differences in the Americas? Aware of the urgency of self-definition, some U.S. Latinos/as have turned to self-categorizations like Chicano/a, Mexican American, La Raza, Nuyorican, Boricua, and Pueltorro in the struggle to articulate their differences.[16]

As a whole, self-categorization is a situational and relational dynamic. Individuals can name themselves according to an array of identities. It is possible to choose a label that connotes different arenas: (1) hemispheric and continental: "Americano"; (2) national: Mexican, Chilean, Cuban; (3) regional: suramericano, centroamericano, caribeño; and (4) personal. At the personal level, individuals are free to use whatever term that is available in a given context. At times, "Latino" and "Hispanic" are interchangeable, depending on the dialogic situation, the topic in progress, and the semantic exchange between speakers. Once a term is first used, there is a tendency to continue using it in a conversation until one of the speakers changes the term.

There is another term that needs to be explained, and that is "Latin." I define "Latin" as a denomination imposed by an Anglo-American system of power. Being "Latin" means to come from a Spanish-speaking country, to be an immigrant whose identity as "Latin foreign other" is marked by, and anchored in, a Spanish accent and exotic looks. Such conceptions of the "foreign other" are perpetuated by ready-made stereotypes: the Latin bombshell, the Latin lover, Latin music, Latin rhythm, Latin dance, Latin type, Latin temper, Latin time. These ideological constructs confine Spanish-speaking immigrants to a politics of representation that often racializes them and perpetuates racist practices. The same dynamic applies when "Latin" is used to refer to the "Latin domestic ethnic and racial other"—such as Chicanos/as and Puerto Ricans. Within the Anglo-American cultural imaginary, all ways of conceiving, perceiving, and representing the "Latin other" constitute a discursive web that I call "Latinness." A major constituent of "Latinness" is what the mainstream calls "Latinization." I in turn see "Latinization" as a process of cultural appropriation. The dominant Anglo-American system of power accepts Latinos/as and their cultural productions and social interaction, as long as Latinos/as accommodate Anglo-American ways of seeing and cultural discursive models of the other.[17] In these terms, as Frances Aparicio and Susana Chávez-Silverman have theorized, "Latinization is limited to reformulations of cultural icons by the dominant sector: it is, thus, synonymous with commodification."[18] Under these circumstances, "Latinization" is not a product of transculturation and hybridization.[19] It is an act of cultural appropriation that "involves *taking* something, often from someone, and it is rarely an isolated gesture. . . . [This] act of taking is marked by a legacy of violence, and of forced adaptation to imposed symbolic orders and the loss of the colonized's right to name things as their own."[20]

"Latinization" differs from "Latinidad" in that the latter results from Latino/a agency and intervention when U.S. Latinos/as articulate and construct cultural expressions and identity formations that come from a conscious political act of self-affirmation.[21] Hence, any Latino cultural performance and ritualistic enactment constitutes an affirmation of "Latinidad." From this perspective, all kinds of activities—exhibits of ethnocultural symbols and icons, celebrations, parades, street fairs, festivals, *fiestas patrias* (national holidays), religious ceremonies, literary readings, political manifestations and activism, college courses and student organizations, and the broadcasting of Spanish television shows—constantly reactivate and mobilize "Latinidad."[22] In these activities, mainly through music, dance, theater, literature, and food, "Latinidad" is circulated in an evolving process that facilitates the invention of U.S. Latino/a identities, Latino local and national imagined communities, and "Latinidad" itself. One result of such celebrations and rituals is an increasing consciousness and affinity among U.S. Latinos/as (and other Latin Americans). There is no doubt that this collective sharing of cultural values, which promotes ethnic self-affirmation, ethnic pride, and the institutionalization of political agendas, functions within the parameters of cultural performances and artistic expressions. For example, when Latina singer Selena was assassinated in 1995, the Latino communities in the U.S. mourned her death for months. Selena's death brought Chicanos/as and Latinos/as together in a unique manner, because she emblematized a new bilingual/bicultural/border identity. Latino audiences also identified with her humble "migrant" roots, her *mestizaje* (mixed-blood heritage) and her ability to not only cross over borders, but to blur *las fronteras* with her singing in both Spanish and English. Her tragic death made Selena a mythical figure, the most avant icon of "Latinidad." At the same time, ironically, Selena's early death served as the most visible cultural performance of "Latinidad" in the U.S. With Selena, "Latinidad" has found its furthest articulation and its most complete national cognition and consciousness. For many Chicanos/as and Latinos/as, the Holy Trinity has become La Virgen de Guadalupe, Frida Kahlo, and Selena.

Some final thoughts on the usage of terminology: I reserve the term "Latino/a" for (1) a second generation, and previous generations in the case of Chicanos/as; (2) for Puerto Ricans living in the U.S. (the peculiarities of their colonial situation and circuit of migration have problematized identity issues between first and later generations); and (3) first-generation Latin American immigrants who consciously and intentionally recognize bicultural/bilingual identities that oscillate between a Latin American past and a new, U.S. Latino/a present.

In the context of the formation of a new Latino/a identity in the U.S., the term "Latino/a" constitutes an act of political consciousness that is a response to U.S. imperial practices and internal colonialism.[23] There are additional factors, such as race, class, gender, and pigmentation that determine hierarchical relations of power within that system of domestic colonialism. In short, a Latino is an American in the U.S. who demands ethnic differentiation from all other U.S. Americans, while at the same time reaffirming a cultural heritage and political alliance with all other Latino Americanos in the hemisphere.

Another problem embedded in identity labels is what has been called the *burden of representation:* as Kobena Mercer has theorized, "[I]f there is only one black voice in the public discourse it is assumed that that voice in the public discourse 'speaks for' and thereby 'represents' the *many* voices and viewpoints of the entire community that is marginalized from the means of representation in society."[24] It is not only an issue of who speaks for whom, but *where* someone speaks from; as Mercer observes, "to speak *from* [means to speak from] the specificity of one's circumstances and experiences, rather than the attempt, impossible in any case, to speak *for* the entire social category in which one's experience is constituted."[25] Such a burden reinforces the assumption that all minorities are the same and that one person of color speaks for all of them. In the case of U.S. Latinos/as, given the plurality of national origins and Latino/a identities, the burden of representation causes major generalizations that do not apply to each particular experience of Latinos/as. This burden is most damaging in tokenism. Assuming that one representative can speak for the whole community or for all minorities "not only creates a burden that is logically impossible for any one individual to bear, but which is also integral to the iron law of the stereotype that reinforces the view from the majority culture that every minority subject is, essentially, the same."[26]

Clearly, the issue of which term you choose is connected with the issues of *to whom* you are speaking, *for whom* you speak, and *from where* you speak. Each individual has the choice to use whichever label according to his political views and historical experiences. Some will use "Latino" in their affirmation of a "Hispanic" identity; some will use "Latino" as an umbrella term, in their pursuit of solidarity; some will use "Hispanic" because they have internalized governmental categories or because they translate it as "Hispano"; some may detest the term "Hispanic" because it has associations with the "ghetto," people of color, and the working class; some will prefer "Chicano" to "Mexican American."

The use of any label is a political act that contributes to identity formation in given social confrontations, interactions, transactions, negotiations, and accommodations. I am a Puerto Rican, I am a caribeño, I am a latinoamericano, I am americano and, according to legal papers, I am an American citizen (although of a second-class status). I have consciously advocated that I am a "Latino" with Hispanic roots. Presently, I see myself more as a U.S. Latino than a Puerto Rican. I am not subjected to a national identity from which I have been at a distance since my migration to the U.S. in 1973. I am minimally informed about the politics back on the island. My existence and political praxis are grounded *here,* in the U.S. Being a Latino connects me to my past with Latin America and the Caribbean and positions me in the Anglo-American political and social arena with other Latinos/as who have recently migrated, or with those for whom the U.S. is *home.* As a Puerto Rican immigrant I have a common history with other U.S. Latinos/as, a history whose coordinates are colonialism, violence, and diaspora. The irony is that recent and first-generation immigrants do not realize that they were emigrants who became immigrants, and that they have become the subjects of a domestic colonialism. We are here to stay and to share a common history of oppression and exploitation with a second generation, and many generations to come, for whom *home is the U.S., here and now,—aquí y ahora.*

ACT ONE

A CRITICAL READING OF LATINO/A
REPRESENTATIONS ON BROADWAY

1

Carmen Miranda and Desi Arnaz
Foundational Images of "Latinidad" on Broadway and in Hollywood

Any attempt at mapping the politics of representation of Latinos/as on Broadway and in Hollywood must have as its foundation two artistic figures: Carmen Miranda and Desi Arnaz. Both immigrants have contributed significantly to the contemporary stereotypical characterizations of U.S. Latinos/as. Miranda and Arnaz materialize the inaugural depictions of our present preconceptions and visualizations of "Latinidad" in the U.S. cultural collective imaginary. Given the political landscape, particularly Franklin D. Roosevelt's Good Neighbor policy, both performers embodied the artistic translation and mediation of political relations with Latin America in the 1930s. What, at first glance, appears to be vivid entertainment and a naive exhibition of otherness constitutes, rather, a conscious and premeditated mode of representation and stereotypization of "Latinidad." Miranda's and Arnaz's performances were loaded with political and ideological practices, maneuvers, and strategies.

My goal in this first chapter is to examine critically the first fleeting theatrical instances of each of the two performers, who appeared "coincidentally" in the same season (1939–1940) on Broadway. My archeological project will center on reconstructing Miranda's and Arnaz's performances on Broadway. By analyzing their theatrical performances as interpolated, imported cultural units inscribed as exotic markers and signifiers of otherness, I will demonstrate how their performances laid the foundations for contemporary stereotypes of Latinos/as in the U.S. theatrical and cultural imaginary. My reading will be documented with the films *Down Argentina Way* and *Too Many Girls* (both 1940), which incorporated, almost in their entirety, the stars' original and ephemeral theatrical acts. Initially produced on Broadway, Hollywood fixed these performances on film for future audiences. As a result, the borders between Broadway and Hollywood are blurred: each genre and cultural model (staged musical comedy and musical film) comple-ments and replicates the other. Accepting that Broadway and Holly-wood constitute an uninterrupted imaginary horizon in a cultural discursive continuum, it will be possible to examine the dominant stereotypical representations of Latinos/as.

To begin, are Miranda and Arnaz "Latinos" or "Hispanics"? The answer is, neither. At the historic moment of their arrival, both were seen as Latin American immigrants, from Brazil and Cuba, respec-tively. After migration, their nationalities were the determining factor of their identities in the U.S. The dominant Anglo-American sociocul-tural world denominated and recognized them only as "Latins," and, like many other Spanish-speaking immigrants, they called themselves "Latins" and/or "Spanish," as in "Spanish Harlem." Miranda and Ar-naz were first-generation immigrants who before migration had no consciousness of being a minority solely defined by race and ethnicity. Now, if I were to situate them within the framework of a political act of recovery, reclamation, and reappropriation of "all things Latin" be-fore the emergence of a U.S. Latino/a consciousness in the mid-1960s, in that act of recovery and re-visioning of the past Miranda and Arnaz would become integral components of the history of "Latinidad" in the U.S. Their incorporation, presence, and existence in a common U.S. Latino/a past would concretize a political action embedded in a histori-cal process of Latino/a self-determination, self-affirmation, and ethnic pride. Consequently, as we revise our past from a critical perspective, we regain our agency by questioning and reclaiming our history, which, in turn, confers a sense of being Latino/a and belonging to an imagined Latino national community. By exercising a retroactive move, and practicing a critical retrospective gaze that positions the past within a present perspective, we will enable ourselves to reevaluate the stereotypical representation of our cultural past and reaffirm the articulation of self-representation through the process of deconstruct-ing those stereotypical images. As a result, our act of consciousness-changing and intervention will provide us the tools to retrocede in time and space while looking forward, in order to articulate new identities and foster an imagined U.S. Latino community under the umbrella category of "Latinidad."

Charting a Genealogy

It is not useful to approach the theatrical performances of Miranda and Arnaz in isolation. Their ethnic performances on Broadway must be located within a continuum of dominant cultural images of Latinos/ as in the U.S. To examine the role and function of their performances in the hegemonic cultural imaginary of Broadway and Hollywood, it is crucial to look at the Anglo-American discursive and representational landscape of the "Latin other." My task will be to chart Anglo-American repertoires of the cultural imaginary and geographies of Latin America to demonstrate how stereotypical modes of representation operate, and how meaning is produced and circulated. In order to describe and examine the politics of representation and location of the "Latin other" in the dominant cultural discursive web, a distinction must be made between the "Latin foreign other" and the "Latin domestic ethnic and racial other." "Foreign other" refers to immigrants coming from Latin America. For them, home is abroad, and they are constricted to articulating their identity according to the nationality of their country of origin. They are marked by their heavy Spanish accents. "Domestic ethnic and racial other" designates those Latinos/as who have been born or raised in the U.S. and who are fluent in English. For them, home is here. People of color within this group also experience a history of racism, disenfranchisement, exploitation, and marginalization as a result of the internal colonization of the subaltern in the U.S.: Chicanos/as, Puerto Ricans, African Americans, Asian Americans, and the like. Both categories of otherness operate within an "imagined geography" that can be conceptualized as a socioideological discursive "topo(s)graphy."[1] By "topo(s)graphy" I mean a cultural geographical map in which I chart forms and models of representation in order to display the places and regions of given territorial, visual, mental, and ideological constructs of the "Latin other." Such a topo(s)graphy includes the discursive positions and situations in which the imagined other inhabits and transacts. These constructs read as a topos—a rhetorical discursive convention composed of an ensemble of common places, motifs, themes, tropes, symbols, icons, and metonymical and metaphorical relations.

I will demonstrate how this rhetorical topo(s)graphy structures the Anglo-American model of imagining the "Latin other." I will make evident how ethnicity and race are discursively articulated, rhetorically constituted, and performed through certain stereotypical loca-tions—that is, *locus exoticus, locus tropicus,* and *locus urbanus.* I aim to demonstrate (1) how discursive representations function when por-traying the "Latin other"; (2) how dominant ideologies register racist and racialized discursive modes and practices in the representation of the other; and (3) how ideology interpellates and positions individuals in given social and historical contexts and power relations. The topo(s)-graphy of this ideological apparatus can be mapped in four coor-dinates: spectacle, exoticism, an inventory of agricultural and raw materials, and tourism.

The imagined topo(s)graphy of Latin America as a whole has its own continental umbrella designation of being "south of the border." Only a handful of countries compose this imaginary geopolitical map: Cuba, Mexico, Argentina, and Brazil. Anything can happen, anything goes south of the border, for Latin America provides a carnivalesque atmosphere, the ideal space for romance, leisure, and sexual excite-ment. The inhabitants of this imaginary land, at times interacting in the liminal zone of the border itself, exist for the sole purpose of en-tertaining Anglo-Americans by playing whatever roles they have been assigned: performer, bandit, Latin lover, delinquent, or spitfire. "Latins'" raison d'être is to sing, dance, romance, be comical, and live from fiesta to siesta. Neither time nor history regulates this exotic and mythical spatial terrain. In the 1930s and 1940s, Latin America became a postcard, a photograph, a tourist attraction, a night club, a type of theme park where fantasy and fun were guaranteed and escapism as-sured while U.S. national security interests were guarded. "Putting on a show" meant impersonating stereotypes in which and by which the "Latin other" is objectified, depicted in demeaning or excessive ways, and/or made into a spectacle.

Women have been a traditional source of spectacle in patriarchal society, and that misogynist tradition continues in this domain. Images of virginity, penetration, and fecundity abound in the descriptions of landscapes in the chronicles of the conquest of America. Like the Span-iards and other explorers, who in their conquests and colonizations perceived the New World as a foreign body (that of a woman), the United States has its own history of feminizing the South American continent.[2] Patriarchal and imperial U.S. discourse represents Latin America as a feminized and sexualized other who must be controlled, tamed, and possessed. For example, in a political cartoon published in the *Philadelphia Evening Public Ledger* in 1923 and entitled "My, How You Have Grown," Uncle Sam courts a Latin America personified as a white Spanish lady who is wearing a mantilla and shawl and using a

1.1 Caricature: "My, How You Have Grown!"

fan all stereotypical props of "Latinness" (fig. 1.1).[3] Uncle Sam, as potential suitor, displaces Europe, the previous patriarchal possessor. Europe has been replaced and Latin American men have been displaced. They have been silenced, castrated, and left out of all affairs, political and otherwise.

Representation of Latin America as a woman continued, but changed in the 1940s, when Latin America was personified as a fertile woman. It was now Carmen Miranda who emblematized Latin America's production of agricultural goods. As historian Eduardo Galeano has stated, "Carmen is the chief export of Brazil. Next comes coffee."[4]

Miranda was the queen of all "banana republics" (the predominant epithet used to brand Latin American countries as incompetent and ineffective in a modern capitalist world). It is ironic that the very same people who negatively stereotyped Central American countries as "banana republics" were the ones (like Rockefeller and the United Fruit Company) who turned these countries into "banana republics" in the first place.

Miranda's exhibitionism was restricted to the spectacular staging of a cornucopia of agricultural commodities. Out of sight of the voyeur, however, was the mineral extraction that has been veiled and silenced. Rockefeller, coordinator of Inter-American Affairs for the State Department during Roosevelt's presidency, made it quite clear that the U.S. economic interest in Latin America was not limited to fruits:

Our lines of security are not only military, they are also economic. Outward from our shores in wartime go men and finished materials. Inward must flow the raw materials to feed our factories and stock our arsenals. That demand could never have been fully met without the raw materials of our neighbors.

From them our production lines needed, and got, manganese and chromium and tungsten for the many kinds of steel alloys used in mechanized warfare. Tin for containers and copper for munitions. And bauxite for aluminum for our planes; quartz crystal for radio communications systems to lead those planes to their targets; oil to fuel the bombers, and mica for detection devices to protect us from the planes of the enemy—these and a wide variety of other strategic materials our production lines needed, and got.[5]

Uncle Sam's relations with Latin America are not only sexist and chauvinistic, but also paternalistic and racist. In numerous caricatures in the first decades of the twentieth century, the Latin American countries appear as a child for whom the United States must baby-sit, as seen in a cartoon published in the *Columbus (Ohio) Dispatch* in 1902, in which Cuba is portrayed as a black child (fig. 1.2).[6] The subordination inherent in such infantilization provided justification for the Anglo-American military interference in Latin American politics and economies. By infantilizing Latin America, the U.S. assumed a position of power that confined the countries and its people to viewing themselves as incompetent and in need of guidance.

Dominant cultural representations of Latinos/as were not limited to Latin Americans in their home countries. In the U.S., the "Latin domestic ethnic and racial others" have their own histories of misrepresentations and underrepresentations. Both Mexican Americans and Native Americans were targets for ridicule, stereotyping, and racism in theater and film—let's not forget Tonto! In the film industry, there was a tradition of portraying Latinos/as as dark-skinned bandidos, villains,

1.2 Caricature: "I'll give you one teaspoonful, Cuby. More of it might make you sick.

and greasers. These cinematic depictions are negative and derogatory images based on ethnic and racial stereotypes.[7]

In contrast, light-skinned Latinos—Ramón Novarro, César Romero, and Gilbert Roland—portrayed gracious Latin lovers, following the steps of all-time sex idol Rudolph Valentino, who played the role of a lustful gaucho in *Four Horsemen of the Apocalypse* in 1921. These "gay caballeros" qualify as romantic heroes whose aristocratic heritage, sex appeal, and eroticism were celluloid magnets for female audiences. Other Latinos were recruited simply as extras and used to reflect the ethnic and racial representation needed to portray a given foreign locale.[8]

In the representational ethnic spectrum displayed in Hollywood and on Broadway (and eventually on television), the locales evolved from the wild frontiers of the West and Southwest to the jungles of the modern-day city. A new topo(s)graphy appeared in the late 1950s in the cultural imaginary of the "Latin domestic ethnic and racial other," when illegal aliens, criminals, gangsters, and drug addicts were used to stereotype Latinos/as. Cisco Kid, Speedy Gonzalez, and Tonto were displaced and replaced by juvenile delinquents and dysfunctional gang members in the ghettos of cities with large Latino/a populations: Los Angeles, Miami, Chicago, and New York. Settings such as the Alamo and the Mexican Revolution, and themes such as conquest, the Wild West, machismo, and bullfighting ceded in the 1950s to new ethnic and cultural representations.[9] At this time, a new film genre emerged: the "social problem" film.[10] The most visible example on Broadway and film is *West Side Story*, in which Puerto Ricans, who belong to a gang called the Sharks, constitute a threat to the U.S. national order. Since the 1960s, "Latin" stereotypical representations and locales have been perpetuated in the mythic derogatory constructs of the "[b]anana republics, the sleepy villages with lazy peons basking in the sun, uncivilized half-naked Indians, violent government coups spearheaded by cruel dictators, mustachioed bandits and beautiful señoritas."[11] In other words, the bandidos, the greasers, the *vaqueros* (cow boys), and the lazy peons became the drug dealers, the drug addicts, and the gang members. The new topo(s)graphy offered a range of urban spaces—the *locus urbanus, locus barbarus*, the street and jail—where the protagonists were illegal aliens, evildoers, and sinister criminals.[12]

The representation of Latinas is similar to the male stereotypical trajectory. Latinas are trapped in the stereotypes of angel, virgin, mother, whore, *cantinera* (tavern keeper), maid, and, most frequently, vamp, seductress, or spitfire. Frivolity, sensuality, and passion define women's fiery, tempestuous, and explosive personalities.[13] If "Latin" men are reduced to being "Latin lovers," "Latin" women reach fame through other epithets: Lupe Vélez, "the flamboyant hot tamale" and "the Mexican Spitfire;" Burnu Acquanetta, "the Venezuelan Volcano;" Olga San Juan, "The Puerto Rican Pepperpot;" María Antonieta Pons, "the Cuban Hurricane;" Rita Moreno, "the Puerto Rican Firecracker;" and Carmen Miranda, "the Brazilian Bombshell."[14] Such degrading and sexist labels clearly signal the exploitation of the female body and its commodification in patriarchal voyeuristic and misogynist practices. "Latin" women, or "señoritas," are objects of desire, available for romance, to satisfy the male gaze and sexual desire, they are registered in the Anglo-American cultural imaginary in the form of woman-as-spectacle.[15]

In the 1940s, no image of "Latin" women was disseminated and circulated as thoroughly as that of Chiquita Banana. Chiquita comically parodied Miranda, exposing the sociocultural construction of Latin America as a female, as a banana, as a commodity. Such impudent objectification and commodification of Latin American women and Latin America placed gender at center stage, as an instrument of commercial exchange and as a means to promote the financial investments and interests of U.S. multinationals like the United Fruit Company. Chiquita was a woman and a fruit: a hybrid monster, a half-breed whose performance became an Anglo-American cultural icon. In commercials, Chiquita delivered the message that bananas should be a part of the U.S. diet and menu. She had to sell herself with a touch of "Latin" flavor, referring to her tropical nature. The ad's jingle narrates how she comes in a banana boat from a little island south of the equator in order to help the Good Neighbor policy.[16]

Chiquita's native home is the tropics, a symbol of exoticism that actualizes the stereotype of the "Latin foreign other" in the U.S. cultural imaginary. Undoubtedly, she is a component of the U.S. cultural topo(s)graphy of Latin America and, as such, inhabits the realm of exoticism, tropical rhythm, local color, visual pleasure, and romantic spectacle. The commercial jingle was successful because it duplicated a cartoonish version of Carmen Miranda, who was then at the top of her career. Chiquita's eagerness to advance the Good Neighbor policy demonstrates how the advertisement transmitted a propagandistic political message about issues of foreign policy. Without Miranda there would have never been a Chiquita Banana; without the Good Neighbor policy there would have never been a famous Carmen Miranda; without Chiquita Banana, United Fruit would have never made big profits.

The Good Neighbor Policy

Franklin D. Roosevelt, the Good Neighbor policy, and "Latin" musicals constituted an inseparable triad in the 1930s and 1940s. Their ideological platform depended on the existence of each component, which in exchange validated the political, economic, and cultural crusade against the Axis powers and potential Nazi penetration of the Americas. In order to secure U.S. national interests, Roosevelt sought a hemispheric alliance. He concentrated on accomplishing Pan-American unity through diplomacy, economic policies, strategic military agreements, and cultural exchanges. The Good Neighbor policy's primary purpose was to safeguard foreign markets and sources, and to guarantee profitable investments "south of the border." The hardest aspect of this was having to change the image of the U.S. A succession of interventions, invasions, and military occupations in Mexico, Cuba, the Dominican Republic, Haiti, Nicaragua, and Costa Rica had made the image of "good neighbor" a hard sell.[17] An agreement was made between the U.S. and most Latin American nations that no country was to intervene militarily in another's domestic affairs. Although the U.S. abstained from explicit interference and intervention, it made sure to maintain a few strategic territories—the Canal Zone, and military bases in Guantanamo, Cuba, and Puerto Rico.

The primary U.S. policies and initiatives in Latin America concentrated on introducing industrialization, making profitable markets available to U.S. investors, promoting commercial interchange, and developing tourism.[18] One of the most active architects of the plan was Nelson Rockefeller, in his position of coordinator of Inter-American Affairs.[19] Rockefeller's work on hemispheric coordination and cooperation led to the implementation of cultural relations and exchange programs. In order to preserve in situ strategic and security interests, a massive campaign promoted Pan-Americanism in the cultural domain. Many programs mobilized and circulated a cultural agenda that would benefit U.S. capitalist, military, and national interests.[20] No other cultural medium collaborated with the goodwill campaign to the extent that the entertainment industry did, in all its aspects: music, dance, theater, and film. Hollywood embraced the hemispheric partnership, creating films such as Walt Disney's *The Three Caballeros* (1945).[21]

Interest in Latin America had already been shown in the 1930s, with movies such as *The Cuban Love Song* (1931); *Flying Down to Rio* (1933); *La Cucaracha* (1934); *Under the Pampas Moon* (1935); *Headin' for the Rio Grande* (1936); *Tropic Holiday* and *Old Mexico* (1938); *South of the Border, Mexicali Rose,* and *Old Caliente* (1939); and *Gaucho Serenade* (1940). Such infatuation with the "Latin other" had been launched and officially endorsed in Franklin D. Roosevelt's inaugural speech of 4 March 1933, in which he explicitly addressed his political interest in Latin America, saying, "In the field of world policy I would dedicate this Nation to the policy of the good neighbor—the neighbor who resolutely respects himself and, because he does so, respects the rights of others—the neighbor who respects his obligations and respects the sanctity of his agreements in and with a world of neighbors."[22]

During the years of the Good Neighbor policy, it was not only film that played a significant role in defining the Latin American as "Latin foreign other;" music also became a prominent feature on the Anglo-American cultural imaginary topo(s)graphic map. "Latin" song and dance had entered the U.S. in the 1920s, when Valentino started a tango craze with his sexy and seductive dance scene in *Four Horsemen of the Apocalypse*. In the 1930s, there was a rumba craze, modeled after the Cuban *son*.[23] In the 1940s, Miranda and Arnaz popularized the samba and the conga, respectively; in the 1950s it was to be the mambo. No other artist was as instrumental in propagating the "Latin" rhythm craze as the Spanish-born Xavier Cugat. Desi Arnaz began his career with Cugat's band; Miranda costarred with Cugat in *Date with Judy*; his music vitalized many Hollywood "Latin" musical films.[24]

On the Anglo-American airwaves, "Latin" rhythms provided the desired escapism, exoticism, and potential for fantasy which was yearned for after the Depression and during World War II. An international language, music easily crossed the border and "Latinized" the Anglo-American world.[25] "Latin" styles and melodies spread through all forms of Anglo-American cultural expression: the cinema, Broadway revues and musical comedies, and popular songs.[26]

The impact of "Latin" music was seductive and contagious.[27] Broadway welcomed the rumba craze by interpolating "Latin" rhythms and songs in musicals such as *The Third Little Show* (1931); *Anything Goes* (1934); *Jubilee* (1935); *Panama Hattie* and *Louisiana Purchase* (1940); and *Mexican Hayride* and *Let's Face It* (1941). The placing at center stage of "Latin" song and dance reached its pinnacle with the introduction of Miranda in two Broadway musicals—*The Streets of Paris* (1939) and *Sons o' Fun* (1941)—and Desi Arnaz in one—*Too Many Girls* (1939). With the "Latin" craze, in crescendo, New York City night clubs like the Copacabana, La Conga, and the Latin Quarter featured "Latin" stars.

"Play Latin for Me"

In the 1930s and 1940s, "Latin" rhythm swept America. Rumba and conga produced a dance craze that no one could escape; it was as if everyone had dancing feet. However, it must not be overlooked that, in many of the popular songs, Latin American rhythms evoked primitivism, liberation of the instincts and the body, and pervasive sexuality. Rhythm transported dancers to exotic and erotic locations where love affairs awaited them.

In an article entitled "The Rumba is Here to Stay," published in *Song Hits Magazine* in 1941, José Morand gives the following explanation for the genealogy of the rumba:

What is this music and in what way does it differ from the ordinary American Jazz? I believe the answer lies in its racial origin. The story probably goes back to the Moors in Spain. Take some of your beautiful Latin American tunes and if you have studied the subject you can feel that Moorish influence in many of the melodies, especially those with a minor strain in them. The melodic qualities of the Moors and Spanish gypsies combined with some rhythmic ideas from the great continent of Africa just across the straits—that seems to have been the parentage of the rumba, and geographically it seems logical, though nobody seems able to produce definite proof. Mixing of races often produces unusual combinations of rhythm and melody.[28]

While speculating, Morand connects rhythm with Africa, revealing a racial origin. Both "Latin" rhythm and the peoples of Latin America are hybrid, mestizos, mulattos—in his own words, "unusual." Morand's observation shows that music can be racialized and, at the same time, rhythm can mobilize racist conceptions and attitudes. In these terms, rhythm and exoticism connote race—specifically African race—and race can be musically performed.

It was through dance bands, the radio, and the recording industry that "Latin" songs became popular and in demand. And, of course, there was Hollywood to put these songs in circulation within the practice of ethnic simulacrum. In the cultural topo(s)graphical map that I am charting, the songs themselves, in this era of cultural exchange fostered by the Good Neighbor policy, re-present how the "Latin foreign other" is conceived and how stereotypical "Latin" images were propagated. Indeed, music was one of the discursive formations through which Latin American culture became visible and, most of the time, stereotyped.[29] The medium of music was especially powerful because it was everywhere: on stage, in film, on the radio, in the dancehall, and in everybody's memory.

The "Good Neighbor" song (in the film *Panama Hattie*), though it was a parody of the Good Neighbor policy, clearly illustrates the stereotyping of Latin Americans. It inscribes the limited vocabulary with which Anglo-Americans communicate with "Latins": "amiga/o, muchos amigos, hasta mañana, adiós, sí sí, macho amigo, mucho macho." It is astonishing and illustrative that this lexicon embodies a series of images that perpetuate how "Latins" are conceived: mañana—the concept of time is fundamental to expose the differences between "Latin" and Anglo-American cultures; sí sí—the "other" is always expected to accept Uncle Sam's will; and macho amigo, mucho macho—"Latin" men are frozen in time as machistas. These linguistic cultural constructs—and others, such as fiesta, siesta, gaucho, señor, caballero, chiquita, señorita, patio, maracas—constitute the vocabulary, a kind of

Spanish 101 dictionary that will be used repeatedly in other songs, musicals, and films. Such a limited vocabulary presupposes instant and effective communication with "Latins," as well as assuming that Anglo-Americans understand Spanish language and Latin American cultural reality.

The Anglo-American musical discursive topo(s)graphy of Latin America would find its maximum expression in the Broadway performances of Miranda and Arnaz in 1939. After debuting on the Great White Way, their successful showmanship and charismatic personalities took them immediately to Hollywood. Furthermore, Miranda and Arnaz became the iconic mediators and cultural promoters of the Good Neighbor policy. *Variety* of 19 February 1941 made it clear that Anglo-American film stars would advance the politics of the Good Neighbor policy "south of the border": "Film star shuttle service between Hollywood and South America, at least partially at the expense of the United States government, is in prospect starting this spring. It will be the result of a survey by Nelson Rockefeller committee to cement goodwill between the continents."[30]

Miranda and Arnaz became embodiments of the goodwill political strategy of the time, which intended to imprint ethnic authenticity on the movies set in Latin America and to capture the Latin American movie markets. There was some unease about Miranda's successful appropriation, with concerns about U.S. reaction to her humor; as *Variety* of 6 November 1940 put it, "Carmen Miranda is being featured in the new 'Down Argentine Way,' and while she's known in Buenos Aires and Rio de Janeiro, she is little known in the interior or in Chile, Peru or elsewhere in South America. What will happen when the film gets here no one knows but advance press notices that Miss Miranda is 'the idol of South America' have brought nothing but laughs—laughs of the kind that don't bring biz."[31]

Little did they know: instantly, Miranda took El Norte like a storm, by surprise. She became a superstar, earning at least $200,000 a year, becoming the highest paid female star at the time.

Unlike Miranda's, Arnaz's career did not flourish until 1951, when he created the situation comedy *I Love Lucy* with his wife Lucille Ball. Although he was one of the original stars who promoted the Good Neighbor policy, in his autobiography, *A Book*, Arnaz expresses resentment that he was invited with other actors on a goodwill tour to Mexico not for his talent but because he spoke Spanish. His presence was used to get a reaction from the Mexican people about the Good Neighbor policy.[32]

Amazingly, the *Variety* article from 6 November 1940, in its last two paragraphs, opened the door to the issue of stereotyping the "Latin other" in the Anglo-American cultural imaginary:

Mexicans are frequently cast as South Americans, and nothing brings more grumbling. A Hollywood writer, here recently, explained that seeing the tremendous number of European types, he had an entirely new conception of casting possibilities for authentic South American locale pix. Nothing draws more resentment than the impression that North Americans believe South Americans are part Indian.

All over South America, dress is similar to that in the States and Europe. Yet films come here showing "South American characters" in tight laced pants and long sideburns or shawls and mantillas. That's museum stuff, film men here argue, and it has no excuse.[33]

This comment points to the complexity of the politics of ethnic representation. First, it shows how ignorant Anglo-Americans are in their depictions of Latin Americans. Second, it introduces the issue of race and mestizaje in Latin America. Third, it brings to the forefront the problematics of authenticity. From this vantage point, an interrogative positioning emerges, facilitating a critical reading: Where do Miranda and Arnaz fit in this model? How authentic are their performances? How do race, ethnicity, class, and gender determine their own representation and performance as "other"? How is the "other" portrayed through costumes, locale, body gestures, song and dance, and foreign accent? Do Miranda and Arnaz accommodate their performance acts within the Anglo-American cultural models of the representation of the "Latin foreign other" and within the horizon of expectations of the Anglo-American audiences on Broadway and in Hollywood? Do Miranda and Arnaz continue to involuntarily perpetuate the dominant stereotypes of the "Latin other"?

The Brazilian Bombshell: Carmen Miranda

Down Argentine Way (1940) was the product of the marriage between the Good Neighbor policy and Hollywood. Responding to the U.S. urgency to establish hemispheric ties, the movie was an ideological and political package used in initiating a new covenant with Latin America. With the goal of making the film more attractive and pleasing to Latin American audiences, Hollywood interpolated Carmen Miranda's Broadway performance in *The Streets of Paris*, which had been a rousing box office success (fig. 1.3). Thanks to Hollywood's effort to bring a touch of ethnic authenticity to the screen, Miranda's performance was preserved almost in its entirety. It must be noted that this

1.3 Carmen Miranda in *The Streets of Paris*. (Billy Rose Theatre Collection, The New York Public Library for the Performing Arts, Astor, Lenox and Tilden Foundations.)

attempt at authenticity is also registered in the Latin American location of the film; as Luis Reyes and Peter Rubie have noted, "*Down Argentine Way* (1940) is notable for being the first in a series of Technicolor musicals at Fox that utilized "Latin" background and themes."[34] The movie is essential to a critical examination of the ethnic representation of Latinos/as on Broadway and in Hollywood. Although I am focusing primarily on Miranda's act, the movie as a whole constitutes a great example of Hollywood's "othering" practices.

Down Argentine Way's plot is simple and superficial: a young Anglo-American woman (Glenda), a rich New Yorker whose hobby is collecting horses, falls in love with a rich Argentine (Ricardo), who is attending a horse show in the U.S. Ricardo refuses to sell Glenda a horse after finding out that she is a Crawford. His father, who has had a long-standing family feud with the Crawfords, has instructed him not to sell them any of his horses. After Ricardo's return to Argentina, Glenda flies to Buenos Aires with her aunt to acquire a new horse and to conquer Ricardo. Her interest in horses parallels her search for a husband. But there is an inconvenience: the romance gets complicated when Ricardo's father discovers that Glenda is a Crawford. In order to gain his father's consent for his relationship with Glenda, Ricardo decides to enter the best horse in a race. After intensive training, the horse wins. The victory convinces the father to change his mind. In the end, the father accepts Glenda and the couple lives happily ever after.

How does Carmen Miranda fit in this Anglo-American imaginary topo(s)graphy of Latin America? After Miranda's success on Broadway, Twentieth Century Fox foresaw the lucrative potential of her act. Precisely, she incarnated the ideal symbolization of the Good Neighbor policy. Miranda's cameo appearance in the film was viable through the inclusion of a Buenos Aires night club performance. This scene occurs as part of a tour of the city's night life, given to Glenda by Tito, a "Latin hustler." The Club Rendezvous, featuring Miranda, was among the clubs visited. In this club scene, Miranda's Broadway act was transplanted to Hollywood, revealing the ideological discursive continuum between the Great White Way and the Factory of Dreams.

Down Argentine Way opens with the song "South American Way" and immediately exposes the limited and stereotypical ways through which Hollywood visualizes and characterizes Latin Americans. This song, in both the Broadway performance and the movie, circulates and reinforces the stereotypical Anglo-American representations of South America. As on Broadway, Miranda mesmerizes the film audience. She appears in the Technicolor brilliance of colorful costumes and glittering jewelry. In this opening scene, Miranda introduces the dazzled audience to the flavor, glitter, rhythm, and vivaciousness of Latin American culture. Her song, "South American Way," maps the stereotypical representation of Latin America as the land of romance where all worries are forgotten.[35] The tropics signal sexual liberation and leisure time. South America offers a "crazy" good time, and dreams of love.

As the opening number of the film, this song is out of place, since the action takes place in Argentina. Shouldn't Miranda, have been singing in Spanish instead of Portuguese? Such an error of ethnicity/language was not well received in Latin American movie markets. Miranda's introduction of Argentina was a total embarrassment for the Anglo-American film industry and exposed Anglo-American misunderstanding of nationalist, ethnic, and racial differences in Latin America. Miranda's act at the night club is credible, but rumba and samba are not dances native to Argentina. This opening scene registers the confusion within the Anglo-American cultural imaginary regarding the representation of the "Latin foreign other" and its geography: one signifier is same as the other and the other and the other. All geographic locations become a conflation of different exotic sites: the tropics, the pampas, the Andes—where romance, comfort, fiesta, and siesta are forever guaranteed.

Within this prejudiced and racist way of seeing, "Latins" in the film are one-dimensional. Miranda stands for the "Latin" stereotype of the gayest señorita who is always dancing and advocating the enjoyment of life, inciting passion and sexual desire through her exotic looks. Other "Latins" in the movie are experts in romance or known for their laziness and slow-paced life. As "South American Way" demonstrates, "Latins" ride on mules, signaling primitiveness and farcical behavior; the chauffeur is always taking a siesta; the caretaker of the horses is a grotesque and comical character; the servants and villagers look like condescending caricatures of Mexican peasants; Tito is an opportunistic hustler who takes advantage of the tourists; Ricardo crystallizes the image of the handsome Latin lover, the courteous and charming rich caballero, the colorful gaucho.[36] No wonder, given all the above offenses, that the spectators in Buenos Aires protested the film and Twentieth Century Fox had to reedit and reshoot some scenes that were degrading and insulting to Argentines.[37]

It is important to note that Miranda's first appearance in a Hollywood film was her broadway act per se. This not only confirms her tangentiality to the film, but, most important, it anchors Miranda in her Broadway experience.[38] Why did she become such an immediate sensation and a cultural icon for the audiences and theater critics?

Carmen Miranda was no newcomer to the entertainment industry;

she was an experienced performer. Before her arrival on Broadway, she had been a star in Brazil. She had recorded more than three hundred records and had been featured in five films. On a cruise to South America, Lee Shubert, after seeing her performance at the Casino de Urca, recruited Miranda to appear in his latest musical revue, *Streets of Paris*, which opened on Broadway on 19 June 1939. Her performance stopped the show at the end of the first act. Though she sang in Portuguese, communication through language was not necessary as long as there was music and spectacle. As one critic noted, "The language of Brazil is Portugese. Maybe you no spikka. But let Miranda sing to you and you're practically a native. For her language doesn't need an interpreter. Her flashing smile, those what-big-eyes-you-have, a shrug or two and those marvelously expressive hands, ring the bell the world round. Call it 'oomph,' 'yumph,' or go way back to Elinor Glyn and call it 'it.' That's Miranda."[39] Miranda's rendition of "South American Way" (which, with her heavily accented pronunciation as "Souse American Way," became her signature tune) was one of the musical numbers.

For Broadway audiences, Miranda constituted the most eccentric, exuberant, and popular cultural manifestation of Latin America. Theater critics described her as a fiery Brazilian singer and dancer, with picaresque eye movements, hips in motion, sensual hand gestures, and exotic language, a woman who hypnotized and electrified audiences on Broadway and in Hollywood. She impersonated not only Latin American women but Latin America itself, becoming both the "ambassadress of Brazil" and the "ambassadress for the Good Neighbor policy." Critics were well aware of Miranda's political role:

As an advertisement for Roosevelt's good-neighbor policy, she is worth half a hundred diplomatic delegations. It's that 'Sous American way.'[40]

Miss Miranda is the greatest event in our relations with South America since the Panama Canal.[41]

Here is a fine advertisement for the good-neighbor policy, here is a superb neighbor. Last night the audience hailed her raptuously.[42]

Miranda, a foreigner singing in a foreign language, became such a visual spectacle that the Portugese lyrics did not interfere with the reception process at all. Indeed, some critics assumed that she was singing in Spanish:

The Miranda sings rapid-rhythmed songs in Spanish to the accompaniment of a Brazilian band. . . . But she radiates heat that will tax the Broadhurst air-conditioning plant this Summer."[43]

Her name is Carmen Miranda. Señorita Miranda sings three Spanish songs to the accompaniment of her own sextet of guitarists.[44]

Spanish has always been a blessing of a language. . . . For Miss Miranda, the chief good in the present good neighbor policy, is the chica who in six sizzling minutes, the finale to the first act, star-spangles The Streets of Paris.
    "Nobody here knows what I sing. All they can do is understand from my tone. From my movement. It is a maravilla."[45]

Not only did Miranda make a spectacle of herself, of Latin American women, and Latin America, but critics and audiences glamorized her as a tropical bird with all its plumage and splendor, a native of the jungles:

Enveloped in beads, swaying and wriggling, chattering macawlike Portuguese songs, skewering the audience with a merry, mischievous eye, the Miranda performs only once, but she stops the show.[46]

She is an astonishingly gracious singer, making lively, limpid, sweet, enchanting sounds. No rarer bird has come here in years.[47]

The critics did not hesitate to make metaphor of Miranda's difference and sexuality through animalization and monstrous objectification:

[W]hen she insinuates one of her Brazilian ditties into the audience with the dexterity of a snake charmer, the effect is devastating.[48]

She has the face of an animated gargoyle and entrancing movements and whatever else it is that makes the toasts of towns.[49]

It appears that critics lacked the words to describe Miranda's performance: it was her difference that obstructed language; she was too slippery to be classified:

What it is that Carmen has is difficult to describe; so difficult, in fact, that dramatic critics have grown neurotic in their attempts to get it into words that would make sense and at the same time not brand them as mad sex fiends. Nevertheless, it must be attempted again. First, there is the impact on the eye of Carmen's costumes, always barbaric and brilliant, but nearly always covering her thoroughly with exception of a space between the seventh rib and a point at about the waistline. This expanse is known as the Torrid Zone. It does not move, but gives off invisible emanations of Roentgen rays.[50]

In the absence of words, critics confuse race and ethnicity. Miranda personifies, in its entirety, the racial, ethnic, and sexual "barbaric other" in the Anglo-American cultural imaginary as informed by the topo(s)graphical discursive repertoire of Latin America as the "Torrid Zone." Miranda's place of origin adjudicates her the epithet of "hot tamale," with all its erotic connotations, in addition to locating her in the racial constituencies of the Latin American native peoples:

When Carmen Miranda joined the cast of The Streets of Paris the boys and girls of the ensemble adopted her as their Inca Goddess of Good Fortune and token of a lengthy run.[51]

She seengs song from Brazeel and her body sings with her—eyes, hands, hips, feet—a princess out of an Aztec frieze with a panther's grace, the plumage of a bird of paradise and the wiles of Eve and Lilith combined.[52]

[The] public . . . adored her hot tamale outbursts, and wildly fun knack for chewing the English language around until it came out sounding like an ancient Inca dialect.[53]

These racialized and racist images (Inca, Aztec) combined with the animalization (panther, bird of paradise) perpetuate the stereotype of Latinos/as as exotic racial "others." Miranda, a native Portuguese whose name was Maria de Carmo Miranda da Cunha, becomes the personification of all native Americans; even her singing becomes an Inca dialect. This act of ignorance, resulting from misperceptions and cultural misrepresentations of the "Latin foreign other," occurs because Miranda, an immigrant from Latin America, inhabits and validates the Anglo-American cultural imaginary alongside Incas, Aztecs, and the wild fauna and flora of the tropics and jungles. In these circumstances, Miranda's linguistic play with words and exaggerated accent are markers of race and ethnicity. Although her singing is delectable, it is incomprehensible noise, nothing is said.[54] Moreover, her accent registers a sense of artificiality; as Ana M. López has noted, "At once a sign of her otherness as well as of the artificiality of all otherness, her accent ultimately became an efficient marketing device, exploited in advertisements and publicity campaigns.[55]

Within this perspective, Miranda's performance displays a simulacrum where ethnic and national identities are in constant construction and negotiation. In fact, she stages a spectacle of ethnicity and femininity. Shari Roberts, in a 1993 Cinema Journal article, explains that "because Miranda so exaggerates signifiers of ethnicity and femininity, her star text suggests that they exist only as surface, that they do not refer, and in this way Miranda can become sheer spectacle."[56]

Carmen Miranda was transfigured into a stereotype and a caricature that not only embodied the construction of "Latinness" / "South Americanness" in the Anglo-American cultural imaginary of the 1940s and thereafter, but also registered a spectacle of difference, using her body and sexuality as a site of exoticism and racial and ethnic otherness.[57]

Film scholar Ana López has precisely interpreted Miranda's function as a spectacle of ethnicity and sexuality, explaining that

> Miranda functions narratively . . . and discursively as a sexual fetish, freezing the narrative and the pleasures of the voyeuristic gaze and provoking a regime of spectacle and specularity. She acknowledges and openly participates in her fetishization, staring back at the camera, implicating the audience in her sexual display. But she is also an ethnic fetish. The look she returns is also that of the ethnographer and its colonial spectator stand-in. Her Latin Americanness is displaced in all its visual splendor for simultaneous colonial appropriation and denial.[58]

After becoming a sensational celebrity, Carmen Miranda became part of the Anglo-American cultural imaginary as a vivacious and beautiful señorita who would always entertain. Her image, quite a queer act, has continued to be imitated in campy cross-dressing performance acts by male actors or parodied by females in the theater, movies, commercials, and TV: As John Kobal, the author of *Gotta Sing Gotta Dance*, points out, "her exaggerated mannerisms and clothing became a female impersonator's delight" (fig. 1.4).[59]

Bananas Is My Business, a film documentary released in 1994, illustrates how Miranda invented her stage persona.[60] As her popularity wore off, Miranda began to parody her own self-creation: the more she performed her ethnic invention, the more she became a clownish caricature. Indeed, when she returned to Brazil in 1940, Brazilians did not accept her performance. They felt betrayed by Miranda, who had sold her act out to Hollywood; they accused her of being Americanized. In Miranda's effort to construct her ethnic and nationalist persona in the U.S., she had undoubtedly became "Hollywoodized." Her musical act was a fake, an act of mimicry, a carnivalesque spectacle addressed to satisfy the horizon of expectations of Anglo-American audiences. Rejection by her people led Miranda to respond with the song "They say I came back Americanized." She left Brazil with a broken heart. Over time, Brazilians have reconciled with her Hollywood image and U.S. audiences still worship the "lady with the tutti-frutti hat."[61] As Sara J. Welch observes in "The Mirandification of America," "only in retrospect is it clear that she Mirandified America as much as it Americanized her."[62] Let me clarify that the "Mirandification" of America cannot be confused with transculturation. The cultural exchange is limited to the Anglo appropriation of rhythm and image within a carnivalesque setting; Miranda's Portugese language is reduced to noise. Under these circumstances, her accent drives home the fact that Miranda functions primarily within the parameters of "Latin-

1.4 Willard Scott on the *Today* show, impersonating Carmen Miranda.

ization." The "Latin exotic foreign other" in the U.S. is only assimilated as long it plays the function of entertainment (music, song, dance, and comedy), and when Miranda's look and fashion are objects of consumerism and spectacle.

With the passage of time, Miranda has become more complicated, more campy, more postmodern. Miranda's performances will always be remembered as the most outrageous and hilarious representation of "Latinidad" in Hollywood and in the U.S. cultural imaginary.[63] She became the pseudostereotypical image that would define the Latin American/U.S. Latina identity. Her obituary in the *New York Times* acknowledged this: "Miss Miranda, whose explosive, hippy dancing, thick-accented singing and garish costumes, became a prototype of the dynamic 'Latin' female."[64] An unforgettable parody of Miranda was Betty Garrett's imitation, with her rendition "South America, Take It Away" in *Call Me Mister* (1946).[65] The song pokes fun at the implementation of the Good Neighbor policy and the Latin rumba, samba, and conga crazes. It also refers to Miranda's hypnotizing hip movements and stylized mannerisms. Although this parody is a response to Miranda's Broadway performance and popularity, it also registers the presence on Broadway of another Latino. In the refrain "South America! Babalú! Babalú ay yay, babalú!" none other than Desi Arnaz was parodied.

It is the word "babalú" that refers to Arnaz's performance, a musical act that, like Carmen Miranda's, would activate and mobilize the Anglo-American topo(s)graphical imaginary of the "Latin other." At this discursive intersection, the Queen of Samba and the King of Rumba were the spokespersons for the Good Neighbor policy and shared the cultural pedestal on Broadway as the sole representatives of Latin Americans and performers of "Latinness." Miranda and Arnaz were onstage representing, performing, and speaking for all Latin Americans and U.S. Latinos/as. Their vocabulary may have been limited to bizarre, primitive, exotic, and incomprehensible sounds, but they spoke more than words. "Babalú" and "ay ay" said it all about Latin America and its peoples. The sound and musical interpretation of "babalú" and "ay ay" were powerful evidence for Anglo-American audiences that these performances were indisputably ethnic, authentic, and exotic. With Miranda's and Arnaz's debuts on Broadway in 1939, the Anglo-American cultural representation of the "Latin foreign other" was here to stay. Miranda and Arnaz were predestined to become the foundational images of "Latinidad" in the U.S. topo(s)graphical cultural imaginary of Latin America.

The Latin Lover: Desi Arnaz

Unlike Carmen Miranda, the daughter of migrant Portuguese working-class parents, Desiderio Alberto Arnaz y de Acha III, better known as Desi Arnaz, was the son of one of the wealthiest political families in Cuba. After a group of military men, among them Fulgencio

Batista y Zaldívar, overthrew Gerardo Machado's dictatorship in 1933, Arnaz's father was jailed and the family property was confiscated. Arnaz and his parents went to Miami in exile. Arnaz, whose life story is a riches-to-rags-to-riches one, was not embarrassed to admit publicly the menial jobs he had taken to earn a living, and he willingly expressed his gratitude to the U.S. for his fortune and success: "I really wanna tell you my first job in this country was cleaning bird cages. It's very true. We came to this country, we didn't have a cent in our pockets. From cleaning canary cages to this night here in New York, it's a long ways and I don't think there is any other country in the world that could give you that opportunity. I wanna say thank you, thank you America, thank you." [66]

Arnaz's artistic career began in 1936 at the Roney Plaza Hotel in Miami Beach, when he joined a rumba band, the Siboney Sextet. He was discovered by Xavier Cugat, who, after seeing him perform, asked Arnaz to join his band. In a short time, Arnaz learned the art of show business from Cugat and, in 1937, put together his own band, which became a great sensation after introducing the conga line. When the band reached New York, Broadway's musical director and producer George Abbott and the musical team of Richard Rodgers and Lorenz Hart (who had a new show, *Too Many Girls*, in the works) were attracted to Arnaz's charismatic and artistic potential. [67]

On 14 October 1939, Arnaz appeared on Broadway as Manuelito in *Too Many Girls* (figs. 1.5 and 1.6), a role he would later reprise in the film version. This musical tells the story of young Consuelo (played by Lucille Ball), whose wealthy father hires four young men to guard her while she attends the fictional Pottawatomie College in New Mexico, his alma mater. The all-American boys, whose contract forbids any romantic involvement with Consuelo, get involved in college life, join the football team, and bring about a winning football season. The student body does not know that these four are ringers: three have previously played in the Ivy League, and Manuelito has played in Argentina. As the plot advances, Consuelo falls in love with one of the boys, who struggles with his decision to break the contract. In the end, romance wins and Consuelo marries her bodyguard.

During the filming of *Too Many Girls* Arnaz met Lucille Ball, whom he married. Together they later produced and starred in the most popular situation comedy television series of all time, *I Love Lucy*. [68] What is Arnaz's role in this film? His Manuelito is not critical to the development of the plot; he is simply a minor character whose accent is explained by giving him an Argentine nationality. Manuelito's presence is required to add a touch of "authenticity"; not only is he a hotshot football player, he is a hot "Latin" obsessed with Anglo-American

1.5 Desi Arnaz on Broadway in *Too Many Girls*. (Vandamm Collection, Billy Rose Theatre Collection, The New York Public Library for the Performing Arts, Astor, Lenox, and Tilden Foundations.)

women. His interpolation in the film reaches its climax when he sings and dances a few musical numbers. In the Broadway production, Arnaz performed "Spic and Spanish," which was ethnicized with sombreros, sarapes, other Mexican costumes, and castanets; "She Could Shake Her Maracas"; and the song that closes the first act, "Babalú," an overwhelming, fiery, erotic, and seductive conga number. Diosa

1.6 The Broadway cast of *Too Many Girls*. (Billy Rose Theatre Collection, The New York Public Library for the Performing Arts, Astor, Lenox, and Tilden Foundations.)

Costello was Arnaz's song-and-dance companion in these numbers, a Puerto Rican actress whose "trademark was that she could swish her derriere at warp speed."[69] This duo's popularity was so immense that they would perform at Club La Conga after the stage show.

In the film version of *Too Many Girls*, Ann Miller took over Costello's role, and Arnaz's performance of "Babalú" was moved to the closing of the film, where a big, loud celebration was needed to mark the victory of the last football game. In this final musical act of the film, Arnaz appears in football regalia with his conga drum hanging around his neck. The scene is energizing and sexy, exploiting Arnaz's vivacity, sex appeal, and virility, which are all corporalized in the exhilarating, impulsive, "savage" movements and sounds of his drum playing. The crescendo of rhythm is accentuated by Arnaz's placement in front of a bonfire that frames him, facilitating close-ups of his agitated, sweaty body. Students are dancing the conga at Arnaz's feet, expressing euphoria and eroticism; the rhythmic drive builds as he furiously pounds his conga.

That same passion made Arnaz a matinee idol on Broadway. Women went crazy for his good looks and sex appeal. Thus, Arnaz embodied a new Rudolph Valentino, an updated version of the "Latin lover." That each played an Argentine (Valentino's being the gaucho in *Four Horsemen of the Apocalypse*) made the connection more explicit. The press did not fail to notice the "Latin lover" aura; Arnaz was hailed as a "terpsichorean Rudolph Valentino" by one critic;[70] another said that "as a South American broken-field runner, Desi Arnaz is a good wooer of women."[71] Obviously, Arnaz was defined in terms of sexuality and his ability to seduce women. Men reacted differently; to them he was merely noise: "Mr Arnaz is a noisy, black-haired Latin whose face, unfortunately, lacks expression and whose performance is devoid of grace."[72]

Arnaz is not the only marker of difference in the musical. The story takes place in New Mexico, and, significantly, the name of the college is Pottawatomie, a word that inscribes difference within the othered space of the Native American. The sets and costumes register difference in terms of Mexican and Native American signs of otherness. This space of otherness is a liminal zone where passion is set loose and morals relaxed. This ambience explains why Consuelo must be guarded under "the law of the father." Also, this layered liminal border allows Arnaz to shout like a "tribal chieftain,"[73] and to "[approximate] a tribal chant to Chango, the African God of War" in the final musical number.[74] The whole scene constructs itself in relation to a primitive worldview in which Native American and African cultures converge at center stage, with tribal rituals, chants, and accessive rhythms.

In the film's opening musical numbers, which take place at the college, the camera deliberately presents a few close-ups of some Native American faces.[75] Furthermore, Arnaz's drum is decorated with "Indian" motifs, revealing how African and Native American cultures are fused in the final musical number of the film.[76] Such moments of pseudotransculturation do not represent the multicultural nightmare Cuban critic Gustavo Pérez Firmat observes in his analysis of the film: "The movie's ignorance is so utterly blissful that I find its mindless agglutinating energy difficult to resist. To be sure, *Too Many Girls* is a multiculturalist's nightmare."[77] Rather, I would say, this is a case of blatant cultural appropriation and "Latinization," given that the final movie scene has been molded and accommodated for the entertainment and enjoyment of an Anglo-American audience. The lyrics have disappeared, thus erasing the Spanish language, which has been replaced by unintelligible sounds signaling generic ethnic otherness and cultural difference. Thus, Spanish language has been reduced to mere noise. The audience does not care about the verbal content; it prefers to enjoy the visual spectacle of difference and the primitive sounds of Arnaz's "oé oé" as the conga beat intensifies, possessing the cast and audience. This exotic and racialized space liberates individuals (actors and audience), unleashing their sexual instincts as they dance a conga until the beating of the drums provoke the explosion of their bodies in a volcanic fury.

On Broadway, "Babalú," sung in Spanish, was a spectacle of otherness because of its exoticism and primitiveness. Arnaz's rendition of "Babalú" located the audiences in the realm of African religious rituals.[78] Those audiences did not understand the relation of the lyrics to Afro-Cuban cultural and religious practices. In Santería, Babalú Ayé is one of the Orichas, a deity in the Yoruba mythological world. The chant functions as a prayer and an offering in exchange for protection and future happiness in love, health, and prosperity. Given the syncretism of African and Catholic religions in Cuba, Santería identifies Babalú Ayé with Saint Lazarus. In the Yoruba mythical world, Babalú was a lascivious and promiscuous man who, after having sex with many women, became ill. His body was covered with lacerations and only dogs, licking his sores, would follow him. When appropriated by Santería, Saint Lazarus became the patron saint of people sick with leprosy, smallpox, venereal diseases and, more recently, AIDS. In "Babalú," Arnaz impersonates and mimics the voice of a black man ("negro") who is worshipping the Orisha to be successful in love with his "negra." The issue of race and racism is embedded in the line "quiero pedir a Babalú una negra bembona" (I want to ask Babalú for a negra with thick-nigger-lips). The spectacle and the vocal impersonation only perpetuated the notion of the racial "other" as performative.[79]

Lacking a translation, the audience had no knowledge of the African origin of the song "Babalú," nor of the African origins of the rumba and the conga; neither were they informed of the African roots of Carmen Miranda's sambas and bahiana outfits.[80] Like Miranda, Arnaz was condemned to communicate through queer sounds, hyperbolic ethnic representations, running gags, and visual spectacle. In this aspect, a statement by Xavier Cugat helps explain the reception process of such ethnic spectacles: "Americans know nothing about Latin music. They neither understand nor feel it. So they have to be given music more for the eyes than the ears. Eighty percent visual, the rest aural."[81]

In films and in song, Miranda's and Arnaz's English was fractured and mangled whenever, in excitement, anger, or frustration, they burst into a chain of incomprehensible noise. Such instances of verbal nonsense were overemphasized by their thick accents. These tongue twisters, plays on words, and linguistic anarchy were major components of their performances and critical to their efforts to please Anglo-American audiences. Their accents and linguistic outbursts translated as markers of exoticism and ethnic difference, and particularly articulated their "fiery Latin temperaments." However, both actors, by refusing to show full command and performance of the English language and grammar, and by insisting on converting it into gibberish once they had learned it, challenge Anglo-American audiences. As they pleased, they imposed their difference and foreignness: within the carnivalesque, they camouflaged their Latin American origins and staged humorously their ethnic identities. Pleasing, in these terms, means to give enjoyment, as well as to perform within one's own will (in spite of how constrained one may be by stereotypes). On the stage, Arnaz and Miranda did as they pleased.

Significantly, their accents limited Miranda and Arnaz to playing the roles of marginal characters. Arnaz's accent would haunt him throughout his life, and was emphasized in his famous recurring line as Ricky Ricardo in *I Love Lucy:* "Honey, I'm home!" In an episode after his Little Ricky was born, Lucy is afraid their son will have his father's accent. She tells Ricky, "Please promise me you won't speak to our child until he's nineteen or twenty." Throughout *I Love Lucy*'s TV run, Arnaz's accent was not only in a comic context but in a cruel reality: his accent was a form of embarassment, one that impeded the progress of his artistic career. Even within the domestic sphere, Arnaz as Ricky Ricardo must clean up his ethnic act; his accent must be exiled from the home, because it is a marker of difference. It is allowed only in the public sphere, as a form of entertainment in his night club, the Tropicana (which would eventually be renamed Babalú). It is ironic that "what we remember most about Ricky is the sound of his voice,"[82] that is, his accent, and his "Babalú" cries.

As the years passed, Arnaz sounded like a broken record, always performing "Babalú" on *I Love Lucy*. This repetitiveness paralleled the evolution of Miranda's singing and performance into comedy and parody. Through the years, Miranda's voice became squeaky, her exaggerated, accented broken English, over-pronounced *r*s, and plays on words became monotonous, nonsensical, predictable, and sometimes annoying. When her film *If I'm Lucky* (1946) was released, critic Bosley Crowther of the *New York Times* reduced her performance act to "animated noise."[83] Her act ceased to develop; it became more artificial, excessive, grotesque, clownish, and farcical. Indeed, her bahiana turbans and hats became a comic amalgamation of fruits, as in *The Gang's All Here* (1943).

In this aspect, Miranda and Arnaz were condemned to repeatedly enact their performances as pure ethnic entertainment. They had no choice other than to make the best of the "Latin foreign other" roles Hollywood had for them. Arnaz was very conscious of his limitations, as he confessed in his autobiography. Referring to the auditions for *Too Many Girls*, he said, "At that time the Latin type they were describing, [able to handle comedy, song, and dance] was not easy to find in this country. . . . The only ones who were known then were the romantic Rudolph Valentino types and the George Raft types, or the other extreme, the Crispin Martin lazy Mexican character or the Leo Carrillos."[84] "Latin" roles were so scarce in Hollywood that when Arnaz returned from military service in 1945, he had already been replaced with Ricardo Montalbán.

Broadway and Hollywood's racist practices were apparent in producers' initial refusals to televise a situation comedy with the characters Lucy and Ricky as protagonists who had an interethnic marriage: "The big brass at CBS thought he was not the type to play a typical American husband."[85] Ball and Arnaz were well aware of the difficulties of doing a show together: "[E]xperts insisted the program was doomed to fail. They said 'a foreigner' with an accent wouldn't be believable, playing an average American husband."[86] There is no doubt that race was a subtext: Arnaz was the other, the "Latin" type; although Caucasian, his origins were "south of the border." Furthermore, Cuba was seen in racial terms, linked to Africa culturally and ethnically, as we saw earlier in the 1902 political cartoon about Cuba. Precisely because of his Cuban ethnicity, it was inconceivable that Arnaz could play certain roles, including the husband in *I Love Lucy*. Arnaz once declared, "You know, I think if it wouldn't have been for Lucy, I would have stopped trying a long time ago because I was always the guy that didn't fit. When she did 'My Favorite Husband' on radio they said I wasn't the type to play the part. Then finally she wanted to do the television show and she said 'Well, I want to do it with Desi.' So everybody again said, 'Well he doesn't . . . he is not right to play your husband.'"[87] At work here are racist practices. The Hays Code stated that "miscegeneration (sex relationship between the white and black races) is forbidden."[88] This prohibition included half-breeds, mulattos, Native Americans, African Americans, Asians, Arabs, and, of course, "Latins."

Even off stage, Arnaz was not the type to receive an invitation to join the most prestigious golf course in Palm Springs, the Thunderbird.[89] Arnaz's racial and ethnic roots were exposed and overtly devalued on another occasion. In a television appearance on *The Ed Wynn Show*, in which Lucille Ball was being interviewed, Arnaz interrupted by playing the drums. After a series of interruptions Wynn finally said, "You'll ruin the whole show playing those drums. They'll think it's some African show."[90] These comments not only racialize Arnaz's performance, but also register blatant racism. This appraisal of Arnaz's performance supports the idea that, since his first appearance on Broadway, Arnaz's musical number "Babalú" was read as a racial and ethnic performance. The "savage" percussion, the rapturous music, and the loud tribal chanting transported the audiences to Cuba and specifically to the topo(s)graphical Afro-Cuban discursive location as represented in the Anglo-American cultural collective imaginary.

The convergence of race and ethnicity is also crystallized in "She Could Shake Her Maracas," one of the songs Arnaz performed in *Too Many Girls*.[91] This song stereotypes Latin American culture and comically degrades Latinos/as by attributing to them a bad temper and lack of intelligence. It tells the story of Pepito and Pepita, who fall in love despite their national origins—he is from Cuba and she is from Rio del Mar. (Notice how these locations echo Arnaz and Miranda's homelands.) Furthermore, like Arnaz and Miranda, both Pepito and Pepita are entertainers: Pepito plays the guitar, and Pepita shakes the maracas. Of all places, they end up in Harlem, where they can consummate their love. In these terms, the location of the protagonists in Harlem signals their position in the U.S. as "Latin foreign ethnic and racial others": They are allocated to the othered space of African Americans, since race determines a priori their identity in the U.S.

Arnaz also activated and perpetuated the stereotyped imaginary construction of Cuba as the land of romance and mañana with another song, "Cuban Pete."[92] With this song, he is self-proclaimed as the "king of the rumba beat" and exalts his expertise as a "Latin lover"; he sends the señoritas dancing, and people can forget their worries if they dance to his tune all day long. How, then, can we separate the Latin American ethnic identity from the Anglo-American stereotype of the "Latin other"?

Moreover, Arnaz goes farther in his representation of the "Latin other" as a *racial* other. If, in his rendition of "Babalú," he impersonated the African race and Cuban ethnicity through music and sound, and "Cuban Pete" shamelessly stereotyped "Latins," it would not be until 1953 that Arnaz carried his ethnic and racial act to its maximum expression. It is only reading backwards that "Babalú" exposes its full meaning: the visual representation of the racial other, which had been partially silenced and camouflaged, is disclosed in the 19 January 1953 *I Love Lucy* episode, "Lucy Goes to the Hospital" (figs. 1.7 and 1.8).[93]

The episode opens with the character Ricky holding a book that has a photo of an African with a painted face on one page and a photo of an African mask on the other. As Ricky intensely studies the photos, he makes faces in imitation of what he imagines to be African: he opens wide his mouth and eyes and grimaces. It is not until later in the episode that the audience learns that he is rehearsing a voodoo act. This is a new act, and Ricky's performative act of creation parallels Lucy's act of giving birth. When Lucy and Ricky arrive at the hospital,

1.7 Desi Arnaz in blackface in the *I Love Lucy* episode "Lucy Goes to the Hospital."

Ricky realizes that he has to get ready for the new voodoo number at his night club. He calls his friend Fred to ask him to bring over his makeup kit. Once Fred returns, Ricky goes to the bathroom to put the makeup on. Ricky comes out in blackface and goes to the fathers' waiting room, where he scares a nurse because "the voodoo make-up is a grotesque amalgam of whitened eye sockets, darkened skin, painted-on fangs and a fright wig of black hair."[94] The terrified nurse calls a policeman and Ricky leaves for the club. During his performance, Fred calls and informs him that the baby is born. Still with his makeup on, Ricky heads back to the hospital. Chaos reigns when he terrorizes the staff and the policeman tries to arrest him. Ricky clarifies his identity as a performer, thus justifying the blackface, to the policeman. Nevertheless, when a nurse comes to the waiting room to announce that Lucy delivered a baby boy, Ricky responds as the father and she is shocked, paralyzed, and speechless.

As a whole, the blackface episode is a distorted and grotesque masquerade that articulates racist practices within the domain of comedy and performance. Blackface impersonation converts the racial other into an object of humor. What attempts to be amusing and entertaining

1.8 Desi Arnaz in blackface performing at the cabaret in the *I Love Lucy* episode "Lucy Goes to the Hospital."

inscribes a vulgar and demeaning deformation of the racial other, and establishes power relations. As Eric Lott has aptly observed in "Love and Theft: The Racial Unconscious of Blackface Minstrelsy": "'Black' figures were to *be looked at*, shaped to the demands of desire; they were screens on which audience fantasy could rest, securing white spectators' position as superior, controlling, not to say owning, figures."[95]

Ricky's impersonation of the racial other positions his voodoo act within a discursive web where Africans incarnate primitiveness and cannibalism. Yet I would like to go a step further. Race is a significant element in this episode, from the opening to the closing frame. It is crucial to examine the spectacle of blackface because, at this moment, when Little Ricky is being born, ethnicity and race intersect. The racist practices that confined Arnaz are now made visible in his character Ricky's blackface. It can be read that Ricky/Arnaz is parodying, subverting, and transgressing the Hays Code, which banned miscegenation. It is obvious that an interracial marriage was not a usual occurrence in the hospital, which explains why the nurse was so taken aback. A black man was not expected to be in that space. Ricky/Arnaz was able to bring a black man into a forbidden zone by means of blackface, just as he had been able to bring a "Latin" man into the forbidden zone of an interethnic marriage, one which was perceived as an interracial marriage. I interpret this moment of ethnic, racial, and sexual intersection as Arnaz's effort to perform race as spectacle through blackface. Ironically, underneath all that makeup, there is a *white* man. Consequently, the baby will be white. Similar to the function of masquerade at carnival, the blackface functions as a catalyst to expose and then subdue all fears and suspicions that the baby was the offspring of an interracial marriage. In these terms, Ricky's enactment of race at the moment of his son's birth is pure masquerade, just as it was when Arnaz sang "Babalú" on Broadway in 1939. His blackface musical number is all simulacrum, held up by the scaffolding of racist stereotypes and practices, and continuing the Broadway tradition of "racialized entertainment as [a cultural] commodity."[96]

Authenticity and the Burden of Representation

In *The Latin Tinge*, John S. Roberts quotes Xavier Cugat as saying, "To succeed in America I gave the Americans a Latin music that had nothing authentic about it."[97] This declaration is loaded with all kinds of issues. How authentic are cultural, ethnic, and racial representations? Up to what point do Latin American migrant entertainers—like Miranda and Arnaz—have to accommodate their performances according to the Anglo-American stereotypical representations of the "Latin foreign other" and to satisfy the Anglo-American horizon of expectations? Why, above all, do artistic performances like music and dance embody and activate national identities? In the cases of Miranda and Arnaz, why are they singing in Portuguese and Spanish when they are not being understood? Are they speaking to themselves, to reassure their belonging to an imaginary nationhood abroad? From where are they speaking? Who are they representing; for whom are they speaking?

Nobody questions Miranda's and Arnaz's nationalities. They are the quintessential personifications and emblems of Brazilian and Cuban national identities. It seems as if, after migration, Miranda and Arnaz had to objectify their ethnicities in order to stage them and to reaffirm their national differences. Yet such a task requires a process of selection of national traits and symbols, through which a new identity is forged and made visible. This process mobilizes an inventory of "national things" containing all elements native to a given nation: music, dance, rhythms, typical costumes, folklore, foods, national holidays, religions, and art. This inventory is charged with ideological and political views as well as with class, racial, gender, and sexual biases. Undoubtedly, it is the entertainment industry that serves best to stage, perform, and enact national, cultural, racial, and ethnic identities. In these terms, Miranda personifies the samba and Arnaz the rumba and the conga.

When examined closely, both entertainers appropriated music and rhythms from the African components of the socionational spectrum of ethnic identities, social classes, and races that constitute the imaginary national communities of Brazil and Cuba. Although there is a high degree of transculturation and hybridization, what is absent here is the self-representation of and by the African constituency. Consequently, Miranda's and Arnaz's ethnoracial spectacles must be approached with caution. When analyzed their performances reveal the institutional ideological apparatus and social practices of racism in Latin America, translocated to the U.S.

Both Miranda and Arnaz are Caucasians who simulate blackness. Their performances of blackness speak for the African demographic component of both countries, but, in both musical acts, the African is made invisible. The African is unrepresentable because the racist dominant culture has not opened a space of or for African self-representation. There is no room for the subjugated and the subaltern to speak, to perform, and to re-present himself. Instead, two successful entertainers who are white have taken African culture and have appropriated their own re-presentation. Miranda and Arnaz have turned African culture into a performance and an impersonation of the other with their staging of blackness as simulacra. In this sense, their performances function in accordance with given relations of cultural hegemony, social power, and racialized/racist practices at home and abroad. This means that the Afro-Brazilian and the Afro-Cuban are left out, silenced, and relegated to the margin. As a result, a black physical body marked by race has no "authentic" representation or voice in the sociocultural arena. Afro-Cuban and Afro-Brazilian representations are acceptable as long as the performers *perform* blackness—that is, put at the forefront the *performance* of blackface.

When considering that Miranda's and Arnaz's theatrical acts inscribe signs of otherness and racial markers of difference, it must be asked: whose culture is being represented? Whose race is being performed? Both entertainers invent an ethnic spectacle of the African racial other: Miranda does this through both her costumes and her samba;[98] Arnaz does this with his drum and voice, performing a Santería ritual incorporating the rumba and the conga. In this process of cultural appropriation of the African other, a process that keeps at a distance the legacy of transculturation in their native countries, Miranda and Arnaz represent and perform the African components of their respective countries by using stereotypical elements that define the African other: vivacity, vitality, rhythm, brilliant colors and exoticism. Additionally, both the samba and the conga incarnate the carnival tradition of Brazil and Cuba. In the evolution of the Brazilian and Cuban national identities, these festive forms of music and dance were popularized, giving voice to the marginalized lower classes composed mainly of African descendants and mulattos. For each respective nation, these national constructions became cultural icons that signified and emblematized a populist representation of what it is to be Brazilian, or Cuban within the parameters of transculturation.

Once Miranda and Arnaz emigrated, they entered the Anglo-American topo(s)graphical cultural domain of the representation of Latin America, primarily as racialized and exoticized others. It is here that the "authenticity" of their ethnicity metamorphoses into a stereotype. With the passage of time, both performers had to hold on to their memories and constantly reenact and reaffirm their foreignness, nationality, and ethnicity. At this intersection of nationalism and migration (always constructed within the realm of the memory of what was ethnic or racial in their homelands) Miranda's and Arnaz's musical performances convert, over time, into parody. This process applies to their "Latin" accents and their overemphasized mispronunciation, exemplified predominantly in the extravagant and exaggerated rolling of the letter *r*. This is most noticeable in Arnaz's musical rendition of a Spanish popular tongue twister that overpronounces the *r*: "r con r cacharro con r barril, rrr, rrr, rrr." In Miranda's case, at the beginning of her career her songs delivered the softness, gentleness, and musicality of the Portuguese language ("Mama eu Quero" and "Bambu, Bambu"); later, she was overemphasizing syllabic repetitions and atypical sounds, turning herself into a caricature. Her *r*s and plays on words became her signature in songs like "I yi yi yi yi (I Like You Very Much)," "Chica Chica Boom Chic," "Chattanooga Choo Choo," and "Weekend in Havana." In her recordings with the Andrew Sisters, "Cuanto le gusta," "The Wedding Samba," "I See, I See," and "The Matador," Miranda's pronounciation locates her in the realm of comedy, clownishness, and laughter. More surprising is that her lyrics refer to Mexico instead of Brazil. In "The Wedding Samba" she sings about the land of the Río, and in "The Matador" the lyrics refer to a utopic love relationship in the Rancho Grande. Obviously, Miranda's way of seeing Latin America has been influenced and shaped by the Anglo-American topo(s)graphical discursive construction of the nations "south of the border." It is ironic that Miranda's assimilation of the Anglo-American imagined topo(s)graphy of Latin America, her heavy and faked accent, her compelling charisma, and her breathtaking talent made her *more* "authentic" according to the Anglo-American ways of seeing the "Latin other". Her presence accurately corroborated and validated dominant Anglo-American stereotypes of Latin America and Latin Americans.

The ultimate irony is that native Brazilians and Cubans see and identify with, respectively, Miranda's and Arnaz's cultural performances and ethnic and racial impersonations as accurate representations of their national identities. Miranda and Arnaz appear to consolidate a national identity that can only be seen, objectified, and projected from a distance, particularly when that national identity is reenacted and exported by emigrants. Indeed, these emigrants became the guardians, preservers, bearers, and transmitters of nationalism. They became the cultural ambassadors of their country of origin and its people. Thus, Carmen Miranda, according to Heitor Villa-Lobos, represents Brazil at its best: "Carmen Miranda carried her country in her luggage, and taught people who had no idea of our existence to adore our music and our rhythm. Brazil will always have an unpayable debt to Carmen Miranda."[99]

Miranda's and Arnaz's authenticity was not questioned by U.S. audiences, who assumed that, since the two were native Latin Americans, they automatically embodied a native Latin American nationality. In both cases, their representations of ethnicity in the domain of performance were equivalent to ethnic Latin American realities. This was not true, however, for their representation of race. As discussed above, Miranda's and Arnaz's musical acts appropriated African elements that relegated Afro-Brazilians and Afro-Cubans to the margins. In this sense, their performances staged a partial blackface minstrel show that perpetuated the racist stereotypes within the Anglo-American cultural imaginary.[100] Furthermore, their ethnicity, which converged in the Anglo-American cultural imaginary with race, restricted them from acting in any roles that signified white ethnicity and race. Of course, their accents, not their skin color, were the main obstacles. However, they were considered ideal actors for impersonating any nationality marked by race or "Latin" ethnicity: for example, Miranda played Cubans and Brazilians and Arnaz played Argentines and Cubans. Hoping to get more serious acting roles, Miranda even dyed her hair blond. Unfortunately, her efforts to whiten her performance never succeeded. In contrast, white actors were allowed to play "Latins"; for example, Don Ameche played an Argentine in *Down Argentine Way*. Given these racist practices in which the other plays the imagined "Latin other,"

1.9 The *I Love Lucy* episode "Be a Pal."

Miranda and Arnaz shared the *burden of representation:* any roles they played represented all "Latins." Given that their ethnic performances situated them within the Anglo-American cultural imaginary, both had to enact ethnicity according to the Anglo-American stereotypical constructs and expected behavior of the "Latin other."

No image puts into question the authenticity of Miranda's and Arnaz's ethnicity as much as the stereotypical portrayal of both of them in the 22 October 1951 third episode of *I Love Lucy,* "Be a Pal" (fig. 1.9.). When Lucy is afraid that Ricky is losing his interest in her, her friend Ethel suggests a Dr. Humphrey book, *Keep the Honeymoon from Ending.* Its third chapter suggests "that the wife surround the husband 'with things that remind him of his childhood.'"[101] Lucy, in her effort to recreate the authenticity of Ricky's homeland and childhood, decorates the living room with all kinds of things that she thinks are Cuban: palm trees, bananas, sombreros, sarapes, a flock of chickens, a mule.

There is also a sleepy Mexican peon, a character with a sarape, and Lucy impersonating Carmen Miranda by wearing a Mirandaesque costume and lip-synching to "Mama eu Quero."[102] This scene is of vital importance in understanding Miranda's and Arnaz's position in the Anglo-American cultural imaginary. First, it displays an inventory of what Anglo-Americans (Lucy) consider Latin America to be. Second, it puts all Latin American countries in the same shopping bag (Cuba, Brazil, Mexico). Third, it reveals the dominant stereotypes of the "Latin other": the beautiful señorita, the sleeping peon, and, although absent at the moment, Arnaz's "Babalú" act, which is silently present and associated with these dominant representations. Lucy's display concretizes how all these stereotypical objects constitute the "Latin other." Within this Anglo-American cultural, racial, and ethnic construction of the "Latin other," the world of entertainment converges with the world of the sleepy and lazy peon. This conflation crystallizes how, for Anglo-Americans, the concept of "Latinness" exists as a conglomeration of "Latin" things and peoples. Within this Anglo-American cultural imaginary construction, the "Latin foreign other" intersects with the "Latin domestic ethnic and racial other," the Mexican American. As a whole, this episode stages, activates, and mobilizes the Anglo-American stereotype of a Latin American primitive world "south of the border" and in the Southwest.

With this episode, such a semiotic representation of "Latinness" inaugurates a historical moment through which a foundational image of "Latinidad" emerges as a stereotype. This image exemplifies how, within the Anglo-American cultural and topo(s)graphical imaginary of Latin America and the Southwest, the "Latin other" can be represented and objectified with a given number of "authentic" props. Critic Gustavo Pérez Firmat, in his analysis of the episode and the song, concludes that "Lucy momentarily turns the living room into a womb, or at least a maternal space."[103] I believe that this scene signifies more than an attempt to bring Ricky to his childhood, to the world of the mother; it also signifies a new mode of representing and performing the "Latin other." Pérez Firmat also states that Lucy turns the living room into a Little Havana. Such an interpretation, from Pérez Firmat's Cubancentric perspective, fails to see the new representation of "Latinidad." No Little Havana would make room for Mexican cultural icons, for a primitive and underdeveloped economy with lazy peasants and mules, nor claim Miranda's performance in Portuguese and her queer costume.

Ricky's response to Lucy's act of ethnic impersonation is direct and plain: "Lucy honey, if I wanted things Cuban, I'd have stayed in Havana."[104] This declaration reveals how conscious Arnaz was of his migration and of what he had left behind. He had no intention of living within a nostalgic re-creation of Cuba, because that would be an imposture; all replicas are fake. Nevertheless, Arnaz seemed to have found a way to deal with his past through his music. He erased any symptoms of nostalgia, which would have led to a representation of authenticity by placing ethnicity and nationality within a sacred domain, untouchable and unchangeable. He was then able to perform Cuban ethnicity within the Anglo-American cultural construction of the "Latin other." In this scene, Arnaz was conscious of his stereotyping, participation in, and propagation of "Latinness" and "Latinidad" in the U.S. Pérez Firmat finds it "odd that Ricky does not notice the inappropriateness of sombreros, sarapes, and Carmen Miranda as metonyms of his childhood."[105] But Arnaz did not react to these props, because those stereotypes were not his true self; he was capable of staying at a distance. He knew (as did Miranda) that he was performing for an Anglo-American audience and that stereotypes would sell. Thus, "authenticity" was not a *performance* issue onstage for either Arnaz or Miranda but it might have been a personal identity issue offstage.

As a whole, this episode of *I Love Lucy* functions as a palimpsest of Latin American ethnic, racial and national identities.[106] What has happened is that this symbolic Anglo-American representation of "Latinness" has been written and superimposed over the ethnic, racial, and national identities of Latin Americans. That is to say, in this collage, those previous identities are only registered as Anglo-American stereotypical representations of the "Latin other." Yet the original identities are not completely erased, are still legible. They can be (t)raced. Since Miranda and Arnaz incarnate in their performances the presence of given Latin American national authenticity, for Anglo-American audiences that presence as "Latin foreign other" authenticates Miranda's and Arnaz's original national, racial, and ethnic identities. It is necessary to scrape those stereotypes in order to dismantle them. In this process, the true meaning of "palimpsestos" in Greek—to scrape again—registers its whole significance: it is urgent to scrape stereotypes, to deconstruct them again and again in order to do away with them.

After migration, both Arnaz and Miranda had to reinvent themselves according to the Anglo-American cultural imaginary of the "Latin other" and their horizon of expectations. By doing so, they appropriated those stereotypes, making possible the execution of their own agency and articulating contestatory discursive strategies as they negotiated with the dominant stereotypical representations of the "Latin other." In these terms, Miranda and Arnaz's exaggerated accents can be read as resistance. This is the reason why Arnaz is wearing a suit in the "Be a Pal" episode. If he had worn a "Babalú" costume, he would have acted in complicity with the dominant practices of stereotyping.

Reading Miranda and Arnaz superficially erases their agency and their complex negotiations with the dominant Anglo-American culture. Hence, authenticity itself must be questioned: how "authentic" are immigrants after they leave their homeland? How "authentic" are ethnic performances? Up to what point did Miranda and Arnaz perform the artificiality of authenticity that Anglo-American stereotypes provided them? Although their authenticity may be argued, it is certain that Miranda and Arnaz constituted a new mode of representing "Latinidad." These new representations were propagated through theater, music, film, and television in a moment in U.S. history when popular culture was intersecting with mass culture. The commodification and mass-marketing of these images magnified their power and reach, transforming them into foundational images of "Latinidad" in the U.S.

2

A Puerto Rican Reading of the America of *West Side Story*

My final prayer: O my body, make of me always
a man who questions.
—Frantz Fanon, *Black Skin, White Masks*

After my immigration to Wisconsin in 1973 to attend college, the musical film *West Side Story* was frequently imposed upon me as a model of/for my Puerto Rican ethnic identity. Certainly it was a strange and foreign model for a newcomer, but not for the Anglo-Americans who actualized, with my bodily presence, their stereotypes of Latino otherness. Over and over again, to make me feel comfortable in their family rooms and to tell me of their knowledge about Puerto Ricans, they would start their conversations with *West Side Story:* "Al, we loved *West Side Story."* "Have you seen the movie?" "Did you like it?" On other occasions, some people even sang parodically in my ears: "Alberto, I've just met a guy named Alberto." And, how can I forget those who, upon my arrival, would start tapping flamenco steps and squealing: "I like to be in America! / Everything free in America."[1]

As it happened, I moved to New York City in 1983, to the Hell's Kitchen neighborhood, which borders the area where the film takes place, an area better known today as Lincoln Center. I lived in the neighborhood for eight months with "Nuyoricans."[2] At this time, I had the opportunity to see the movie, which was showing at the Hollywood Theater on Eighth Avenue between Forty-seventh and Forty-eighth Streets. Since I was becoming acquainted with New York neighborhoods and sharing daily the socioeconomic reality of immigrant

Puerto Ricans and their offspring, I became interested in correlating and contrasting the musical film with the historical reality of the immigrants. There had been a massive exodus from the island in the late 1940s. At the time the musical was produced, in 1957, the Puerto Rican diaspora had already penetrated the Anglo-American cultural imaginary. This massive migration would become one of the major constituents of the "Latin other" in the U.S. Puerto Ricans would occupy a position at the intersection of the "Latin foreign other" and the "Latin domestic ethnic and racial other." Such an overlapping of categories resulted from the fact that Puerto Ricans have been American citizens since 1917, but also have their own national identity, defined primarily by their Hispanic roots and values and by having Spanish as their language. In this sense, like Carmen Miranda and Desi Arnaz, they were perceived as a "Latin foreign other," exotic "Latins" with accents. However, in contrast to Miranda and Arnaz, given their colonial and minority status, defined by race and class—Puerto Ricans also became representative of the "Latin domestic ethnic and racial other."

West Side Story was staged at the Winter Garden Theater in 1957, and the film released in 1961 mirrors with great accuracy the original stage production. In this essay, I alternate the theatrical text with the movie script, which was partially revised. By using both versions, just as in the cases of Miranda and Arnaz, my goal is to make of both renditions a single ideological and political text that registers the cultural continuum of Broadway and Hollywood.

My interest in decentering, demythifying, and deconstructing ethnic, social, and racial stereotypes of Latinos/as inscribed in the musical was the result of witnessing the reaction of an Anglo-American audience that applauded euphorically after the number "America." Only then did I understand the power and vitality of the musical, not just as pure entertainment, but as an iconic ideological construction of the stereotype and identity of Puerto Rican immigrants, and all other Latino/a immigrants, in the U.S. I also realized, at the same time, that, in the musical number "America," there is a political campaign in favor of assimilation. Such assimilation is pronounced by a Puerto Rican herself, Rita Moreno, whose acting was awarded the coveted Oscar.[3] The audience's reception, which was manipulated by an Anglo-American patriotic discourse generated and transmitted through the song, led me to question and problematize how the musical configures, produces, and reproduces a racist discourse of Latino otherness in the U.S. How does the musical project ethnic difference as a threat to the territorial, racial, and linguistic identity, as well as to the national and imperial subjectivity, of Anglo-Americans? From such a questioning posture, we should examine how the musical, through its music, dances, romantic melodrama, and exoticism of cultural otherness distracts from the racism within it. We should also examine how it attracts, interpellates, and positions the perceiving spectator—whose social construction of reality and racial differences constitute the Anglo-American dominant ideology—by dividing spatially Puerto Ricans from Anglo-Americans, Puerto Rico from the U.S., the West Side from the East Side, the Latino ethnicity from the Anglo-American Eurocentric, white ethnicity, the Puerto Rican cultural reality from the Anglo-American one, the poor from the rich. These binary oppositions produce a political, patriotic, and mythifying discourse in which the Puerto Ricans, as intruders and invaders of the U.S. mainland, confront the Anglo-American system of power.

The Politics of Space

West Side Story depicts a fight for urban space, a space that has already been impregnated with Anglo-American cultural symbols and political significations for power relations, interactions, and social actions. In this sense, the musical projects how the Puerto Rican migration to New York City in the 1940s and 1950s not only usurps the order and the semiotic spatial organization of Anglo-Americans, but how it also constitutes a threat to the assumed coherent and monolithic identity of the Anglo-American subject. I am interested in highlighting how the Puerto Rican immigration, from the margins of the "ghetto," threatens to disarticulate, according to Anglo-Americans, their sociopolitical system at the capitalist center of New York City.

Manhattan is divided territorially, economically, racially, and ethnically. Each socioeconomic and ethnoracial group inhabits a space concretely demarcated, and even neighborhood border crossings are avoided. Specifically, it has been the musical *West Side Story* that has contributed to the perpetuation of the image of the West Side as a site of urban, ethnic, and racial tensions. The plot of the musical presents the hostility, hatred, and confrontations between two gangs. Those gangs—"The Sharks are Puerto Ricans, the Jets an anthology of what is called 'American'" (137)—reveal, as the action develops, not a mere struggle for territory but, rather, a socioeconomic and racial confrontation. Although the Jets constitute an anthology of "Americans," the gang is made up solely of the children of white European immigrants. Their actions and values embody the ideological apparatus of the Anglo-American national subjectivity—that is, the ideological program and ways of doing of the "all-American boy." Although they belong to the working class, it is obvious that the Jets act according to the "American dream." They have an ideological and political consciousness of both their nationality and imperial superiority, as shown by their competitive desire to be "number one." For this reason, they emblematized the ideology of the all-American boy, a totally white identity that does not leave room for any other ethnoracial groups in the gang. The Jets define themselves in the first song—"Jet Song"—in terms of their own sociopolitical and personal superiority, confidence, and arrogance. In this song, they claim to be the greatest, those who want to be number one and hold the sky. (Indeed, they dream high.) It should be emphasized that blacks have no representation or participation in this "anthology of Americans." Is it because they had already been confined to their own space in Harlem? Hence, the Anglo-American power confrontation is limited to the recently migrated ethnoracial minority group, the Puerto Ricans: "Against the Sharks we need every man we got" (143).

In its historical specificity, the space of the West Side obtains its total meaning when the "not-said" space is read. The "not-said" space is the Upper East Side, which is present because of its topographical contiguity. The Upper East Side is the center of Anglo-American white power, for the upper bourgeois class resides there. At the same time, the action in the West Side is referred to as a "story." In this way, the title silences the dynamic, processual, and dialectical concept of history. It postulates a binary opposition marked by the presence and absence of economic, ethnic, and racial differences: West/East; story/history; Sharks/Jets; spics/white Anglo-Americans. In the above terms, the title *West Side Story* expresses a merely superficial structure at the level of its enunciation—a story of love. However, when the title is read in metonymical relation to the center of power, an absent structure is registered under the textual surface of the story of love; that is, the film has as its deep structure an explicit discourse of discrimination and racial prejudices toward immigrant Latinos/as.

From a questioning perspective, I propose to examine how the absence of the East Side—a geopolitical absence that is signaled metonymically in the title—becomes present. It displaces and decenters the story of love between Maria and Tony on the West Side. Indeed, my alternative reading, by centering on the absent action on the East Side, concentrates on the ideological production of a political and racist discourse that could as easily be entitled "East Side History of Hatred/Racism." With this title I name the ideological discourse of the deep structures of the text; by doing so I decenter the melodramatic and romantic title *West Side Story*.

Furthermore, when the play was restaged at the Kennedy Center in 1985, the correlation between West Side and East Side surfaced once again. The East Side imposed itself as the always-absent presence; as one critic saw it, the actress Katherine Buffaloe "looks and sounds more like an East Side debutante than a West Side Puerto Rican girl . . ."[4] It is evident in this comparison that there is a specific sociocultural and ideological configuration of the East Side and the West Side in terms of class, race, and ethnicity. Such a contrast and worldview are embodied in the silences, omissions, and gaps of the East Side in *West Side Story*.

My alternative reading, based on the binary opposition between West Side and East Side, is more fully understood when it is realized that the original title, considered in 1949, was to be *East Side Story*. The play was supposed to take place on the Lower East Side, as a love story between a Jewish girl and an Italian Catholic boy. However, with Puerto Rican migration, the idea became dated. As a result, the production team even considered Chicano gangs in their search for some exoticism and "color"; as Arthur Laurents, who wrote the book for *West Side Story* has stated, "My reaction was, it was *Abie's Irish Rose*, and that's why we didn't go ahead with it. . . . Then by some coincidence, Lenny [Leonard Bernstein] and I were at the Beverly Hills pool, and Lenny said: 'What about doing it about the Chicanos?' In New York we had the Puerto Ricans, and at that time the papers were full of stories about juvenile delinquents and gangs. We got really excited and phoned Jerry [Jerome Robbins], and that started the whole thing."[5] Bernstein became really inspired by the Chicano gangs; later explaining that "while we were talking, we noticed the *L.A. Times* had a headline of gang fights breaking out. And this was in Los Angeles with Mexicans fighting so-called Americans. Arthur and I looked at one another and all I can say is that there are moments which are right for certain things and that moment seemed to have come."[6]

Laurents had suggested the idea of blacks and Puerto Ricans in New York "because this was the time of the appearance there of teenage gangs, and the problem of juvenile delinquency was very much in the news. It started to work."[7]

Although the team was clearly interested in juvenile delinquency, it is interesting to observe how the "domestic ethnic and racial others" interact and replace each other.[8] The writers moved comfortably from Jews and Italians, to Chicanos, to blacks, and finally to Puerto Ricans. They were simply searching for a confrontation between peoples of color and Caucasian Anglo-Americans. The assumptions of such a script reveal a priori the attitudes and prejudices against racial minori-

2.1 The Broadway production of *West Side Story.* (Vandamm Collection, Billy Rose Theatre Collection, The New York Public Library for the Performing Arts, Astor, Lenox, and Tilden Foundations.)

ties in the U.S. at different historical moments. These prejudices constitute a discourse of racism by framing the "racial other" in stereotypes of delinquency, poverty, and crime; it is, indeed, how Puerto Ricans were conceived and portrayed in *West Side Story,* which re-presents the new spatial paradigm, the *locus urbanus,* for people of color.[9]

Drawing the Line

The first scenes of *West Side Story* establish the dramatic conflict: two gangs fight for social spaces, public territories, and institutions (fig. 2.1). The first to appear are the Anglo-Americans, the absolute owners of the open spaces, that is, the streets and the basketball court. The original text specifies the ownership of the space by the Jets: "The action begins with the Jets in possession of the area: owning, enjoying, loving their 'home'" (137). The crisis surges from the fact that the Jets do not allow the settlement of the Sharks in their territory or home. As a result, the drama articulates a binary and hierarchical opposition of power relations, and this binarism establishes the dominant paradigms of the musical: Jets/Sharks; U.S./Puerto Rico; center/periphery; empire/colony; native/alien; identity/alterity; sameness/difference.

This polarity becomes further materialized iconically in the names of the gangs: Jets/Sharks. When the film starts, in the scene in which the Sharks are pursuing the Jets, on a wall in the background appears the drawing of a shark with its mouth wide open, exposing its sharp teeth. Such an iconic representation emphasizes the "criminal" and "barbaric" potential of all Puerto Ricans. Such Puerto Rican barbarism is confirmed when one of the Jets pronounces, "The Sharks bite hard ... and ... we must stop them now." Clearly, the bite has metonymic implications of cannibalism and of sharks' horrifying ferocity. For this reason, sharks are used as a metaphor to denominate the immigrant Latino otherness coming from the Caribbean. The opposition of Jets versus Sharks reproduces an ideological configuration that opposes cultural technology to nature, aerial military techniques to primitive and savage instincts, civilization to barbarity. In this context, the musical could also be read as an imperialist discourse in which the colonized are represented as a threat to the process and progress of the imperialist and civilizing enterprise.

In this first scene, the two gangs have contrasting physical and racial appearances. Most of the Anglo-Americans are blond, strong, dynamic, and healthy and so embody the ideologeme of the all-American boy. On the other hand, the Puerto Ricans are black-haired and skinny, with "greasy, tanned faces."[10] This first representation installs the perceiving spectator within ready-made stereotypical models of race and sociocultural behavior.[11] In the scene, the Puerto Ricans provoke the Anglo-Americans, and for such actions the Jets expel the Puerto Ricans from their territory. The rejection and exclusion of the "racial and cultural other" is made totally explicit with a graffito stating "Sharks stink." Later, this insult becomes monumentalized when the Jets associate the Puerto Ricans with cockroaches: when Anita, looking for Tony, enters the candy store, one of the Jets whistles the song "La Cucaracha."

After a rigorous examination of the opening scenes, one can detect that the Anglo-Americans generally establish command by speaking first and defining the Puerto Ricans in a pejorative way. Take, for example, a policeman's arrival at the basketball court in the first scene, and later at the candy store. In both scenes, the Puerto Ricans are ordered to leave; the policeman wants to talk only to the Jets. In this way, the immigrants' voices become silenced and marginalized. The policeman says, "Get your friends out of here, Bernardo, and stay out! ... Please! ... Boy, oh, boy. ... As if this neighborhood wasn't crummy enough." Indeed, the original text reads: "Boy, what you Puerto Ricans have done to this neighborhood. . . . All right, Bernardo, get your trash outa here" (138–39). Although the policeman's statement registers the abuse of power by an agent of power, his individualization as a character does not excuse him from participating in the blatant racism in the apparatus of power. He consciously favors the expulsion of the Latinos: "I gotta put up with them and so do you" (139); it is never a matter of acceptance or integration. The Jets also make use of a racist and discriminatory discourse in order to expel the Sharks: "We do own [the streets]. . . . We fought hard for this territory and it's ours . . . the PR's can move in right under our noses and take it away" (140–41). They propose to hang a sign forbidding trespassers; *they* are the ones who draw the line.

Between the two gangs erupts a hostile confrontation and warlike intensity because the Jets want to maintain their territory and sociopolitical order. The "other" threatens to snatch away their spaces and institutions (the gymnasium, the basketball court, the streets, and the candy store). The Jets are not willing to give up: "We fought hard for this turf, and we ain't just going to give it up. . . . These PR's are different. They keep on coming like cockroaches." Clearly, the Jets judge the Puerto Rican migration to the urban center as an invasion of cockroaches that reproduces without control and infects the territory. In order to exterminate them, the Jets prepare for a war: the rumble. These scenes conceive the Puerto Ricans only in their criminal and barbaric nature. The Jets skillfully transfer the concept of deadly weapons to the Puerto Ricans: "They might ask for blades, zip guns. . . . But if they say blades, I say blades. . . ." Those in power enunciate the discourse of the "other." By using such an ideological strategy of transference and transposition, the script, in the lines assigned to the Jets, accentuates and perpetuates stereotypes of Latinos/as, their ways of doing things, and the image of them as criminals. The Puerto Ricans are defined only in their criminal potentiality, as carrying weapons that the Jets will have to face and to match. Indeed, when the rumble takes place, the Puerto Ricans' disposition to fight (and to assassinate) is augmented by their arriving first at the location. In the scene in which Tony tries to make peace, Bernardo refuses reconciliation. This stereotype of Puerto Rican aggression and violence becomes further emphasized when the Sharks are the first to kill. In addition, it cannot be forgotten that, in the prelude to the song "América," one of the young women jokingly defines the Puerto Ricans as criminals: "You'll go back with handcuffs!" (165). In this manner, an assumed criminality of Puerto Ricans becomes stereotyped in the eyes of the Anglo-American audience.[12]

Somewhere Other than Here

The musical's dance scene in the gymnasium is vital for visualizing the divisive frontier line between the two gangs. In the original text, a stage direction states, "the line between the two groups is sharply defined by the colors they wear" (152). The two gangs are defined both by their dress code, which refers to cultural codes (particularly for the women), and by their styles of dancing. They are also defined by the color of their skin. It is in this dance scene that the action changes its course: the hatred between the gangs is open to the possibility of communication and living together, a possibility that arises from the physical attraction between Tony and Maria. Their relationship will become a story of love (albeit a doomed love), and it will predominate from then on as the principal plot of the dramatic text.

This first encounter between Maria and Tony is love at first sight. The camera captures them exchanging glances, and these glances erase ethnic and racial differences. Such an effacement is duplicated in the camera focus: the space (and gang members) surrounding Tony and Maria are blurred. This juxtaposition situates their love relationship in a utopian space: the newly fallen-in-love couple ignore and absent themselves from the immediate reality. From then on, Tony and Maria face a dilemma of trying to locate themselves in a historical, urban space that will permit and respect their interracial relationship.[13] Undoubtedly, Tony and Maria,—and the audience,—expect this relationship to result in marriage. Both of them are conscious of their ethnic and racial difference; as Maria says, "[Y]ou're not one of us . . . and I am not one of yours." Tony will express later, in the song "Somewhere," their search for such an ideal place and future time when they will be accepted for what they are: an interracial and interethnic couple.

An interracial marriage is possible only through erasing the historical present and creating a utopia (in the time of the movie).[14] Romantic melodrama is a strategy of power used to hide and soften the racist discourse. The narrative detour from warfare to love story functions as a camouflage. In these terms, the system of power disassociates itself from any consciousness of racial prejudice and discrimination. Indeed, Tony and Maria become the scapegoats of a racist discourse, because their relationship must end in tragedy. (Of course, if there's anybody to be blamed for this tragedy, it is Shakespeare, who wrote *Romeo and Juliet*, the model for *West Side Story*.) Although their utopian interracial marriage cannot take place, the apparatus of power does not take any responsibility for it. Instead, blame falls on the Puerto Ricans, because Chino assassinates Tony in revenge for Bernardo's death. Hence, Latino otherness functions within a chain reaction of provocation: the Puerto Ricans provoke the Jets by killing one of them, Tony responds by killing Bernardo, and the chain is closed when Chino kills Tony. With this final death, the happily-ever-after outcome for Maria (and the audience) is impossible. In addition, in this last scene, the apparatus of power exercises its authority and control by arresting Chino; prison is the only space available for criminal immigrants.[15] Thus, the chain reaction is, in fact, a circuit that begins and ends with the policeman as the representative of power.

In the final scene, the audience identifies with Maria, whose role is that of a mediator. The spectator disidentifies with Chino and, although viewers may feel some compassion, clearly only Chino bears the blame for the tragedy; it does not cross the viewer's mind that Tony is also a criminal. His crime is obscured by Maria's love when she sings the song "I Have a Love": it is a kind of love that is too strong to be rational. Ironically, although Tony has killed her brother, she cannot stop adoring him: "Te adoro, Anton" (224). In this scene, Maria evokes La Pietá while holding Tony's corpse in her arms. This image activates a Christian cultural repertoire that depends on melodrama for its lachrymose manipulation. It also articulates a series of connotations about women as submissive and suffering mothers, as mothers of sorrow and solitude.[16]

Given that Chino will be incarcerated and that Tony is dead, the film's ideological message implies the extermination of all Puerto Ricans and a desire for them to return to their place of origin.[17] Is there no possibility for a future Puerto Rican generation in the U.S.? The answer is provided by the text itself, when Maria sings that last song. Clearly she states that there is no place for her integration:

> Hold my hand and we're halfway there
> Hold my hand and I'll take you there
> Some day
> Somehow
> Some . . . (223)

Maria cannot mention a place for her future happiness; in this way her love remains suspended. She dreams about a utopia of love after life, because the "where" cannot be located either in her utopia, her present, or her place of origin. This "would-be world" does not exist in the text, and tragedy, instead of marriage, is the only possible closure. In the tragic finale, Maria remains on the threshold of "America." She is marginalized, hysterical, and hateful: "WE ALL KILLED HIM; and my brother and Riff, I, too. I CAN KILL NOW BECAUSE I HATE NOW"

(223). At the end, while holding Tony's corpse, she becomes delirious, wishing to join him in the utopian space of eternal love.[18]

There is no doubt that the space without sociohistorical contradictions for which Maria longs is beyond the grave. There she would meet with Romeo and Juliet, the literary prototypes of the bourgeois melodrama of impossible love. Such a transcendental and assumed universality in the ending erases all historicity. What it reproduces is a mythification whereby *West Side Story* perpetuates its aesthetic, literary, and apolitical values. Take, for example, the following comment from film critic Stanley Kauffmann: "*West Side Story* has been over-burdened with discussion about its comment on our society. It offers no such comment. As a sociological study, it is of no use: in fact, it is somewhat facile. What it does is to utilize certain conditions artistically—a vastly different process. Through much of the work, dance and song and cinematic skill fuse into a contemporary theatrical poem."[19]

The Politics of Race

There is no doubt that the song "America" and its choreography constitute one of the most rhythmic, energetic, and vital hits in the history of Broadway musical comedy.[20] Although it is a Puerto Rican who sings it, the patriotic message is delivered by an assimilated immigrant who despises her origin and autochthonous culture and prefers the comfort of the "American way of life." This song, with Spanish rhythm and a "typical Spanish" choreography, centers the audience in the exoticism and spontaneity of Latino otherness. Nevertheless, the lyrics make the audience concentrate on the patriotic message exposed in the political exchange between Anita and Bernardo. The song, performed by the Puerto Ricans on the roof of a building, (notice how they are confined to a building), pretends to be a Puerto Rican self-definition or enunciation. The song's confrontation of identities takes place when the Puerto Ricans consciously take sides on issues of nationalist politics and assimilation.[21] The importance of this scene does not derive simply from its comical aspect, but rather, from the fact that the Puerto Ricans insult each other for being divided politically and ideologically between the nationalists and the assimilated.

In the film version, this scene, which, in the original text is a racist and defamatory articulation toward Puerto Rico, was revised in order to soften the negative attitude toward Puerto Rico and Puerto Rican immigrants. Indeed, the song "America" in its two versions consolidates the political and ideological nucleus of the drama. While in the original version Anita proclaims openly her total assimilation and scorns her native land and its historicocultural reality, the cinematographic version makes use of irony when she sings "My heart's devotion." Immediately, the line is followed by a statement of contempt, "Let it sink back in the ocean."

Original Text:	Cinematographic Text:
Puerto Rico . . .	Puerto Rico . . .
You ugly island . . .	My heart's devotion . . .
Island of tropic diseases.	Let it sink back in the ocean.
Always the hurricanes blowing,	Always the hurricanes blowing,
Always the population growing . . .	Always the population growing,
And the money owing,	And money owing,
And the babies crying,	And the sunlight streaming,
and the bullets flying. (167)	And the natives steaming.

Anita enunciates Puerto Rican reality as an underdeveloped country with all kinds of natural disasters, socioeconomic and demographic problems, and crime. Although Bernardo discredits and demythifies Anita's exaltation of the American dream, his comments are subordinated and silenced by the patriotic pro-U.S. propaganda. Anita expels any dissidence against the American dream in "the land of opportunity": "If it's so nice at home, why don't you go back there / I know a boat you can get on" (167). Furthermore, Anita echoes the dominant ideology as she advocates total assimilation according to the example of other immigrant people in the past: "Ai! Here comes the whole commercial. The mother of Tony was born in Poland; the father still goes to night school. Tony was born in America, so that makes him an American. But us? Foreigners!" (165). In this way, the myth of immigration to the U.S. is actualized anew, and those who may not like it can leave the land of Uncle Sam. In such terms, the prejudices, discrimination, and racism that Latinos/as face in the U.S. are eliminated and silenced. What the song emphasizes and expresses is the economic prosperity and the instant material gratification of immigrants. Anita voices the dominant imperial ideology in the original text as she exalts the material consumerism and comfort in the U.S.: automobiles, chromium steel, wire-spoke wheels, knobs on the doors, and wall-to-wall floors are all signs of prosperity and industrialization in "America." Clearly, in this parodic inventory of U.S.—manufactured goods, Puerto Rico stands for the economy of an underdeveloped country.

In spite of Anita's assimilation, once she finds out that Bernardo is dead, she changes her attitude toward the Anglo-American system of power. Ironically, Anita, who is the most assimilated, ends up being the most ethnic by affirming her cultural difference. Such difference becomes so impregnated with hatred that she tells the Jets, without fear and in total challenge, that "Bernardo was right . . . If one of you was bleeding in the street, I'd walk by and spit on you" (219). From a position of pain and rage, Anita advises Maria to forget Tony: "Stick to your own kind!" (212). In this scene, now it is Anita who is advocating racial and ethnic segregation. Thus, the system of power does not need to acknowledge any responsibility or guilt for its racial discrimination. Instead, it posits that Puerto Ricans will always be Puerto Ricans, and in instances of crisis, no matter how assimilated they are, they will always side with their own people. The threat of racial otherness is concretized in Anita's self-conscious difference, and, by extension, the potential of rebellion and sociopolitical subversion.[22] Now that Anita opposes Maria's and Tony's interracial marriage, the system of power exempts itself from preventing such a marriage. In the end, it is the Puerto Ricans themselves who advocate getting married to members of the same race, ethnicity, and culture. This is how the hegemonic power pretends to give agency to the marginalized and disenfranchised.

The Practices of Racism

West Side Story has had international fame and success. I have demonstrated how the universal plot of a love story registers a racist discourse in its historical specificity. Even the critics elided the racist issue, concentrating on the urban problem of juvenile delinquency. The choreography was highly praised, and a critic even proclaimed the conservation of the film as a cultural monument, saying, "If a time-capsule is about to be buried anywhere, this film ought to be included, so that possible future generations can know how an artist of ours [Jerome Robbins, the choreographer], made our most congenial theatrical form respond to some of the beauty in our time and to the humanity in some of its ugliness."[23] This "ugliness" cannot be verbalized, because it would uncover the truth, that West Side Story is a discursive articulation of racial discrimination in the U.S. The fact that there is not a single black person acting in the film makes evident another element of its racism; the only black character that I have been able to detect stands in the background of the dance scene (a pseudo-mambo) in the gymnasium.

However, the racist discourse is not totally silenced in the textual surface. In one scene, the practice of racism flourishes when Anita enters the candy store. While stopping her, one of the Jets says openly, "She's too *dark* to pass" (217; emphasis added). Such a declaration confirms that the struggle for territorial supremacy is truly based on racial discrimination of a sort that is not always euphemistic. In this way, the text contains its own representation of racism, which it locates in several domains: adolescence, juvenile delinquency, agents of power, and even in the spectator's political point of view.

Another act of racism appears in the film version of the musical, when policeman Schrank kicks the Puerto Ricans out of the candy store and proposes a deal to get along in the neighborhood: "I get a promotion, and you Puerto Ricans get what you've been itching for . . . use of the playground, use of the gym, the streets, the candy store. So what if they do turn this whole town into a stinking pig sty? . . . What I mean is . . . Clear out, you! I said, Clear out! . . . Oh yeah, sure, I know. It's a free country and I ain't got no right. But I got a badge. What do you got? Things are tough all over. Beat it!" There is no doubt that Schrank has the power and the laws to protect the country from any threat, usurpation, disorder, or terrorist act. Although he rationalizes his abuse, Schrank is applying the national law that legitimates his abusive actions. From such a hegemonic, hierarchical, and racist position, the badge gives him power and legitimization. The badge is the emblem that endorses his own racism and discrimination toward the racial "others" whom he calls openly—and insolently—"Spics." He has the badge, a symbol of power, superiority, and official law; all that the Puerto Ricans have is their skin. The blanks must be filled in so that one can read explicitly the inscribed racism in the actions of the agent of power: "You got the [dark] skin." It cannot be clearer: the racist discourse does not disappear at all from the textual surface. Once you fill in the blanks, that discourse reappears and erupts, subverting the policeman as well as the institutions of legal justice—the maximum representatives of Anglo-American power and law—in their own practices of racism.

If the critics silenced the racist discourse inscribed in the movie and in the theatrical production, the creators also did not care to rectify the negative and pejorative image of Latino otherness.[24] Concerning a protest against the song "America" by "real" Puerto Ricans, two of the creators, Stephen Sondheim and Leonard Bernstein, said in an interview,

[We] got a letter complaining about the one line "Island of tropic diseases," outraged on behalf of Puerto Rico, claiming that we were making fun of Puerto Rico and being sarcastic about it. But I didn't change it.

Opening night in Washington we had a telephone message from *La Prensa* saying that they'd heard about this song and we would be picketed when we came to New York unless we omitted or changed the song. They made particular reference to "Island of tropic diseases," telling us everybody knows Puerto Rico is free of disease. And it wasn't just that line they objected to. We were insulting not only Puerto Rico but the Puerto Ricans and all immigrants. They didn't hear "Nobody knows in America / Puerto Rico's in America"—it's a little hard to hear at that tempo. We met that threat by doing nothing about it, not changing a syllable, and we were not picketed.[25]

Obviously, the system of power—ideologically institutionalized in Broadway's official theater—has the final word and authority to silence the inferior "other," to subdue and stereotype the subaltern. Such practices embody an imperialist and ethnocentric posture that makes evident the latent racism inscribed in the text. So, then, how could an immigrant minority that had just arrived be heard or even dare to protest against a song entitled "America" in the fascist McCarthy era? The song "America" had quite a patriotic and propagandistic message, although it was parodic and carnivalesque. Indeed, the song itself can be considered as a fleeting paradigm of "God Bless America," the "second national anthem" of the U.S. Nor should it be forgotten that the same patriotic message is activated in Neil Diamond's "America," which was used in the 1980s by Ronald Reagan's conservative and reactionary campaign to revitalize, propagate, and solidify the myth of immigration to "the land of opportunity." Perhaps it is not pure coincidence that in 1985 a nostalgic and operatic version of the original text of *West Side Story* was put into circulation.[26] Once again, in this version the song "America" promotes the immigrants' assimilation and propagates the myths of immigration to the U.S. And, once again, it achieves this by degrading those Puerto Ricans who are not willing to assimilate, and by demeaning their native land: "Puerto Rico . . . / You ugly island . . . / Island of tropic diseases."

The Reception of *West Side Story*

". . . the colonial child was made to see the world and where he stands in it as seen and defined by or reflected in the culture of the language of imposition."
—Ngugi wa Thiong'o, *Decolonising the Mind*

"*West Side Story*'s liberalism is so ingenious that the show is embarrassing to revive."
—Martin Gottfried, *Broadway Musicals*

I do not deny it at all: after decades of living in the U.S., my own personal experience as an ethnic minority has led me to question the U.S. cultural and political system. I, who upon my arrival was an assimilated "American" and more Anglo-American than many "Americans," became more Puerto Rican and more Latin American in the U.S. as the years passed. This process of disassimilation and decolonization informs this experiential and testimonial reading of *West Side Story*, an alternative, provocative, and ex-centric reading. I do not deny that this is an ideological and political reading, but so are those that pretend to be neutral, such as traditional scholarship in academia. My aim has been to question, to read from the margin, and to fill in the blanks with the "not-said" in order to decenter, subvert, and transgress *West Side Story*'s official ideological discourse. I have tried to demythify and rescue the racist ideology that was silenced, but registered, in the textual interstices. This racist discourse is clearly inscribed in institutions of power such as those in Hollywood and on Broadway, and in their official critical responses.

Finally, I rescue a quotation from Stephen Sondheim. When asked to collaborate on the musical, Sondheim used as an excuse for not getting involved that he had never met a single Puerto Rican, nor had he shared their socioeconomic disadvantages: "I can't do this show. . . . I've never been that poor and I've never even *known* a Puerto Rican!"[27]

Who are the Puerto Ricans in *West Side Story*? Are they simply literary products, ideological signs, and cultural discursive stereotypes of the Anglo-American sociopolitical system of power? Indeed, *West Side Story*'s cinematographic figurative construction has propagated the image of Puerto Ricans to the extent that it has become the a priori referent, the model of/for immigrant Puerto Rican ethnicity and identity. The reading becomes more complicated when Puerto Ricans themselves identify with this pseudoethnic film image produced by the U.S. cultural-imperial power. This identification reveals the colonial condition of Puerto Ricans. Once they are interpellated by the prefabricated Hollywood image—"made in the U.S.A."—of their ethnicity, they identify with the imperial object/image projected on the screen. This results in their appropriation of that image as their own, and acceptance of it as the enunciation of their own sociohistorical and cultural subjectivity. For example, in 1960, an article in the Puerto Rican newspaper *El Mundo*—"*West Side Story* Continues To Be a Triumph on Broadway"—praises the musical for the positive representation of Puerto Rican immigrants in New York City: "Although the Hispanic newspapers threatened to boycott and protest the show, *West Side Story* continued its run after the approval of the Puerto Rican Resident Commissioner in Congress, Dr. Antonio Fernós Isern. After seeing the show he declared that there was nothing in it that could be harmful or injurious to the Puerto Rican image. I would add that this production really shows understanding and affection towards our people."[28]

While migrant Puerto Ricans protested demeaning representations since the show's opening in 1957, Puerto Ricans on the island seemed to be ignorant of and distanced from the U.S. Puerto Rican experience. For example, Nilita Vientós Gastón, a prominent Puerto Rican intellectual and guardian of national culture and Spanish language, endorsed and exalted the human values inscribed in the production. In her 1961 review of the production in San Juan, she addressed the issue of violence, gangs, and juvenile delinquency, but, as she did so, universalized the social crisis in the musical as an urban condition in which individuals have lost all capacity to behave in a civilized way. Her reading, which is divorced from the Puerto Rican migrant community that experiences exploitation, marginality, and racism, did not consider how class and race articulate the ideological structure of the musical. Her political position was that the musical did not insult Puerto Ricans:

It has been said that the piece is an insult to Puerto Ricans. It is not the truth. The authors, Arthur Laurents and Stephen Sondheim, present a real and urgent problem and dramatize an actual situation. In the characterization of the two gangs, they do not favor one to put down the other. This opinion is supported by the song, "Puerto Rico, you ugly island . . . ," but, the circumstances in which these words are sung—with sarcasm, by a Puerto Rican woman who believes that she has already adapted to the U.S. to another woman who dreams about returning to Puerto Rico—and the context of the whole piece belies any evil intention [on the part of the authors]. I believe, on the contrary, that the Puerto Ricans are portrayed with sympathy.[29]

This interpretation reveals the lack of understanding of the racial site of Puerto Ricans in the Anglo-American cultural imaginary. Given that Vientós Gastón reads only the surface text—that is, the love story—she becomes captive to the romantic melodrama of the story. Vientós Gastón misses the racial discourse that inscribes racist and exclusionary practices against Puerto Ricans. To validate her political assertion, she proposes the following evidence to salvage the musical: Maria is a positive example of innocence, purity, and poetry, and the Puerto Ricans have a concept of family ties that the Anglo-Americans lack. Obviously Vientós Gastón identifies with the idealization of women's virginal status in patriarchy, and defines the structure of the family and Hispanic household as the core and haven of Puerto Rican culture. She dismisses the historical forces of change that altered the Puerto Rican family after migration, and the crisis of patriarchy that Puerto Rican men experienced. Indeed, the truth is that Maria betrays the father and loses her virginity, usurping in this way all kinds of traditional family values and beliefs.[30]

In the 1980s, with the staging of *Jerome Robbins's Broadway,* an anthology of dance scenes choreographed by Robbins, once again the musical number "America" from *West Side Story* was staged. The prominent Puerto Rican writer Luis Rafael Sánchez, as if interpellated by magic, fascinated by the spectacle, or hypnotized by the phenomenal dancing, went in search of the meaning of the dances. He seemed to be trapped in the cultural reflection that Broadway offered him as a mirror of Puerto Rican ethnicity and identity, saying that

"for fifteen or twenty minutes in the *West Side Story* scenes . . . you attend an empire of the senses which modifies and biographs Latinos, Hispanics . . . you attend the colossal uncovering of being and living of Latinos, of Hispanics. . . . It would be unnecessary to insist on the response of gratitude and satisfaction that the audience finds in Jerome Robbins' choreography. It is a kind of ontology of New York streets . . . and it is an open heart to the understanding of Latinos, of Hispanics. It is all understanding and respect."[31]

Both Puerto Rican and Anglo-American spectators ignore the discriminatory practices and racist implications of the techniques Robbins used in order to create and achieve the perfect rivalry and hatred the Sharks and the Jets. These practices contributed to the success of the theatrical and cinematographic productions and can easily be reactualized and reactivated in every single staging and screening, thus perpetuating the racism. "Jerry Robbins started West Side with a bunch of amateurs who had never played roles anywhere—just a bunch of kids who danced in shows," explained the producer, Harold Prince. "He would always call them in groups, 'You're the Jets,' and 'You're the Sharks.' He would put up articles about interracial street fighting all over the bulletin boards where he was rehearsing. He would encourage them not to eat lunch together, but to stay in [separate] groups."[32]

And, if those practices were not enough for the staging of the musical, the actress who played Maria had to dye her skin dark if she was "too white" to embody the Puerto Rican race. Such an action is the result of the Anglo-American sociocultural and political system, which conceptualizes all Puerto Ricans as a "Latin domestic ethnic and racial other" and stereotypes them as black. They did not have to darken Debbie Allen, a black actress who once played Anita, nor Rita Moreno in the film version. However, when Jossie de Guzmán, a light-skinned Puerto Rican, played the role of Maria in the 1980 production on Broadway, she had to be darkened. De Guzmán's first reaction to the darkening was, "Oh, my God, I *am* Puerto Rican—why do they have to darken my hair?" Yet later, "they darkened her pale skin too, and after a bit she liked that, wanting literally to 'get into the skin of Maria.'"[33]

This reaction reveals the complex dynamics of blackface and the politics of representation. Not all Puerto Ricans are black, but on the stage, in order to satisfy the horizon of expectations of Broadway audiences, some performers will or must engage in appropriating the "racial other" as stereotyped in the Anglo-American cultural imaginary. Within these racist practices, de Guzmán is forced to pass as an authentic Puerto Rican determined only by race: to be a Puerto Rican is to be a person of color. Such a performance of race and ethnicity, under these specific theatrical racist practices, reveals that in representing the "other," race is performative. Race is historically, politically, ideologically, and culturally constituted, produced and represented in given social formations, power relations, and discursive practices.

The reception of *West Side Story* is another story for U.S. Puerto Ricans, the so-called Nuyoricans. Particularly, it is women who have challenged the stereotype of Latina representations in the musical. For example, writer Nicholasa Mohr has deconstructed the stereotypes and demythified the ideological underpinning of Latina women, always represented as passive and virginal, or as spitfires and whores. She emphasizes the fact that women were totally nonexistent as positive role models and were silenced when she was growing up. Indeed, one of her primary goals in her writing praxis is to recover that legacy in her culture, and to contest the "Maria syndrome":

> Maria the virgin of María de Magdalena. The "Maria syndrome" had even been immortalized in that great American musical classic *West Side Story.* Beautiful music, exquisite dancing, the entire production conceived, arranged, choreographed and presented by successful white men, not one of them Hispanic. Here, we have María, the virgin, ready to sacrifice all, and the other side of the Latina, Anita, the "loose one" who sings "I want to be in America," meaning not in Puerto Rico, "that ain't America and it ain't good enough!" . . . Where were the rest of us? Where was my own mother and aunt? And all those valiant women who left Puerto Rico out of necessity, for the most part by themselves bringing small children to a cold and hostile city. They came with thousands of others, driven out by poverty, ill-equipped with little education and no knowledge of English. But they were determined to give their children a better life, and the hope of a future. This is where I had come from, and it was these women who became my heroes. When I looked for role models that symbolized strength, when I looked for subjects to paint and stories to write, I had only to look at my own. And my source was boundless, my folklore rich and the work to be done would consume an eternity."[34]

In sharp contrast to the native Puerto Ricans' reception of the musical, Mohr locates herself, her writing, and her Latina women's history within a political arena where migration, sexism, and racism constitute the fundamental coordinates of a history of marginalization and oppression.

In a similar vein, another U.S. Puerto Rican writer, Judith Ortiz Cofer, in her collection of essays, stories, and poems *The Latin Deli*, takes a political stand in relation to Maria in *West Side Story*. Her personal story, "The Myth of the Latin Woman: I Just Met a Girl Named María" narrates how Maria has haunted her all her life. Not even in Europe could she escape the stereotype, as "María had followed me to London, reminding me of a prime fact of my life: you can leave the Island, master the English language, and travel as far as you can, but if you are a Latina, especially one like me who so obviously belongs to Rita Moreno's gene pool, the Island travels with you."[35] Like Mohr, Ortiz Cofer uses the term "Latina" as an identity marker. In that way, she not only embraces other Latino ethnicities in the U.S., she also engages in the deconstruction of Latina stereotypes in Hollywood and in the media. Throughout her life, she has been harassed by people singing "Maria," "La Bamba," and "Don't Cry for Me, Argentina" to her after they discover her ethnic background. As she examines the Anglo-American sociocultural attitudes toward her, Ortiz Cofer arrives at the most problematic stereotypical construction: all Latinas work at domestic, waitress, and factory jobs. At this point, her testimonial reaches a political positioning that unveils Anglo-American practices of racism and classism. Having set the stage, Ortiz Cofer presents an incredible autobiographical experience: at her first public poetry reading, one of the guests assumed that she was one of the waitresses and asked her for a cup of coffee. She rationalizes the experience as an act of ignorance, not of cruelty. That scene would continue to remind her of what she needed to overcome to be taken seriously as a writer. Ortiz Cofer's anger at the incident gave fire to her reading, making it a powerful performance. As she read, she addressed her poetry to that woman who had made an unforgettable mistake. "That day," she says, "I read to that woman and her lowered eyes told me that she was embarrassed at her little faux pas, and when I willed her to look up at me, it was my victory, and she graciously allowed me to punish her with my full attention."[36] Ortiz Cofer transformed this incident into a source of empowerment, but, sadly, this occurrence attests to how Latinos/as constantly have to justify and prove who they are. As a result of discrimination and stereotyping of Latinas, Ortiz Cofer was forced to develop a politics of affinity with other Latinas. She now uses her writing as a medium to educate those who are prejudiced and to break away from dominant cultural representations, like that of Maria in *West Side Story*. "Every time I give a reading," she says, "I hope the stories I tell, the dreams and fears I examine in my work, can achieve some universal truth which will get my audience past the particulars of my skin color, my accent, or my clothes."[37]

As the years have passed, *West Side Story* has become a classic of Broadway musical theater. It is repeatedly staged in high school and college productions, and regional theater revivals. With each production, the stereotypical representation of Puerto Ricans is activated and circulated. Being such a powerful cultural and ideological artifact in the dominant Anglo-American imaginary, it is not easy to ignore. *West Side Story* is not merely a period piece; it is a theatrical work that continues to sustain the dominant ideology. These elements draw the territorial boundaries between peoples of color, the working class, and the white constituency of "America." Indeed, in an article in the *New York Times* in 1991, "Old Film Mirrors New Immigrant Life," we are told the film is used to educate the children of immigrants on the vicissitudes of migration and cultural survival, and to instruct them on the problems faced in the contemporary urban multicultural city.[38]

Undoubtedly, any time that *West Side Story* is recycled in its theatrical productions and screen showings, we could find ourselves once again questioning, deconstructing, and demythifying the dominant Anglo-American discursive representation of the "Latin domestic ethnic and racial other." Therefore, for a critical reading the following issues must be tackled: where do the Anglo-American practices of racism, registered in the cultural imaginary, start or end? In the conception of the piece? In the selection of the cast? In the rehearsals? In the theatrical productions? In the screenings of the film after translating the theatrical production into the cinematographic medium? Or in the reception of the audiences and the critics?

3

A Chorus Line
Not Such a "One, Singular Sensation" for U.S. Puerto Rican Crossovers

Whenever we think about mainstream representations of Latinos/as on Broadway, we see a flashing marquee reading *West Side Story*. Indeed, as shown in the previous chapter, Puerto Ricans became internationally famous because of the success of that theatrical production and its later film version. However, when we try to name other representations of Latinos/as on Broadway, either in Anglo-American works or in theatrical productions by Latinos/as themselves, there is a long, long silence. Whenever I ask in which plays or musicals have Latinos/as been represented on Broadway, the answer is the following: "Let me see . . . well . . . I really cannot think of any." And I hear over and over again: "Are there any other shows besides *West Side Story*?" It took even me by surprise to realize that there is another production that has taken the Puerto Ricans around the world. The show was *A Chorus Line*, the second longest running musical on Broadway history (1975 to 1990, surpassed by *Cats* in 1997), which had two Puerto Rican protagonists, Diana and Paul (fig. 3.1). But the story does not end there. Once I started my research, I found out that one of the authors of *A Chorus Line* was a Puerto Rican. Born Conrado Morales in Spanish Harlem, he renamed himself Nicholas (Nick) Dante.

3.1 The *Playbill* for *A Chorus Line*. (PLAYBILL® is a registered trademark of Playbill Incorporated, N.Y.C. All rights reserved. Used by permission.)

A Critical Approach

In this chapter, I aim to examine the politics of participation and representation of Latinos/as in *A Chorus Line*. Doing so, I will analyze how Puerto Ricans, both author and characters, are positioned in *A Chorus Line*. I have more questions than answers: Who was Nicholas Dante? Can I rescue him from oblivion and acknowledge his theatrical merits?[1] What are the practices of cultural and ethnic representation in the musical that permit the Puerto Rican identity and subjectivity to be articulated? What are the cultural politics and strategies that frame and anchor their inclusion in the musical? Do Dante and Priscilla López, a Puerto Rican who also collaborated on the musical, enunciate themselves in the characters of Paul and Diana, or do they simply become an enunciated objectivized "other" inscribed in a dominant cultural text as tokens? Are they plainly representing stereotypes according to the Anglo-American dominant models of the "Latin foreign other" and the "Latin domestic ethnic and racial other?" Given that subjectivity and identity formation are constructed and articulated in relation to race, class, ethnicity, gender, and sexuality in a given sociohistorical context, how is difference constructed and mediated in *A Chorus Line*? What does mainstreaming and crossing over mean in this musical for Dante, López, and their fictional/autobiographical characters? Does this musical open a space for a multicultural and multiracial representation that functions as an act of ideological contestation, transgression of identity categories, and development of agency that in one way or another subverts or resists stereotypical representations of Latinos/as in the Anglo-American cultural imaginary? And finally, how does Dante's character Paul intercept and intersect his Puerto Rican ethnicity with his gay sexuality, both of which mirror Dante's own reality as a Puerto Rican and a homosexual? Using these questions as a springboard, my goal in this chapter is to show how Puerto Rican participation, representation, and dramatic constituency was predominant and crucial in the making of the musical. I will not only examine Broadway's cultural practices of appropriating, commodifying, and commercializing minority experiences, but I will locate the musical as the first Latino crossover theatrical piece on the Great White Way.

I will focus on Dante's role in the writing process of the musical and the ways in which his "difference" is constituted and articulated in the musical. This same process applies to the character Diana, who was modeled after López, a dancer and actress who participated in the original planning of the musical and who acted in the original theatrical production.[2]

An Archeological Quest

Those who have seen *A Chorus Line* want to return and experience it over and over again. Over the years I must have seen it more than seven times; each time I would get more involved with the confessions and psychological struggles of the characters who were enduring the process of elimination while auditioning for a chorus line in a mythical Broadway show.[3] This backstage musical develops as the dancers reveal their identities, career backgrounds, and sexual orientations, and frankly voice their differences, histories, personal problems, and failures. These confessions are in response to the character Zach, the director of the future musical, who asks the dancers to say something about their lives and ambitions in order to unveil their personalities.

In the opening scene, there are some twenty-four candidates, of whom only seventeen will stay; of those, eight dancers—four men and four women—will finally be selected for the musical. All the dancers are unemployed, and the plot centers on the urgency to get a job. The musical opens with the number "I Hope I Get It," in which the aspiring dancers confess how needy they are, how desperate they are to get a job. The dancers' autobiographies become a collage of self-revelation, motivation, fear, anxiety, emotion, aspiration, and dreams that puts their bodies on the line. The audience sees the long, horizontal white line painted across the floor of the bare stage where the chorus line will stand. Indeed, the line has multiple meanings, such as the dancers returning to the unemployment line; their desire to cross the line of success and make it to stardom; their putting themselves on the line— at risk—as they narrate their insecurities; and the literal meaning of the all-American show stopper, the chorus line of a Broadway musical.[4]

How were all these testimonial materials put together? In 1974, Michael Bennett met with a group of dancers for more than twenty-four hours and recorded their interviews and stories. Later, the actual monologues and dialogues were transcribed from the taped sessions. At this initial stage, Priscilla López participated, and Nicholas Dante was the transcriber of the trials and tribulations of these Broadway gypsies. Dante also prepared dossiers, based on the workshop, for each potential *dramatis persona*, and polished the stories as well. It happened that Dante's own story was very dramatic and, as a powerful monologue, it became the heart and soul for the musical in progress. His confessional piece contained his life story as a timid Puerto Rican and a sexually molested child who ended up performing as a transvestite. The story materialized the compelling realism, dramatic impetus, and emotional appeal of the musical in its preliminary phase. This monologue was the only piece of the original script that remained almost intact in the final version of the show. It was so moving and breathtaking that Dante's soliloquy was to be dramatically recited instead of turning it into a song.

Although *A Chorus Line* was a team effort, Dante seems to have been the main writer in the original collaborative script. Dante, a dancer himself, really aspired to being a writer, and *A Chorus Line* offered him the opportunity to fulfill his writing aspirations. Little did he know, however, that he would later be upstaged by Michael Bennett, a known manipulator, and by the entrance of another playwright, James Kirkwood, who would later receive most of the credit for writing the book.[5] Kirkwood edited the script, quietly appropriated the authorial rights, and gained fame by being advertised as coauthor. Kirkwood's name eclipsed Dante's, and even appeared before Dante's in promotional materials: "Book by James Kirkwood and Nicholas Dante." In reference to this, Dante stated,

I worked on the show eight months before Jimmy came in. I wrote more than he did, but he got more credit and more money than I did. . . . I felt like the secret writer, which in a sense was my own fault. . . . I made the least amount of money of all the collaborators. In my ninth year I had reached the $1-million mark. All the others reached it a lot sooner than that. . . . I would go to my lawyer, and he'd talk to me in figures that scared me to death. I mean, please! I was born in Spanish Harlem![6]

It is clear that alphabetical ordering was not taken into account; Dante was simply considered a nobody in the theater business, and his contribution went overlooked.[7] He was also aware that he was at a disadvantage for not having completed a formal education, for having a working-class background, and for being a marginal Puerto Rican raised in el barrio:

I figured out later, he didn't even want me. *He wanted my story!* I kept saying to him I was into writing now. I mean, I was an aging dancer, thirty-two. I wasn't going to be a star or anything. I'd dabbled at writing early in my life, and had thought about becoming a writer. But later—after I'd quit high school—I'd put it aside because I felt you couldn't be a writer without an education. I pretty much stopped, became a drag queen and all that. Once in a while I'd scribble something.[8]

Years later, Dante discovered that Neil Simon had been asked to contribute lines, without Dante's approval.[9] The situation became worse when Michael Bennett himself took all honors for being the one who conceived, choreographed, and directed the show.[10]

Nevertheless, Dante always wanted to be a writer and he always considered *A Chorus Line* to be his main creation. He dared to denounce Bennett openly in the following bitter statement:

Look, I was part of the inner circle before they fucked me over and refused me credit for *Chorus Line*. So much of *Chorus Line* is mine, outright mine! Sure, with contributions from Michael and Bob Avian. Jimmy Kirkwood wound up with more than I did, more money, credit, everything! I was responsible for Paul's monologue. That's my story! I was that faggot, that drag queen discovered by his parents. It all happened to *me!* I came up with the conceptual idea of the montage, and it says—right there, in every program ever printed!—"Conceived by Michael Bennett!" My Idea! I was a dancer just like Michael, and of course he made me fall in love with him, got what he wanted out of me, then basically threw me out like so much garbage, the way he did with everybody except Bobby, who is, truly, a wonderful man."[11]

In another interview, Dante said, "Now, I think the whole show hangs on that monologue and I'm thrilled with it. I think now it paved the way for *Torch Song Trilogy* and other gay material that reached Broadway."[12]

Indeed, Dante defiantly challenged Bennett by demanding authorial recognition and ownership. Most important, in this passage, Dante positions himself as the founder of gay theater on Broadway. Although Mart Crowley's *The Boys in the Band* (1968) predates *A Chorus Line*, Dante discards this piece, which focused on neurotic, alcoholic, closeted gay men in perpetual crisis. Dante is conscious that his monologue goes further: it represents a site of/for a subjectivity in process that struggles in the construction and articulation of a gay identity. In this sense, Dante's monologue speaks about his own experience in a voice that is one of honesty and impeccable integrity. At work here is a politics of representation: *who* is speaking, and from *where* he is speaking are fundamental questions in the definition of gay theater. Furthermore, his effort to make his protagonist Paul credible, humane, and courageous in his act of coming out shows Dante's primary concern that gay people be represented in an authentic way, and that gay theater be a source of self-respect, empowerment, and pride. After such an indispensable contribution to gay theater, Dante sadly disappeared from the map.

So, whatever happened to Nicholas Dante, a crossover Puerto Rican who cowrote the international megahit *A Chorus Line*? When *A Chorus Line* opened in 1975, Dante declared "It's the first thing I ever wrote. . . . What you saw on stage is 90 per cent true. It's our life stories. I'm 33 and I've been dancing all my life. Now I hope I can be a writer."[13] What happened to Nicholas Dante, the aspiring playwright?

When I decided to do research on *A Chorus Line* and to contact Nick

Dante, it was too late: he had died of AIDS in 1991. Unfortunately, I found a list in a show-business magazine with his name listed among sixty-seven others from the entertainment industry who had died of AIDS that year: "Nicholas Dante, 49, died May 21, 1991. Dancer, Pulitzer and Tony winning playwright who co-wrote the book for *A Chorus Line.*"[14] Now that I had the date of his death, my next step was to find his obituary. The 22 May 1991 *New York Times* obituary contained the information necessary for tracing Dante's life, and for gaining access to his other works, particularly a screenplay entitled *Fake Lady,* based on Paul's story in *A Chorus Line.* Paul's monologue, according to Dante, was a truthful account of his own childhood and adolescence struggling with his homosexuality. I then assumed that *Fake Lady* must have elaborated extensively on Paul's sexuality, female impersonations, and ethnicity. The problem was where to find the script. I went to New York's Library for the Performing Arts at Lincoln Center, but they had no record of Dante's writings. I went to the Public Theater, and they told me that their archives were at Lincoln Center. Finally, they gave me some names of people who had been involved in the original production. When I called them, these people referred me back to the Public Theater. I felt frustrated, going in circles, when I realized that Nick Dante had evaporated from the theater world; sadly, his name was not even *recognized* by some of the people and institutions I contacted.

My last alternative was to return to the obituary and contact the surviving relatives. I was finally successful in reaching his niece, who referred me to his brother, who was in charge of Dante's estate. Surprised by a now-resurgent interest in Dante's writings, his brother mentioned that some people from California were interested in seeing them, and that even the Public Theater's Joseph Papp had wanted access to the scripts before he died. He referred me immediately to the lawyer in charge of Dante's estate. Of course, I made it clear that there was no money involved and that my intentions were to read *Fake Lady* in order to rescue Dante from total oblivion and to do a critical reading of his work. I tried to call the lawyer, but had no success. Sadly, I doubt that I will ever have access to Dante's writings, because, at this point, the issue is that Dante's scripts have become a commodity, and profit making will be the final word.

The Politics of Representation and Identity

A critical study of ethnic diversity and cultural difference in *A Chorus Line,* of course, cannot be limited to Latino/a representation in the work. Despite the fact that there are Asian American and African

American delegates, their participation is more for reasons of tokenism. Their characters do not develop and they are not essential to the
dramatic component and development of the action, as are the characters Diana and Paul. Nevertheless, these ethnic representations are a
gesture of inclusiveness that constitutes a multicultural and multiracial
effort; as one critic has observed, "A variety of ethnic groups is included in this chorus line—Chinese, Puerto Rican, Jewish, Black, Irish,
and what have you. They come in all heights, colors, and sexual per-
suasions. In a sense, the musical is about the diversity of America."[15]
Although the musical proposes to stage a diversified theater community, it cannot be forgotten that *A Chorus Line,* having sexuality as a
major theme, places at center stage three gay protagonists, Paul among
them. Given my interest in the politics of representation, I must examine (1) How Paul's sexual preference is represented; and (2) How that
sexual component intersects with his Latino ethnic self-representation
as he enunciates a subaltern gay and ethnic identity.

From the beginning of the show on, Diana and Paul stick together.
During the audition, they stand together at the far right end of the
chorus line. They have a special friendship, one in which Diana plays a
dominant role because Paul is shy and lacks self-confidence. At various
times she protects him, encourages him, and forces him to make decisions. Paul's insecurity is displayed in the opening scenes, when presenting his photo and résumé he sings:

> WHO AM I ANYWAY?
> AM I MY RESUME?
> THAT IS A PICTURE OF A PERSON I DON'T KNOW
> WHAT DOES HE WANT FROM ME?
> WHAT SHOULD I TRY TO BE? (22)

It is obvious that Paul has an identity crisis. Such a crisis will later
be understood fully when he delivers his soliloquy. In these opening
scenes, his true identity is suspended as he sings: "Secret, my whole
life was a secret." What could the secret be that he so diligently guards
but is so anxious to disclose, to share?

When Paul is called to introduce himself, he states, "Paul San Marco.
It's my stage name. My real name is Ephrain Ramirez. I was born
in Spanish Harlem—October 22, 1947" (28). His identity crisis is accentuated by denial of his Puerto Rican roots and by his adoption of an
Italian stage name. Later, the director, Zach, is curious to know why
he went from Puerto Rican to Italian. At this point, we cannot forget
that Dante himself changed his name from Spanish to Italian, from
Conrado Morales to Nick Dante:

Zach: For one thing, if you're going to change your name—why go from a Puerto Rican name to an Italian one?

Paul: 'Cause I don't look it . . . People say, "You don't look Puerto Rican, you don't look Puerto Rican." But I am.

Zach: So you figured you look Italian?

Paul: No, I, ah—just wanted to be somebody new, so I became Paul San Marco. (98)

Paul explains that he wants to be someone new because he is not proud of himself. This scene also prepares the audience for Paul's monologue, which will reveal his low self-esteem and lack of confidence. For the time being, his only secret is his passing as an Italian; he is ashamed to be a Puerto Rican. Paul believes that he can pass because he does not look like a Puerto Rican. Here, Puerto Rican identity is defined by race—a visible marker—and not by ethnicity. In these terms, by "passing," Paul pretends to leave behind his subaltern status and the marginalization that "Puerto Ricanness" implies in the U.S. Most important, it shows how the Anglo-American hegemonic worldview has racialized Puerto Ricans as it discloses the racism inscribed in such a comment as "You don't look like one of them." That Paul "does not look like" a Puerto Rican is a racist utterance that validates internalized racism. Race is the only factor that determines his inclusion and participation in the Anglo-American world in which whiteness is invisible. Paul's passing occurs at different levels: first of all, Paul has crossed "racial" boundaries; second, he has crossed class boundaries; and third, he has crossed over to a hegemonic space—Broadway—in which Puerto Ricans are not expected to be. His body is not marked by color, and thus his acceptance and integration in a white world is feasible because his epidermal difference has been erased. Given that Paul is a second-generation Puerto Rican (as is Diana), his accent does not attest to his foreign otherness, but there is a speech difference—his barrio dialect, which marks a priori his class origin.

In contrast to Paul, who has an identity crisis and becomes an impostor for trying to pass as Italian, Diana has a strong personality and is not afraid to verbalize her ethnicity: "My name Is Diana Morales. And I didn't change it 'cause I figured ethnic was in" (28). Diana accentuates her difference; for her, being Puerto Rican is an ethnic marker that could be read as a racial marker, given the olive color of her skin. The use of Morales, Nick Dante's real last name, demonstrates how proud Diana is of her own ethnic roots as opposed to Paul, or Dante himself. If Paul has tried to move from the margin to the center, Diana has flaunted her ethnicity, projecting a sense of authenticity. When it comes to her ethnicity, Diana has learned how to laugh at herself and the system. Later, she will joke that she cannot feel the bobsleds in an acting class because of her Puerto Rican origin: "But I said to myself: 'Hey!, it's only the first week. Maybe it's genetic. They don't have bobsleds in San Juan'" (65). In this sense, she is conscious of how mainstream culture objectifies her and how she is represented as an exotic "other." In the film version of *A Chorus Line*, there is a scene in which Paul makes a move to walk away from the audition, after the director threateningly suggests that anybody who cannot handle the tough questions should leave. Diana says to Paul, "Quédate. Somos puertorriqueños. Según ellos nos avergonzamos de todo. Screw them. Stay. We are Puerto Ricans. They think that we are ashamed of everything." From a similar self-consciousness of her ethnic origin, when the director asks her what made her start dancing, she answers jokingly and ironically, "Who knows? I have rhythm—I'm Puerto Rican. I always jumped around and danced" (29). Diana is always standing in quicksand, in a constant balancing act as she deconstructs dominant stereotypes of Latinos/as, dismantles whatever prejudices are at work, and, at the same time, affirms her ethnicity with ironic pride. She employs the same ironic tone when she delivers her song, "Nothing."

"Nothing" was based on Priscilla López's story about a teacher at New York's High School for the Performing Arts who had given her a difficult time through his approach to, and method for, acting; composer Marvin Hamlisch and lyricist Edward Kleban wrote the song based on López's acting-class experience. Through this "cultural appropriation," López's self-enunciation, which is clear in the original taped sessions, becomes a ventriloquized mediation through the character Diana. Her experience is translated and filtered in the song that enunciates her as an "other," while her character Diana pseudoenunciates herself as a speaking subject/object. In spite of this mediation, Diana still projects a strong sense of self-representation as a speaking subject, and is not simply embodied as an object representing the "Latin domestic ethnic and racial other."

In the teacher's acting techniques, Diana finds only nonsense. When he asks her to improvise and to feel the motion, the wind, and the chill, she is incapable of feeling anything. All she knows is that the acting instructions—"this bullshit"—is absurd. She stays in class until she prays to Santa María, who tells her to quit because the teacher and his acting methodology are lousy and irrelevant. The Virgin's advice is for her to quit the course, to find a better class with a better instructor. While Diana is funny in her criticism, she is also very political: her questioning of her teacher's esoteric techniques subverts Broadway's dominant ways of approaching theater and acting. She denounces both her professor's discouraging advice to transfer, and the lack of support from her classmates. Diana's decision to drop out is an act of rebellion that is validated by the Virgin Mary's intercession. Diana reverts to her Latino, Catholic religion in order to transgress and subvert her professor's acting approach and authority. The final irony is her revenge; when she hears that he has died, she feels nothing.

At first sight, Diana could be considered a stereotypical Puerto Rican dropout, but the truth is that she is very courageous and dares to question the system. Maybe, because of such self-confidence, she perseveres in life until she succeeds. For such determination and self-awareness, she will be selected to be in the chorus line at the final call. Unfortunately, Paul's outcome will be the opposite. Because of his fragile personality and a knee injury, Paul will never cross over, will never make it.

The most moving scene in the musical is Paul's life confession.[16] With the other dancers on break, Paul is onstage alone to talk with the director about what he had been reluctant to discuss when the others were around. He tells of his poor upbringing in Spanish Harlem, his troubles in school, his child abuse, his effeminate manners, and his homosexuality. He has dropped out of school after being advised to do so when he openly proclaimed his homosexuality. With his lack of education and self-assurance, Paul has been able to find a steady job only as a dancer with *The Jewel Box Revue*, a drag show. Although he has tried to prevent his parents from discovering his demeaning and humiliating job, they visit him backstage to bring him his luggage before he leaves on a road show. They recognize him in drag and his heart sinks. Yet, as they part later, Paul's father tells the producer, "Take care of my son" (103), never having called him "son" before. Paul has finally been acknowledged and respected by his family. He breaks down in tears; so does the audience.

There is almost no sign of Paul's ethnic identity in this monologue, given that he has constructed his identity primarily on his sexuality— he is gay. On the only occasion in which he refers to Puerto Rican culture, Paul divorces himself from his heritage and his family. When Zach asks him if his parents supported his dancing career, Paul's response immediately disassociates him from home and national roots. "What do Puerto Ricans know about theatre"? he says. "Now they have Channel Forty-Seven—but then they didn't have anything" (99). In this statement, Paul disconnects himself completely from his Hispanic background. After growing up in el barrio, Paul assumes that being poor entails a poverty of culture. His devalued and demeaning perception of Puerto Rican culture clearly materializes his degree of assimilation, his inferiority complex, and his shame of being Puerto Rican.

In his reference to Channel 47, a Spanish-language channel in New York City, Paul once again distances himself from his parents' language and their background. Paul incarnates a new generation whose first language is English, a generation that sees assimilation as the only choice for survival. Such an erasure of ethnicity puts at the forefront the extent of Paul's immersion in the Anglo-American world. Indeed, his idol is Cyd Charisse, and as a boy, he fantasized about impersonating her in a musical.[17] In this sense, Paul appropriates and internalizes white, Anglo-American dominant representations of femininity. Paul's functioning within the Anglo-American cultural imaginary, and passing as a light-skinned Italian, show how race and ethnicity are not the primary markers of his identity.

For Paul, the crucial difference is his sexual orientation. His real problem in life has been how to deal with homophobia in school and at home. Paul's identification and emulation of Cyd Charisse locates him in the domain of transvestism and exposes his degree of "femininity." Growing up in a homophobic environment, Paul has been the victim of hatred and intolerance; his own body language has made him the target of ridicule and harassment. "I was such a sissy. I mean, I was terribly effeminate," he tells Zach and the audience (100). Other boys have tortured him and made fun of him in school: "I wouldn't raise my hand because I would be afraid they would laugh at me. They'd even whistled at me in the halls" (100). His self-consciousness about being a "sissy" and his inability to "act like a man" have led him to question gender roles. Having been called a "faggot," he has a low self-esteem and cannot fit into gender categories: "I always knew I was gay, but that didn't bother me. What bothered me was that I didn't know how to be a boy" (100). He wants to be who he is, but is constantly reminded to comply with heterosexual gender attributes and behavior. His failure to act macho makes him realize that being a man is not performing machismo. "I couldn't take it anymore," he explains. "See, when I quit school, what I was doing was trying to find out who I was and how to be a man. You know, there are a lot of people in this world who don't know how to be men. And since then, I found out that I am one. I was looking for the wrong thing. I was trying to learn how to be butch" (100).

In his rejection of machismo, which required a butch impersonation, Paul defines himself within a new model of gay identity. Indeed, his awareness of his gayness, which he situates around 1962, anticipates the gay movement, gay pride, and a gay identity formation before

Stonewall, before "gay liberation." Paul not only verbalizes his gay pride, but also longs for a gay community. Given that the Village was not the official "mecca" of gay life until 1969, his only choice was to hang around with "strangers" on Seventy-second Street. Paul's painful childhood and adolescence, his willingness to condemn homophobia, his consciousness of homosexual difference, and his articulation of a gay identity are the factors that make the compassionate, tolerant, and liberal members of the audience see him as a young man with respect and dignity. Paul becomes a human being in search of the acceptance of his difference and of a community. What started as a demeaning childhood ends up in a courageous and heroic confession by a sensitive gay man. While his ethnicity is invisible in the beginning of the musical, his sexuality is always visually inscribed on his body. His gayness, a marker of difference, makes it impossible for him to pass as a macho man, Puerto Rican or Anglo. The audience will remember most his gayness and cross-dressing experience because these have upstaged his ethnicity.

Although Paul is no longer willing to impersonate machismo, he is inclined to impersonate "femininity." His act of transvestism goes hand in hand with his love for performance, as he claims "I was always being Cyd Charisse . . . Always. Which I don't really understand because I always wanted to be an actor. I mean, I really wanted to perform" (99–100). If being butch repressed him and marginalized him, female impersonation liberates him. The lesson that we learn from Paul is that gender is a sociocultural construction, and performative; it is not the embodiment of an essentialist or biological nature. As Judith Butler has theorized,

Gender reality is performative which means, quite simply, that it is real only to the extent that it is performed. . . . If gender attributes, however, are not expressive but performative, then these attributes effectively constitute the identity they are said to express or reveal. The distinction between expression and performativeness is quite crucial, for if gender attributes and acts, the various ways in which a body shows or produces its cultural signification, are performative, then there is no preexisting identity by which an act or attribute might be measured. . . .

. . . gender cannot be understood as a *role* which either expresses or disguises an interior "self," whether that "self" is conceived as sexed or not. As performance which is performative, gender is an "act," broadly construed, which constructs the social fiction of its own psychological interiority.[18]

Paul's desire to perform, as well as his lack of a high school diploma, has forced him to apply for the job with the *Jewel Box Revue.* His expectation was to be one of the male (boy) dancers, but he has only been offered a job as a pony, a girl. All of a sudden, after pretending for so many years that he was Cyd Charisse, Paul has been given the opportunity to be in a performance, yet his first reaction is not a positive one; he evaluates the whole situation as a "freaky" experience. It is important to note here that Paul considers himself to be a "pretender." Again, he places himself in the domain of imposture. If before he was passing as an Italian, now he is passing as a woman. Paul's whole life search for an identity has been a continuous performance in which gender and ethnicity are acts of disguise or transvestism.

Soon Paul realizes that life in the drag world is not a bed of roses. He perceives how demeaning it is, saying, "Nobody at the *Jewel Box* had any dignity and most of them were ashamed of themselves and considered themselves freaks. I don't know, I think that it was the lack of dignity that got to me . . ." (102). It is precisely that "dignity" that saves Paul from succumbing; indeed, his dignity crystallizes his gay pride. Paul has engaged and prepared the audience for the climax of his story.

About to go on tour to Chicago, Paul has asked his parents to bring him his suitcase. They have arrived early, and Paul is still in drag. This time he has been impersonating a Chinese woman, passing as Anna May Wong. He has hoped that he would not be recognized by his parents, but the opposite has happened; nevertheless, the show must go on. This final passing has not been successful for Paul. Underneath all the makeup, Paul cannot hide. No matter how hard he has tried to pass ethnically, racially, and in gender, he has found himself essentially naked in front of his parents. It is this nakedness that redeems Paul: underneath all his appearances, masquerades, and impostures is a true self. Paul emerges at the end of the monologue as a human being who does not have to pretend to be what he is not; the monologue has authenticated his true self. The final approval comes from his father, who calls him "son" for the first time. Paul, with pride and dignity, has become a man.

Yet it must be noted that Paul delivers his confession by making use of melodrama. Through the emotional manipulation of melodrama, his story is totally ahistoricized, producing the effect of transcendence and universality. This locates Paul and the audience in an ideal, emotive, imaginary realm in which social reality lacks the historical contradictions of given relations of power.

Once Paul finishes his monologue, it no longer matters that Paul is a Puerto Rican dropout and a drag queen. His acts of simulation and passing have been justified for the audience. His female impersonation and his denial of "Puerto Ricanness" are seen as his struggle to belong. If there is anyone to blame for his failures and insecurities, it is a homophobic society that does not accept his sexuality and is not willing to understand his difference and questioning of masculinity and gender roles. In addition, Paul's failure to finish school can be attributed to an indifferent school system that did not try to retain and nurture him, one in which the school psychologist simply said; "I think you're very well-adjusted for your age and I think you should quit school" (100). This reminds one of the bad advice and lack of interest that minority students coming from low-income sectors face, and of the problems that gay students who come out at school face. In this sense, issues of gender, class, race, and sexuality inform Paul's identity, constituting a new politics of representation.

Paul's character in *A Chorus Line* clearly registers what Stuart Hall has stated about a new politics of minority (black) representation. For Hall, categories of gender and sexuality are made problematic when it is no longer assumed that these categories are the same, that they remain fixed and secured. "What the new politics of representation does is to put that into question, crossing the questions of racism irrevocably with questions of sexuality . . . ," Hall explains. "This double fracturing entails a different kind of politics because, as we know, black radical politics has frequently been stabilized around particular conceptions of black masculinity, which are only now being put into question by black women and black gay men. At certain points, black politics has also been underpinned by a deep absence or more typically an evasive silence with reference to class."[19]

Paul's ultimate secret, which articulates his politics of representation, is his cross-dressing act. The secret of his female impersonation is revealed only to Zach and the audience. In his sad story, Paul unveils his secret, making his gayness visible. Although passing as a woman is an act of imposture, the audience now identifies with his sincerity and honesty. By confessing publicly, Paul authenticates his gay identity. He dares to come out in the most melodramatic fashion. Passing as an Italian meant the erasure of race; in contrast, passing as a woman is an act of courage and survival.

Indeed, Paul's story is so credible that he does not have to be in drag to tell it. At this moment, cross-dressing is made visible through language alone. Paul's sexual preference is not challenged by Zach, who has questioned his ethnicity. This time, Paul's gayness is taken for granted. Without a doubt, Paul's gayness is inscribed on the body of the actor Sammy Williams, who originated the role: his thinness, softness, and effeminate gestures were all signs that stereotypically confirmed his homosexuality.

Although Paul has challenged and surpassed the stereotype that all Puerto Ricans are black, here he perpetuates the stereotype that all gays are sissy and nelly. This perpetuation is made possible through the use of Williams's body as a "gay representation," or prop; this representation depends on the intersection of dramatic text and performance text. In the theatrical production, Williams's body must be read as a semiotic performance. The audience's emotional identification with Paul forgives all acts of imposture and assumed identities: they understand that Paul is passing to survive. The boy that did not fit in anywhere finds his place in the act of performing the story of his life and his marginality. Furthermore, by hearing his confession, the audience experiences both the power of the confessor and the power of catharsis. The whole production becomes a psychological rite of passage through which Paul is redeemed and the audience exercises a degree of cathartic pleasure, pleasure that derives from identification and the power relation of redeemer to redeemed.

Paul was able to pass the color line and the gender boundaries; will he now pass as one of the eight dancers selected for the chorus line? No—Paul fails to pass. Call it poetic justice, deus ex machina, or penance, but Paul has to pay the price for his desire to cross over. After hurting his knee, he is disqualified and must go back to where he came from, a place where identities are impostures, a place where the desire to belong is a continuous process of contradiction, ambiguity, ambivalence, liminality, and transformation. Ironically, Paul's theatrical performance derives its power from his unsuccessful attempt to attain an identity that is monolithic and stable. In this sense, the musical displays Paul's subjectivity in process, in which identity is protean rather than fixed and unitary. Paul destabilizes essentialist notions of racial, class, ethnic, and gender identities. He emblematizes the postmodern dictum: we are all transvestites at one time or another, somewhere, somehow. It is through social performances that we construct and articulate our passing identities. As transvestites, we all undergo a "category crisis" in which identities are determined by our subjectivity in process within specific historical junctures.[20] By impersonating class, race, ethnicity, and gender in given power relations, we explore, experience, experiment, put on the line—in short, we simulate and perform who we are. If identity is a simulacrum, then, who is more authentic in *A Chorus Line*, Paul or Diana?

If the character Paul had been centered exclusively on issues of ethnicity and race, the role would not have been played by an Anglo-American actor such as Sammy Williams, who won a Tony Award for his performance. This pseudoethnic impersonation (an Anglo playing a Latino) exposes the mechanisms of representing the "other" on Broadway: "we can play you, but you can't play us." Of course, which is easier to play within the hegemonic system of ethnocultural representations: a Puerto Rican, a gay Puerto Rican, or a Puerto Rican who has silenced his ethnicity and race to be *only* gay? Is it that easy to erase ethnicity, when the dominant Anglo-American cultural imaginary has only stereotypical constructions of Latino otherness? Frank Rich, the former *New York Times* theater critic, makes explicit that that ethnicity, although not always apparent, is always an issue with Paul. Reviewing the show on its record-breaking 3,389th performance in 1983, with ten Pauls onstage, Rich observed, "There was also Sammy Williams, who originated the role of Paul, the Puerto Rican homosexual. As staged by Mr. Bennett, his confessional monologue became a group recitation—with 10 Pauls forming a phalanx of lost men, like the sharks in *West Side Story,* all sharing their unhappy youthful memories with one another in a tableaux of minority solidarity and mutual support."[21]

Frank Rich cannot distance himself from Anglo-American cultural models of Latinos/as and negative stereotypes once he sees a Puerto Rican onstage. For him, *West Side Story* is the beginning and the end of Latino representation. Once there is more than one Latino, all he can see is a gang of "lost men." The irony is that Paul's gang is composed of gay men, in contrast to the macho roles in the gangs of *West Side Story.*

So, how can U.S. Latinos/as cross over, when dominant cultural stereotypes and prejudices always end up reminding them of their limitations and inferiority? If there was a successful, though difficult, crossover in *A Chorus Line,* it was that of the character Diana. Paul wanted to cross over, worked very hard for it, but never succeeded. Given that much of Dante's life seemed to model Paul's, did Nicholas Dante cross over as a playwright even after being the first Latino to receive the Pulitzer Prize for drama and a Tony for best musical book in 1976? Dante's only option, after numerous rejections, was to give up his dream of becoming a writer and to go back to the theater to play the role of Paul onstage in a touring company. Dante, like Paul, never totally crossed over; nor did Dante's play *Fake Lady.* Dante's ultimate act of impersonation, *Fake Lady,* based on Paul's monologue and Dante's life, was never to become "one singular sensation."

INTERMISSION

4

An Octopus with Many Legs
U.S. Latino Theater and Its Diversity

While attending the Festival Latino of New Plays in San Francisco in August 1993, Ruby Nelda Pérez, well-known Chicana performer, described U.S. Latino theater to me as "an octopus with many legs." Why did she choose the image of an octopus? It is based, obviously, on the comparison of the mollusk's tentacles to the many forms, many "arms" of U.S. Latino theater. Yet Pérez's depiction demands further examination, and this monstrous image invites us to exercise an allegorical reading of Latino theater. For me, the body of this cultural form is a heterogeneous and plural one, comprised of a host of playhouses, playwrights, performances, genres, styles, and histories. Each of these "arms" claims a multiplicity of ethnicities, politics, ideologies, degrees of assimilation, ways of approaching theater, artistic and aesthetic values, audiences, and resistance to and negotiations with the Anglo-American world. Its racial constituency and complexion are made of many colors: Caucasian, African, Native American, Asian, mestizo, and mulatto. Its eyes reflect and refract an assemblage, conflation, and juxtaposition of ways of seeing. The large distinct head of the body of U.S. Latino theater is "Hispanic" culture. Its mouth speaks English, "Spanglish," and Spanish. Which language is used at any given time depends on the specific historical moment of Latino/a migration to the U.S. (as for Chicanos/as, they were always here); the length of time lived in the U.S.; the linguistic and cultural resistance of immigrants to assimilation; the social construction of reality of a second generation conditioned by the experience of bilingualism and biculturalism; the levels of nonformal and formal education; and last, but perhaps most significant, the endorsement and internalization of an English-only, Anglo-American identity by some U.S. Latinos/as.[1] While many of the U.S. Latino plays in the 1980s and 1990s are in English, their content is, above all, bicultural.

Language, after class and economic status, is one of the most critical and controversial components of Latino theater. Language creates boundaries among Latinos/as, as well as between Latinos/as and the dominant Anglo-American culture. The Anglo mainstream assumes that all Latino theater is in Spanish, or that it is from Latin America and needs to be translated, or that it is too bilingual and specifically ethnic to be relevant to Anglo-American audiences. There is little awareness that, although first-generation exiled Cubans write in Spanish (and thus belong to the Cuban canon-in-exile), Chicanos/as, Cuban Americans, and U.S. Puerto Ricans/Nuyoricans write English or bilingual pieces, thus making difficult their inclusion in the official theater canons of Mexico, Cuba and exilic Cuba, Puerto Rico, and even the U.S. It must be understood that U.S. Latino theater emerges as a result of particular geographic (rural or urban), political, historical, and class experiences of individual ethnic groups in this country. Furthermore, it is the nationalistic exclusion of U.S. Latino theater from the Latin American canon (primarily because of the Spanish-only dictum in Latin American countries of origin) that reveals underlying issues of differences in given ideologies, dramatic structures and conventions, characterizations, and aesthetics. As long as there is a place for Cuban exiles and Puerto Rican immigrants in the theatrical canon of their home countries, their theater is *not* U.S. Latino theater; it is Cuban, Puerto Rican, Latin American, or Hispanic American. Critic Eliana Rivero has astutely addressed this issue, explaining that "[f]or some [Hispanic immigrants] . . . a link with the native country and its literature can be maintained if return to the homeland, however short or temporary, is possible. . . . They, as a rule, consider themselves as Latin American 'emigre' [sic] or transplanted writers and have a niche in their own national literatures, whether these are written inside or outside the homeland."[2]

The marginalization of U.S. Latino theater within Latin American theater canons, and its classification within the U.S. as "minority" and "ethnic" inform the ways in which it is located in an interstitial and liminal space. This is a double marginalization and exclusion. By not having an official residence, Latino theater registers its difference, one that eludes the possibility of facile classification and definition. In these terms, it gets lost offstage, overshadowed by the importation of Latin American theatrical pieces in translation—for instance, *Death and the Maiden*. In a similar way, mainstream Anglo-American adaptations of Latin American theatrical or literary pieces (i.e., *Juan Darién, Kiss of the Spider Woman: The Musical,* and *The Chronicle of a Death Foretold*) take center stage and evict U.S. Latino theater.

Through all of this, these many labels and misperceptions add to the confusion of defining this country's Latino theater. This anxiety of categorization not only affects the cultural form itself, but also calls into question the meaning of "American."

U.S. Latino Theater: A Panoramic View from Coast to Coast

If the raza will not come to the theatre, then the theatre must go to the raza.
—Luis Valdez, *Early Works*

U.S. Latino theater is not centralized, as Broadway theater is: its branches are independent, diverse, and dispersed according to the historical and sociopolitical experiences of Latinos/as in the U.S.—usually limited to Chicanos/Mexican Americans, Cuban exiles/Cuban Americans, and U.S. Puerto Ricans/Nuyoricans. Although theatrical productions of Latinos/as can be recovered from an earlier past, I locate the emergence of U.S. Latino theater in the 1960s as the foundational moment of the formation of a U.S. Latino/a ethnic identity.[3] It was specifically in that decade that the presence and visibility of Latino theater began, with the political activism of Chicano/a farmworkers leading to the institutional establishment, in 1965, of Teatro Campesino in California.[4] Teatro Campesino's main paradigm for reaching and attracting community audiences was the creation of the *Actos*. These one-act interlingual performances, created collectively, had well-defined political platforms: "Actos: inspire the audience to social action. Illuminate specific points about social problems. Satirize the opposition. Show or hint at a solution. Express what people are feeling."[5] Among the Actos, *Los Vendidos/The Sell-Out* is the most representative of this art form.

On the East Coast, as a result of an emerging ethnic and racial consciousness instigated by the 1960s civil rights movement and the *lucha* (struggle) against exploitation, racism, and marginalization of people of color, a theater emerged among Nuyoricans that was designed to foment ethnic pride and denounce imperialist oppression. At the same time, Cuban exiles started to produce their own theater (in Spanish) in Florida and New York. "These Cuban theatrical productions were mainly shaped by—and sometimes took their names from—previous popular and bourgeois theatrical models such as *teatro bufo* (a nineteenth-century Cuban minstrel theater form) and Eurocentric ways of approaching theater such as the theater of the vanguard and the theater of the absurd. For Chicanos/as and Nuyoricans there was a trajectory from street, improvisational, and agitprop theater to community-based theater. In sharp contrast to Cuban theater, Chicano/a and Nuyorican theater appropriated Latin American ways of presenting political theater, especially techniques used by *teatro popular; teatro de protesta;* Augusto Boal's theater of the oppressed; and collective creations popularized by *nuevo teatro;* and Brechtian models, in order to mobilize and raise consciousness among working-class audiences in urban barrios and migrant communities in rural areas.

Chicano theater, conceived and delivered as a collective effort on the West Coast and in the Southwest, primarily advocated social change and the fighting of injustice—like Teatro de la Esperanza, which originated in Santa Barbara and moved to San Francisco; Teatro Libertad and Teatro del Sol in Tucson; Teatro del Valle in Phoenix; Su Teatro in Denver; Teatro Guadalupe in San Antonio; and the Border Arts Workshop in San Diego. As for other forms of U.S. Latino theater, a brief inventory reveals how the geopolitical locations of Latinos/as in the U.S. emerged hand in hand with theatrical models, manifestations, and agendas: examples include the Bilingual Foundation of the Arts Theater in Los Angeles; Teatro Avante in Miami; Teatro Bilingue in Houston; and INTAR, Teatro Repertorio Español, Teatro Duo, Thalia, Teatro El Portón, Nuyorican Poet's Café, Teatro Pregones, and Teatro Rodante Puertorriqueño (The Puerto Rican Traveling Theatre, or PRTT) in New York City. Like Teatro Campesino, PRTT's philosophical and ideological platform entailed the staging of plays that were a source of cultural reaffirmation and ethnic pride; among its goals were "[to] promote identification and self-esteem in alienated ethnic minorities . . . bring free, high quality entertainment to neighborhoods which cannot afford to pay Broadway or Off-Broadway prices."[6]

Today, the Latino Chicago Theater Company serves the Latino community in the Midwest, and Washington D.C. is served by Teatro Nuestro, Gala Hispanic Theater, and LatiNegro. In the 1990s, U.S. Latino theater has enjoyed a resurgence in San Francisco with BRAVA! For Women in the Arts, and in Los Angeles at the Mark Taper Forum, its U.S. Latino Theater Initiative; both are powerful community-based theaters focusing on political intervention and activism in order to address significant issues pertinent to the Latino communities at large.

With the leadership of Cherríe Moraga at BRAVA! and Luis Alfaro and Diane Rodríguez at the Mark Taper Forum, Latino theater has been renewed and empowered. Both spaces have opened the door for new directions and new visions, particularly by promoting diversity and fostering professionalization without abandoning U.S. Latino theater's politicoideological commitment. Indeed, it was at the Mark Taper Forum in 1978 that *Zoot Suit*, a box office success, became the first Chicano play to attract Latino urban audiences. Since Teatro Campesino, *Zoot Suit*'s creator, aspired to crossover success, when the play migrated to Broadway, it was a disappointing flop.

U.S. Latino theater is a theater produced mainly by Chicanos/as of many generations, by a Latino second generation, or by what I call the "domestic ethnic and racial other," as defined in the first chapter of this book. This second generation, whose historicity is rooted in the States, engages the U.S. experience; home is the U.S., where being Latino/a or "Hispanic" means belonging to an ethnic minority. Calling the U.S. home entails juggling a bilingual and bicultural identity, comingling languages, coping with the vicissitudes of a hybrid identity, living "on the hyphen," inhabiting the border, and being assigned to the status of minority or "other." Although Latino theater is an integral and intricate part of American theater, like African American and Asian American theater it is a minority art form that is continually marginalized and silenced. The lack of a niche within the national canon and the minority status of this theatrical form explains its existence on the margins.

Since the 1980s, with Latino/a demographic growth and the increase of new migrations from Central America, South America, and the Caribbean to the U.S.,[7] Latino theater here has become more diversified. This "octopus with many legs" now incorporates works of Colombians, Dominicans, and Central Americans who are economic, not political, exiles. Many urban U.S. Latino theaters are undergoing a new kind of transculturation, one that results from the interaction and transaction with other Latinos/as. What was once a unique ethnic theater (i.e., Chicano, Nuyorican), now is a conglomerate and fusion of Latin American ethnonationalist roots and experiences.

U.S. Latino theater is presently experiencing a host of changes and transformations, particularly with new playwrights crossing over. The trend in the 1960s was toward community-based theaters; since the 1980s, the trend has been to move out of the grassroots theaters and into Anglo-American regional theaters; Latino theater has thus moved from being a collective endeavor to the exaltation of the individual, the playwright, a transformation that registers increasing commodification and commercialization; it has moved from community-building to entertainment, with a touch of multiculturalism, practiced mainly in Anglo-American regional theaters desperate for new (ethnic and racial) middle-class audiences. (Here it must be noted too, that the budget cuts in the arts have greatly affected both Latino and minority theater.)

Another factor in these recent changes is the presence of a generation of playwrights who have received a formal education (and degrees in theater arts), and who now adhered to middle-class values. This new generation does not feel compelled to be specifically "ethnic," nor to stage the barrio's dramatic plots. This is the generation advocated in *Time* magazine's special issue "¡Magnifico! Hispanic Culture Breaks Out of the Barrio" (July 1988), in which it was said that "the Hispanics seem to be moving beyond an initial preoccupation with anger, self-pity and reductionist politics toward a stage literature that communicates rather than confronts, that reaches for universality and yet portrays people individually."[8] This political statement is a generalization that reflects a priori how Eurocentric artistic values and bourgeois aesthetics dictate the criteria for evaluating works of art. Aesthetics and agitprop, universality and locality, and authenticity and mimesis are always at odds when it comes to recognizing the artistic and political value of Latino, and other minority, theater. The end result is total depreciation and marginalization, as counter-hegemonic politics and ideologies resist and clash with elitist (mis)conceptions of art. Such a biased value system favors U.S. Latino theatrical productions that enchant Anglo-American audiences with touches of exoticism through the use of magic realism. Limiting magic realism to spectacle and to the use of tricks and technical apparatuses not only constitutes a cultural appropriation, but disfigures the mythical roots of magic realism as a cultural reality. For example, the two most produced Latino plays to date, Milcha Sánchez-Scott's *Roosters* and José Rivera's *Marisol*, entertain Anglo-American audiences with unexplained phenomena (like the character Angela's levitation in *Roosters* and a visiting guardian angel in *Marisol*). As Rivera himself has stated, magic realism has become another form of stereotyping: "[Magic realism] is the new stereotype which has actually replaced Piñero's heroin addicts with levitating virgins and bleeding crucifixes."[9]

In opposition to the Anglo-American mainstream desire to universalize U.S. Latino theater and depoliticize its origins, the image of Latino theater as an "octopus with many legs" undermines any homogenization or categorical conclusions. Latino theater always locates itself within the domain of difference, of hybridity, of monstrosity. We can imagine this gigantic animal, "Hispanic theater," with a huge head, sitting over the U.S., moving its tentacles on a multiplicity of stages and suctioning audiences. It is this image of monstrosity that accurately captures the nature of a U.S. Latino theater that denies all categorization based on superficial resemblances such as labeling and the imposition of rigidly defined and dominant dramatic structures. This theater revels in problematizing and destabilizing the essentialist notion of monolithic Latino experiences, identities, and ways of seeing.

Latino theater as a monstrous creature can be explained with the words of Michel Foucault, who has said that "the monster insures the emergence of difference. This difference is still without law and without any well-defined structure . . . the monster provides an account, as though in caricature, of the genesis of differences."[10] If U.S. Latino theater emerges as a monster in order to signify its difference, its plurality, its heterogeneity, and its contradictions, then by contrast, Anglo-American theater on Broadway appears as a fossil. As a fossil it denies change; it is stagnant. It is lifeless because it is homogeneous and has become a predictable conventional model with its own frozen horizon of expectations. For Foucault, "[the fossil] functions as a distant and approximative form of identity; it marks a quasi-character in the shift of time . . . [it] recalls, in the uncertainty of its resemblances, the first buddings of identity."[11] This fossilized Broadway of the 1990s is condemned to stage revivals, British imports, flops, and Disney spectacles that continually signal Broadway's impending death. David Richards, a *New York Times* theater critic, has addressed Broadway's incapacity to reinvigorate and revitalize itself, saying, "it's long been known as the fabulous invalid and the Great White Way, but we may have to start calling it Six Flags Over Broadway. . . . While there has always been a raffish, thrill-seeking side to theatergoing, the distinction between Broadway and a theme park grew decidedly narrower during the 1993–94 season."[12]

As a theme park, Broadway perpetuates itself as a petrified spectacle of "glitz, special effects, flashing lights and scenery outperforming the performers—all in the service of the enduring American fallacy that bigger is, if not better, at least better for box office."[13] Richards concludes with a pessimistic prediction, one that reveals once and for all the inevitable death of Broadway despite its attempts to overcome its crisis: "Yet, this quest for the experience to end all experiences is suicidal, a death wish in disguise. A taste for sensationalism may be built into the American temperament. But catering to it will not save Broadway."[14]

May I ask, then, what *will* save Broadway? If Broadway is to come to terms with its own anachronism and ahistoricity, the only solution for its survival is to redefine itself, to declare its independence from British musical megahits, to break away from adapting nineteenth-century master narratives and Hollywood films, to confront the infantilization of audiences with Disney's appropriation of Times Square and Broadway as a sanitized theme park, and to become more inclusive of regional theater and minority theater—women's, gay and lesbian, African American, Asian American, and U.S. Latino/a.[15] The existence of these other theaters serves as a constant reminder of Broadway's fossilized, white Eurocentric identity, an identity that is captured in its denomination as the Great White Way, and which confines Broadway to a tourist attraction and a commodified escapism, spectacle, and entertainment. In a multicultural and democratic society that demands the recognition of diversity and difference, "minority" theater is the ultimate alternative for the revitalization and survival of American theater on Broadway and nationwide, and for returning to the theater its ritualistic function in society.

U.S. Latino Theater on Broadway?

But a glance around the lobby at any Broadway show reveals who *isn't* there: any of the city's readily identifiable minorities—blacks, Hispanics, Asians, and the young.
—Thomas M. Disch, "The Death of Broadway"

Is it possible to produce U.S. Latino theater on Broadway? Although it may appear incredible, only four Latino plays have ever crossed over: *Short Eyes, Zoot Suit, Cuba and His Teddy Bear,* and, most recently, John Leguizamo's *Freak.* Miguel Piñero's *Short Eyes,* a play that centers on prison life, racism, sexuality, and inmates' power relations, was awarded two Obies and the best american play award by the New York Drama Critics Circle in the 1973–74 season. Luis Valdez's *Zoot Suit* was produced at the Winter Garden Theater in 1979. Reinaldo Povod's first play, *Cuba and His Teddy Bear,* was staged in 1986 at the Longacre Theater.

Zoot Suit, which was advertised as the first "Hispanic" play ever to come to Broadway, was devalued as a theatrical production because the critics and the audiences did not identify with the acting techniques and the politicoideological content and agenda of Teatro Campesino, the company that produced it. The musical represented a foundational cultural and political moment of the Chicano movement as it promoted the empowerment of Chicano identity and cultural pride. *Zoot Suit* combines history and fiction. It is a musical that retells the events of a murder of a young Mexican American at the Sleepy Lagoon in Los Angeles in 1942. The Sleepy Lagoon which got its name from a Henry James tune and movie, was an irrigation ditch that young Mexican Americans frequented as a result of segregation. Some twenty *pachucos* (urban street boys who distinguished themselves stylistically by wearing zoot suits) were falsely accused and convicted of the murder. This mass conviction led to a witch-hunt of pachucos that culminated with the Zoot Suit Race Riots in 1943, when U.S. servicemen stationed in Los Angeles assaulted Mexican Americans in the streets and in the barrio. In 1944 the verdict was eventually reversed. The case is memorable because of its media sensationalism, blatant racism, and bigotry.

In the musical, El Pachuco is a mythical figure who functions as a mediator between past and present, reality and fiction, as he discloses a truthful account of the Sleepy Lagoon case and narrates the works and tribulations of one of the pachucos, Henry Reyna, leader of the Thirty-eighth Street Club. He follows Reyna's life, arrest, and trial (fig. 4.1). Though *Zoot Suit* was an enormous hit on the West Coast at the Mark Taper Forum, in New York City a series of elitist, xenophobic, and racist reviews damaged its chances for success. *Zoot Suit* became a complete fiasco when neither "Hispanic" audiences nor Anglo-Americans showed up to see it. The main reason that the Latino (mainly working-class) population stayed away is that Broadway is not part of their world; the Anglo-American absence was a result of the musical's mostly unfavorable reviews:

"Zoot Suit" aspires to be a story and symbol, universal message, and popular entertainment all at once; but its creators have failed to join all these things together.[16]

In attempting to present a favorable view of the Chicano culture, Luis Valdez, the author and director of "Zoot Suit," appears not to have been aware of how unpleasant his view of that culture is bound to appear to most contemporary Americans.[17]

The *tribal* energy is expressed by the magnetic pull that Valdez generates among all the performers.[18]

Nobody is likely to doze off during "Zoot Suit," not only because of the decibel count but also on account of its *animal* vitality.[19]

The most devastating review came from *New York Magazine's* John Simon, whose condescending, insulting, and outright elitist attitude toward Latino culture and Teatro Campesino illustrates his lack of decorum and respect. Simon's maneuver was to use the glossary of the play in order to undermine it as a work of art:

4.1 The character El Pachuco in *Zoot Suit* on Broadway. (Copyright © 1999 by
Universal City Studios, Inc. Courtesy of Universal Studios Publishing Rights, a
Division of Universal Studios Licensing, Inc. All rights reserved.)

To espouse the terminology of *Zoot Suit* (a lengthy glossary of *caló* is provided
by the program), I can describe the cheap set by Thomas A. Walsh and Roberto
Morales only as *¡Que desmadre!*, though the costumes of Peter J. Hall rate a
guarded *¡Orale!*, whereas the staging by Luis Valdez is as *pinche* as his dramaturgy. The acting is hard to evaluate, since the writing is mostly *pendejadas*,
although an audience of theatrical *verdolagas* (many more Hispanics than *ga-
bachos*) lapped it all up as if everyone on stage were a *chingón*. I myself could
latch on to merely one line in all this *puro pedo* . . . [20]

4.2 The cast of *Short Eyes* on Broadway. (Friedman Abeles Collection, Billy Rose Theatre Collection, The New York Public Library for the Performing Arts, Astor, Lenox, and Tilden Foundations.)

By calling his review "West Coast Story," Simon reduces *Zoot Suit* to the stereotypes of the "Latin ethnic and racial other" in mainstream Anglo-American culture. Notice Simon's title citation of *West Side Story*; another critic also made a similar analogy, calling *Zoot Suit* a "big, noisy, brightly colored show, . . . a West Coast descendant, broadened and cheapened, of *West Side Story*."[21] These critics can only see through Broadway's dominant cultural representation of the imagined "Latin other," a model that is a stereotype and does not contain a single trace of Latino self-representation or agency.

In contrast, *Short Eyes*, which moved from Joseph Papp's Public Theater to the Vivian Beaumont Theater at Lincoln Center, received the approval of most theatrical mainstream audiences and critics (fig. 4.2). There is no doubt that, in part, the critical success of the play was motivated by the ideological factor that the actors as well as the playwright were reformed ex-convicts; the show was seen as an inspired rehabilitation effort. For example, one critic stated that "this production is significant not only as a theatrical event but also as an act of social redemption."[22] However, the play still did not escape John Simon's harsh criticism. This time his ferocious critical disposition took a sanguinary bite from the audience:

On two separate occasions, downtown and uptown, I watched an audience composed largely of blacks and Puerto Ricans, but containing also a goodly number of more or less hippified whites, behave with abominable inhumanity. The fact that they talked or shouted back at the stage (a barbarous habit, admired, oddly, by such different critics as [Robert] Brustein and [Clive] Barnes) is merely uncivilized. It does express involvement, but involvement that makes it impossible for others to hear, and for its exhibitor to stop and think, is imbecile, antisocial, and worthless. What truly appalled me, though, was the unbridled ecstasy with which these audiences savored—pealingly laughed, deafeningly cheered and applauded—the victim's being hung head down in a filthy toilet, threatened with sexual assault, brutally hounded and mauled, and finally slaughtered. Similar ovations greeted other homosexual acts, fist fights, and even the least show of violence . . . [23]

Obviously, Simon does not identify with the play and its "uncivilized" audience, who, for him, are barbaric and antisocial peoples of color joined by a handful of white liberals. Simon can only identify with the criminal, whom he sees as a "victim," when in reality the protagonist is a different criminal, a child molester, who happens to be white.[24] For the critic, the characters as well as the audiences have trespassed on Broadway. Simon seems to have experienced only sanitized bourgeois theatrical productions with "civilized" white audiences. Can he or other critics in the establishment trespass into the world of the "ghetto" or the prison? Do they recognize other forms of theater besides Broadway and European productions? Have these critics ever crossed over to attend local community-based productions, where performances are a part of life, a ritual in which audience participation defines and complements dialectically the theatrical event? In Simon's case, can he understand how significant it is for an audience to see their own people (of color), their culture, their social world represented, no matter how negative, brutal, or stereotyped it could be? Would Simon locate at the same level of barbarity African American gospel services where audiences carry on a dialogue with the pastor, turning the service into a ritualistic performance that culminates in spiritual extasis? To what extent do race and class worldviews shape and determine theatrical productions and critical reviews? Can Broadway critics make a little bit of room for constructive criticism? Despite its violence and criminal atmosphere, why shouldn't *Short Eyes* be read as an expression of a means of survival?

Reinaldo Povod's *Cuba and His Teddy Bear* was also moved by Joseph Papp from the Public Theater to Broadway. The play sold out its entire run in three hours because it had an all-star cast featuring Robert DeNiro, Ralph Macchio, and Burt Young. While *Cuba and His Teddy Bear* received mixed reviews because of its dramatic flaws and need for editing, the importance of the play is that it echoed and engaged in a dialogue with the "mean street" life and drug environment of *Short Eyes*. It is the story of a father, Cuba, a drug dealer who tries to save his son Teddy from falling into a world of crime. One of Cuba's friend's Che, a junkie poet and playwright coerces Teddy into becoming a writer. Throughout the play, father and son engage in a series of exchanges that reveal the boy's talent, his love for his father, his identity crisis for being a Latino who looks white, and so on. The character Che is modeled after Miguel Piñero.

It is undeniable that three Latino plays on Broadway do not constitute the acceptance and mainstream success of U.S. Latino theater. Even less visible is theater by, for, and about women, lesbians, African Americans, Native Americans, and Asian Americans. An exception to the staging of minority theater is the recent emergence of plays by and about white gay men. It must then be asked, What is minority theater, and how marginal is gay theater? How does Latino theater, which is triply marginalized because of its ethnicity, class view, and aesthetics, fit? The Latino productions staged on Broadway and discussed above are disturbing and problematic regarding issues of representation: they can easily perpetuate the stereotyping of U.S. Latinos as delinquents, gang members, criminals, drug users, or as the underdogs of the disenfranchised American working class. Herein lies the problem of the *burden of representation. One* Latino play is expected to represent and speak for all Latinos/as. It is crucial to make known that not all Cubans are trapped in reactionary nostalgia or are of the upperclass. Not all Chicanos/as are migrant peasants who take pride in a Native American past and legacy or a mythical Aztlán. Not all Puerto Ricans live on welfare or are delinquents in the streets of New York. Not all Dominicans, Colombians, and Central Americans engage in drug trafficking or are illegal aliens. Not all U.S. Latino/a playwrights should be expected to write ethnic specific plays for community-based U.S. Latino theater audiences, to stage sagas of assimilation, or to portray bilingual and bicultural experiences.

There is no doubt that for a general audience these plays crystallize the embodiment of derogatory stereotypes of U.S. Latinos/as. In addition to the violence and criminality in these plays, there is always an urgency that engenders sporadic attempts through which the playwrights and their protagonists struggle to claim their agency. In this sense, this trilogy represents a collective ritualistic effort that can be read as acts of intervention and survival. Yet, these works do not constitute the entire canon of Nuyorican and Chicano theater. There are other Nuyorican playwrights who address life in the barrio and whose protagonists are not drug dealers and heroin addicts. There is room

for compassion, pride, spirituality, hope, and positive identity formation in plays where survival in the barrio is a constant process of negotiation: for example, Juan Shamsul Alám's *Zookeeper;* Miguel Algarín's
and Tato Laviera's *Olú Clemente;* Migdalia Cruz's *Lolita de Lares;* Louis
Delgado, Jr.'s *El Cano;* Federico Fraguada's *Bodega;* Edward Gallardo's
Simpson Street; Richard Irizarry's *Ariano;* Yolanda Rodríguez's *The
Cause;* Edwin Sánchez's *Unmerciful Good Fortune* and *Clean;* and Cándido Tirado's *La Barbería.* It is significant that the first three Latino plays
to have been produced on Broadway are those that confirm and perpetuate the Anglo-American audience's conception of the "other" as abject and subaltern.

Audiences are not informed of a new generation of U.S. Puerto Rican playwrights—those mentioned above and others, such as Carmen
Rivera, Reuben Gonzalez, and José Rivera—who struggle to write
against negative representations of street life in the "ghetto." This new
generation is working hard to move beyond the migration and crisis
of patriarchy that defined the first generation. These new playwrights
revisit, re-vision, and reimagine the history of Latino diaspora, exile,
and nostalgia, as new hybrid identities are articulated and constructed
on the stage. They are professionals who have received a formal education, who are an integral part of the middle class, and whose home is
here in the U.S. Nuyoricans have become the dominant ethnic minority
in New York City (the *West Side Story* nightmare come true!), but the
establishment is simply not interested in Latino/a representations that
do not fit the dominant image of Puerto Ricans as a culture of poverty.
Chicano theater has also evolved: it is no longer restricted to migrant
and/or rural audiences.[25] There is a new middle-class perspective, one
that is rooted in the urban experience and shaped by college education
and the professionalization of Chicanos/as. Among these new Latino/a
voices are those of Luis Alfaro, Roy Conboy, Rodrigo Duarte Clark,
José Cruz González, Evelina Fernández, John and Gabriel Fraire, Arthur Girón, Josefina López, Oliver Mayer, Alicia Mena, Rick Najera,
Monica Palacios, Elaine Romero, Rob Santana, Carlos J. Serrano, Octavio Solis, Richard Tavera, and Edit Villareal.

Reviewing U.S. Latino Theater

Dolores Prida, one of the most prestigious and outspoken Latina playwrights in the U.S., has continually denounced Anglo-American theater critics for their lack of Hispanic cultural knowledge and understanding in their reviews of Latino theatrical productions. In a 1988
interview, she says that "[t]he problem comes when I'm writing in English and I get critics from the *New York Times* or *The Village Voice* com-

menting on them negatively. The discrimination is there. They fail to put the plays in the context of the experience of the Hispanic community. I think they have a pre-conceived notion of what a Hispanic is. If they see a woman with a *peineta* [an ornamental comb] the American critics will say 'This is real Hispanic.'"[26] In her essay "The Show Does Go On," Prida adds that "American critics are, in most instances, either patronizing or insensitive to the work produced by Hispanics, even if it is in English."[27] In this way, Prida questions the exclusion of U.S. Latino plays from Anglo-American theatrical spaces, and thus questions the institutional ethnocentrism and inherent racism inscribed in the official critical response to Latino plays in the mainstream. Indeed, while Prida attempts to open the canon to cultural diversity and difference, such an opening entails crossing over.

Crossing over can signify taking a risk, particularly when putting something into the mainstream implicates the "whitening" of the U.S. Latino experience. For a Latino play to become a success, to have a general audience appeal, and to be acclaimed to the extent that it has mainstream attention certainly depends on issues of content and language, but also of class worldviews. Publication is also a crucial element for the circulation and production of plays.[28] Lately, it seems as if crossing over is an issue of general interest for both Anglo-American and Latino audiences. In this matter, the mainstream critical response is also responsible for a play's impact, success, and acceptance. Critics must consider ethnic diversity, and other ways of both experiencing and undertaking theater. In the last decade, Broadway has included the voices and stories of minorities. We cannot deny the critical praise and ultimate recognition—with Pulitzer Prizes and Tony Awards— of August Wilson's *Fences*, Marsha Norman's *'night, Mother*, and David Henry Hwang's *M. Butterfly*. However, the extremely limited, once-in-a-lifetime presence of such plays demands that the issues of tokenism be raised. In spite of the occasional gendered, black, or Asian presence on Broadway, U.S. Latino theater is still *absent* on the Great White Way.

If the Broadway system of power intends to put into the mainstream Latino plays and actors, a political commitment to cultural diversity and difference is required. The theatrical experience of the "other" is not merely entertainment and escapism; it is an experience used to foster racial and ethnic diversity as well as social change.[29] Only by understanding "diversity" in this context can Latino, and other minority, theater enter the mainstream with respect, self-esteem, and dignity. And only then will the Broadway theatrical canon and its official critical response be opened to the experiences and knowledge of the "other," that is, Latinos/as, blacks, Asians, women, gay men and lesbians, and other minorities; only then can cultural pluralism and ethnic diversity be fully celebrated as difference. All of this will lead to the ultimate "border crossing" for U.S. Latino and other minority theater in the U.S.

Toward an Understanding of U.S. Latino Theater

The whole issue of finding the "authentic" Latino play gets more complicated when one considers that U.S. Latinos/as may refuse to be called "Latinos" and some may endorse the label of "Hispanic"— as discussed in the introduction to this book—or may prefer to label themselves in nationalistic terms (i.e., Cuban, Puerto Rican, Domini- can, etc.). Some may detest the terms "Chicano" or "Nuyorican"; oth- ers may simply consider themselves Americans, revoking any identifi- cation with their native ethnic roots and people. For example, Eduardo Machado has stated, "I think my work is American. It's in English, it's about being here, it's not about being in Havana."[30] It is vital to locate playwrights in given relations of power and discursive formations in order to determine their identity politics. This strategy also applies to the protagonists of their theatrical pieces.

So, is there such a thing as U.S. Latino theater, and if so, where has it been staged? Who is producing this theater? U.S. Latino theater has always existed on the margins, on the periphery of Off-Off-Broadway, on the borders of regional theater and alternative performance spaces. Latino theater is situated at the bottom of the national hierarchical con- stituency of theaters and theatrical companies and is distinguished for its limited financial resources and low-budget productions. Being pri- marily a community-based form of theater with a pedagogical agenda, it has been produced mainly for the Latino community and has been limited to venues that foment "Hispanic" cultural affirmation, ethnic pride, Spanish language and/or bilingualism, and identity politics.[31]

As mentioned earlier, Latino theater production proliferated in the 1960s and 1970s as a political theater of social consciousness that cen- tered on issues of ethnic hybrid identity, discrimination, oppression, exploitation, underrepresentation, and misrepresentation. Since the 1980s, though, attention in Latino theater and (mainstream) regional playhouses and productions has been drawn to marketing, accessibil- ity to the general public, theatrical and artistic professionalization, identifying targeted audiences for sponsorship, and crossing over in order to cater to Anglo-American audiences in English only.[32] It is no surprise that the latest trend in Anglo-American regional theaters is to do staged readings of Latino plays—most of which are written in English—that will never reach the level of full production. However, the work of some U.S. Latino/a playwrights has crossed over to regional and Off-Broadway theater: Elaine Romero's *Walking Home,* at the Planet Earth Multicultural Theatre in Phoenix; Caridad Svich's *Alchemy of Desire/Deadman's Blues,* at the Playhouse in Cincinnati; Octavio Solis's *Man of the Flesh,* at the Magic Theatre of San Francisco; Edwin Sánchez's *Clean,* at the Hartford Stage, and *Unmerciful Good Fortune,* at the Victory Garden Theater in Chicago; José Rivera's *Marisol,* at the Hartford Stage, and *Cloud Tectonics* at the Humana Festival '95 in Louisville; Lynne Alvarez's *Eddie Mundo Edmundo* at the American Conservatory Theater in San Francisco; Migdalia Cruz's *Miriam's Flowers* at Playwrights Horizons in New York City; and Liza Loomer's *The Waiting Room* at the Trinity Repertory Company in Providence.

Since the 1980s, the move for many professional U.S. Latinos/as has been to make it in the mainstream and, in order to do so, the barrio experience and political/social agenda must be displaced and erased. Some playwrights, on their yellow brick road to success, promote hegemonic middle-class values and silence the dramatic plots of "ghetto" realities. There are no roles for losers, delinquents, drug addicts, and "uneducated" Spanish-speaking Latinos/as, primarily because these plays are not written for barrio audiences, migrant workers, illegal aliens, and their concerns. In mainstream productions the act must be cleaned up when the curtain rises. Middle-class Anglo-American audiences expect to be mesmerized with the exoticism of magic realism and to be entertained with rags-to-riches stories or sagas of assimilation and success. Under these circumstances, U.S. Latino theater is presumed to move beyond the ghetto sets and mentality, beyond its politics of the oppressed; as declared by Michael Alassa, a Cuban American playwright, "We're moving away from ghetto theater. When I first came to [Teatro] Duo, I banned all kitchen sink dramas. The Hispanic-American generation that's coming along now doesn't need to see another kitchen sink drama about where they came from. . . . Maybe other theater groups will start realizing that people like us are starting to write something beyond what ghetto-ized minorities write for their theaters."[33]

There is no doubt that "kitchen-sink" drama plots, that is, "people dealing with drugs and welfare,"[34] are being replaced by the experiences of a more prosperous, assimilated, "Anglo-cized," and elitist social group of middle-class Latinos/as that will fulfill the horizon of expectations of the Anglo-American audiences. The desire to move beyond the ghetto experience is a political move to silence oppositional and confrontational theatrical voices that make uncomfortable the white Anglo-American and Latino middle class. And, if I am not mistaken, this is what Anglo-American mass-media, and assimilated Latinos/as who are for the status-quo and belong to an affluent middle class, call "crossing over," or "mainstreaming." If so, which Latino plays are being produced by the dominant institutions of power? Are some Latinos/as tired of being stereotyped as ghetto marginals? Do kitchen-sink dramas reaffirm and reconfirm already-existing prejudices and stereotypes against Latinos/as? Do we take the risk of falling into new ways of stereotyping, and even essentializing, once it has been promulgated that we silence the impoverished living conditions of the majority of Latinos/as in the U.S.? About this matter, Alvan Colón Lespier (at Teatro Pregones in New York City) has observed the dangers of crossing over to mainstream audiences; commenting that "[r]ecently some producers have unsuccessfully tried to insert Latino theater into the mainstream currents of American theater. Latino theater cannot be used as bait. When our theater is presented as an exotic cultural product or when it is watered down to make it palatable to Anglo audiences, the result is a deformed or distorted version of our culture."[35]

Any effort to limit Latino theater to a single definition is reductionist and simplistic. For some, a definition is based solely on political awareness or ethnic authenticity. For others, because of its political agenda, agitprop intentionality, and pedagogical function, Latino theater cannot accommodate a bourgeois aesthetic dimension that would impart to it a universal quality and artistic style. What is at stake here are political worldviews that define what a work of art is. Whose philosophy of theater or taste is to define Latino theater? As Ed Morales, a Latino theater critic, once stated, "[M]aybe we are beyond the distinction [of] aesthetics/agitprop."[36] If this is the case, we must start reformulating the history of U.S. Latino theater, its artistic values, and its audiences from a new perspective that questions Eurocentric, ethnocentric, and phallocentric ways of making theater.

In order to grasp the artistic value of U.S. Latino theater and its politics, we should ask ourselves some basic questions: What is the function of U.S. Latino theater? Where is it produced, and who are our audiences? How can we acknowledge diversity and difference? What kinds of ways of making theater exist in Latino theater? What are the old paradigms? Which plays get produced, and why, and where? Are U.S. Latino/a actors playing roles in productions that have crossed over? Should we move away from community-based theaters and political activism? Should we cross over, at whatever cost, to the mainstream or Broadway? Can this "octopus with many legs" acclaim its diversity without restraining it to a label or categorization that essentializes and homogenizes the Latino/a historical experiences in the U.S.?

In the following chapters I attempt to answer some of these questions. I concentrate on a handful of issues that contribute to the understanding of U.S. Latino theater. By centering on new voices, visions, and directions I examine its constituencies, as playwrights and their protagonists shape and advance a new politics of representation, identity, and ethnicity. As U.S. Latinos/as, gay and lesbian Latinos/as, and Latinos/as with college education claim their agency in order to stage their experiences, contradictions, dislocations, uncertainties, and a spectrum of alternative ways of seeing, Latino theater is experiencing a historical (r)evolution, an exciting process of permutation and creativity. Not only are there new playwrights and performers appearing nationwide, but there are also new audiences (college students and professional Latinos/as) who foment and support Latino theater and performances. The success of John Leguizamo (Off-Broadway *Mambo Mouth* and *Spic-O-Rama,* and later on Broadway with *Freak*); the acclaimed solo performances of Marga Gómez (with *Memory Tricks, Marga Is Pretty, Witty, and Gay,* and *A Line around the Block*); and the awarding of MacArthur awards to Guillermo Gómez-Peña and Luis Alfaro, and Obies to María Irene Fornes, Carmen Rivera, Louis Delgado, Jr., José Rivera, and Leguizamo in the last few years bear witness to the increasing visibility of Latinos/as and the embrace of audiences.

Most important is the rearticulation of U.S. Latino theater by women, and gay and lesbian playwrights, who have taken the lead in redefining the constituencies of this cultural form since the late 1980s. At the historical moment when male playwrights ran out of stories to stage, Latinas stepped in to invigorate the theater with plays that offer new visions and attract new audiences. Playwrights and performers such as Lynne Alvarez, Janis Astor del Valle, Elvira and Hortensia Colorado, Migdalia Cruz, Evelina Fernández, Amparo García, Terry Gómez, Silvia González, Liza Loomer, Josefina López, Alicia Mena, Carmen Rivera, Yolanda Rodríguez, Elaine Romero, Diana Saenz, Caridad Svich, and Edit Villareal have created a new poetics and a new politics of/for approaching theater. It cannot be forgotten that respectable and prolific *mujeres en teatro* have paved the way for these newcomers: Denise Chávez, María Irene Fornes, Cherríe Moraga, Estela Portillo Trambley, Dolores Prida, and Milcha Sánchez-Scott. Gays and lesbians have come out in theatrical and performance pieces to break the silence and dismantle sexual taboos; among them are Alberto Antonio Araiza, Rane Arroyo, Janis Astor del Valle, Ricardo Bracho, Joseph R. Castel,

Nilo Cruz, Manuel Martín, Jorge B. Merced, Pedro R. Monge Rafuls, Manuel Pereiras, Edgar Poma, Alfonso Ramírez, Oscar Reconco, Guillermo Reyes, Edwin Sánchez, Héctor Santiago, and Ana María Simo. In response, heterosexual male playwrights have had to reconsider homophobic, misogynist, sexist, and machista attitudes, positions, and representations of each of these "others."

A new U.S. Latino theater has emerged, with new dramatic structures, new protagonists, new perspectives, and new ways of articulating, negotiating, and accommodating bilingual and bicultural identities. In the 1990s, one of the most successful genres of U.S. Latino theater, besides Latina and gay and lesbian theater, is that of the solo performance. Many U.S. Latino/a performances are autobiographical, and the speaking subject enacts personal memories and voices silenced experiences and lifestyles. Among the many performers of solo works are: Belinda Acosta, Yareli Arizmendi, Beto Arraiza, Wilma Bonet, Nao Bustamante, Laura Esparza, Coco Fusco, María Mar, Monica Palacios, and Ruby Nelda Pérez.

U.S. Latino theater today incorporates a cornucopia of themes, dramatic actions, and issues. The following inventory does not do justice to its plurality, but it portrays the heterogeneity of the art form; among the subjects that Latino theater has addressed are recent immigration; dislocation and reterritorialization; assimilation and social mobility; illegal alien discrimination and deportation; exile; nostalgia; cultural memory; biculturalism; journeys away from home and back home; the staging of the dysfunctional family; crisis of patriarchy; empowerment of women; feminism and body politics; feminism and the deconstruction of machismo; the questioning and reversal of stereotypes; the articulation of gay and lesbian identities; AIDS awareness; environmental consciousness; health issues; confronting homophobia, sexism, and racism; passing, and crossing over; cultural shame; community building; confronting gentrification; internalized racism; political activism; the myth of the eternal return; resistance to "English only"; homelessness; mourning; Latin American politics; border and hybrid identities; revisiting and recovering historical events, re-visioning history, and honoring historical heroes and heroines.

A new trend is to poke fun at cultural icons and institutions, revision traditional values and practices, and perform subjectivities in process as part of claiming agency and empowerment. Comedy groups, like Culture Clash, Latins Anonymous, and Chicano Secret Service have successfully toured the nation. Their satire, irony, and humor makes possible the dismantling of stereotypes by turning them inside out. Cuban Americans like Nilo Cruz and Carmelita Tropicana are reconnecting and building new bridges with Cuba and other Latino communities; other playwrights like Eduardo Machado and Luis Santeiro are portraying protagonists who juggle Cuban American bilingual and bicultural identities. This new generation has moved away from restrictive categories of ethnicity and the rigors of nationalism. Other issues that in the last decade are shaping the politics of U.S. Latino theater are AIDS, and urban uprising and chaos. Once again, Latino theater embraces political activism in order to save our communities from drugs, gang violence, police brutality, and AIDS. When it is a matter of life and death, art is political.

U.S. Latino theater in the 1990s advocates positive self-representations, promotes the tolerance of difference, tackles themes and political issues that affect U.S. Latino communities at large, practices a politics of affinity, and celebrates Latino culture and its peoples. If earlier issues of transculturation and assimilation focused on the relation with the dominant Anglo-American culture, today, with the increased migrations of Latin Americans to cities and the increasing interaction among different Latino/a groups and other peoples of color, the new processes of transculturation are less binary. They are more layered, with cultural/ethnic exchanges between Latinos/as (and Latin Americans) who previously had little contact with each other. Nationalist and ethnic labels are no longer capable of completely representing or defining identities that are plural, hybrid, and in flux. The old paradigms of race, nation, and sexuality are being reconfigured and expanded to include equally meaningful notions of gender and sexuality. At this moment, U.S. Latinos/as, through theater, can articulate new forms of identity that are both sources of and models for agency and empowerment. The presence and visibility of U.S. Latino theater can no longer be ignored. It is here to stay, in all its diversity and difference.

ACT TWO

LATINO/A SELF-REPRESENTATIONS IN THEATRICAL PRODUCTIONS

5

Staging AIDS
What's Latinos/as Got to Do with It?

We don't need a cultural renaissance; we need cultural
practices actively participating in the struggle against AIDS.
We don't need to transcend the epidemic; we need to end it.
—Douglas Crimp, *AIDS: Cultural Analysis/Cultural Activism*

The unspoken rule is that you can exist only as one thing at a
time—a Latino or a gay man—with no recognition of reality's
complexity. Add an H.I.V. diagnosis to this mix and it gets
complicated.
—Dennis deLeon, "My Hopes, My Fears, My Disease"

AIDS is not only a medical crisis but a crisis of representation. Many
issues complicate the AIDS epidemic. Among them are the questions
of who contracts AIDS, and how the person with AIDS is represented.
The diversity of AIDS cases becomes problematic when we consider
that dominant cultural representations of AIDS are produced by a
mainstream Anglo-American population. By the year 2050, when there
will, we hope, be a cure for AIDS and the cultural archives of the
plague can be reviewed, researchers will recover an archipelago of cultural constructions that register who was infected and affected by
AIDS in the 1980s and 1990s. The record will erroneously show that
mainly white, gay, middle-class men contracted, experienced, suffered
from, and died of the virus. Critic Richard Goldstein has acknowledged the silences of all "others" in the arts in his declaration that
"AIDS is increasingly a disease of impoverished people of color. Yet,
if one were to describe this epidemic from works of art alone, one
would have to conclude that only white women and gay men have been
people with AIDS."[1] Regarding this, Michael Cunningham has also
observed that "Still, if you go to a show that touches on AIDS, the odds
are good you're going to be seeing a lot of gay white men."[2] On the
representation of whiteness and AIDS, cultural critic and scholar David
Román has aptly theorized that

[w]hiteness, as an unmarked racial category, presumes a series of universals that disavow the ways that race and ethnicity factor into our understanding and responses to AIDS. The idea that race and ethnicity might shape a person's experience of AIDS was not explored in early AIDS discourse. The elision of the two categories—race and sexuality, or, more precisely, white and gay—sustains the white normativity that defined urban gay culture at the time. Race, as a category of analysis in AIDS performance, would not be forcefully addressed until the early 1990s.[3]

In this chapter, I examine how issues of representation and relations of power, agency, and intervention are important factors that contribute to the response and imagery of AIDS in society at large. I will limit myself to the theatrical space in order to expose how groups with access to power have unintentionally marginalized and silenced other groups such as Latinos/as in general, gay and lesbian Latinos/as, people of color, women, and drug addicts. These groups have been underrepresented—rather, misrepresented—because those with access to power (Broadway and Off-Broadway) have taken the lead and outlined the paradigms of staging AIDS. My goal is to raise consciousness that AIDS as a crisis of representation (of language, imagery, and discourse) is also a crisis of representation in terms of who is represented, when, where, why, and how. To paraphrase Tina Turner, when staging AIDS, what's Latinos/as got to do with it?

The Dominant Paradigm of AIDS Theater

A look at AIDS theater reveals the absence of people of color. Plays about AIDS center on white, gay, often Jewish, men: Larry Kramer's *The Normal Heart* (1985), William M. Hoffman's *As Is* (1985), Harvey Fierstein's *Safe Sex* (1987), Tony Kushner's *Angels in America* (1989–1993), William Finn's *Falsettos* (1992), Kramer's *The Destiny of Me* (1993), Paul Rudnick's *Jeffrey* (1993), Terrence McNally's *Love! Valour! Compassion!* (1995), and Jonathan Larson's *Rent* (1996).[4] All of these plays deal with the personal drama of AIDS in specific communities. Nonetheless, they establish the paradigm of AIDS as a universal experience when, in fact, their particular experience pertains mainly to one ethnic group: white, Jewish, gay men. My point is not that white, Jewish, gay men should not stage their experiences, but that we must recognize that the AIDS activism that first challenged the silence and prejudices surrounding the disease was mobilized by white, Jewish gay men—in particular, by Larry Kramer. Kramer credits his experience as a Jew in touch with the horrors of the holocaust for developing his comparison between gays with AIDS and Jews. His book *Reports from the Holocaust: The Mak-*

ing of an AIDS Activist (1989) outlines his philosophy and position, as he speaks out as a Jew and a gay man:

You can march off now to the gas chambers; just get right in line.
. . . Perhaps because I am both, I find it remarkable how many similarities I notice between homosexuals and Jews. . . . History recently made a pretty good attempt to destroy the Jewish people, and as I think history now has an opportunity to do (and is already doing) pretty much the same to homosexuals. . . .
. . . Only this time the "infernal machine" is the AIDS holocaust.[5]

Kramer's outrage is summarized by his statement that "[i]t's not too early to see AIDS as the homosexuals' holocaust. . . . We are now in a situation historically equivalent to, to, say, the German Jews circa 1938–1940."[6]

Yet as theater on AIDS was defined by gay men, it became a theater of exclusion. The first anthology of AIDS theater, *The Way We Live Now: American Plays and the AIDS Crisis* (1990), does not contain any African American, Asian American, Haitian, or U.S. Latino/a voices.[7] Although Michael Feingold's introduction is well-intentioned, he falls into the trap of universalizing the experience of one ethnic group: "In this volume you will find a range of human possibilities as wide and complex as the reach of the epidemic itself. . . . You will also find a record of the numbness, the shock, the fright, the immobility I have mentioned. There is no way to overcome these things without viewing them straight on."[8] How "wide and complex" is the experience to which he refers, if so many voices were not included?

The second anthology of AIDS theater, *Sharing the Delirium: Second Generation AIDS Plays and Performances,* also does not include any plays by people of color.[9] What is even more amazing and embarrassing is that white America has already proclaimed a "second generation" of AIDS plays and performances. Whose generation is this? Whose theater is this? Why are women and people of color absent? Unquestionably, *Sharing the Delirium,* like *The Way We Live Now,* anthologizes only the white, gay experience and struggle with AIDS. It universalizes this gay experience as the dominant paradigm of AIDS theater and performance. According to the editor, Therese Jones, this second generation is characterized by humor. "Second generation works," she tells us, "represent a radical shift in theatrical representations of AIDS, no longer an event to be comprehended but a reality to be accommodated. . . . Unlike first generation plays, humor is not incidental but essential in second generation theater, an entire spectrum of Comedic drama: satire, farce, romance, slapstick, and burlesque."[10] In other words, gay, white theater on AIDS is funny and can afford to laugh in the 1990s; these people have learned how to cope and survive through camp and irony. Nevertheless, to what extent is class an important factor shaping and framing the perspective and philosophies of life in gay, white theater on AIDS? Can this theater, which is now an integral part of the mainstream, function as a model for minorities? Furthermore, given that people of color have become the fastest-growing population acquiring AIDS, can they afford to laugh at it? If people of color were not acknowledged when the "first generation" of AIDS plays was anthologized, what are their chances of being produced and published in this "second generation?"

There may be room for plenty of laughs in the second generation of AIDS plays and performances for their white, gay audiences, but, once again, can minorities laugh at AIDS? Can people of color just sit there and "share the delirium": After a first generation of anger, activism, militancy, and consciousness-raising, attributing a delirious quality to the second generation conveys that its members have entered a state of hallucination and incoherent speech. "Sharing the delirium" means, literally, to share "a state of mental confusion and clouded consciousness resulting from high fever, intoxication, shock, or other causes."[11] Is the gay community in a state of delirium, or is it simply trying to distance itself from the calamities and atrocities of AIDS? If so, what will the "third generation" of AIDS plays be like? Will it be the theatrical experiences of those who have been marginalized, oppressed, and silenced since AIDS started to be culturally articulated and discursively represented in the 1980s? Can people of color "share the delirium" with "festive laughter, universal laughter, ambivalent laughter" when the statistics show the alarming and increasing spread of AIDS among people of color, women, and children?[12] Let's make this clear: only a small sector of society—gay, white, middle-class men and their liberal white audiences—is "sharing the delirium."

If we trace the history of the oppression of gay people, the issue of class and race cannot be left out; not all of us have access to power. The problem is that gay identity has been universalized and essentialized as a "white" identity, without making room for difference. Not all gay people experience racism and marginalization. The oppression of some tends to be limited to homophobia, as exemplified by Larry Kramer's question, "Why is it that white heterosexuals prefer not to think about or deal with AIDS? For the African and the Black and the Hispanic American cases, it's because of racism. For the gay male cases, it's because of homophobia."[13] The way Kramer defines oppression reveals that "gay male" equals "white male" in a given social class and location—for example, Greenwich Village, in New York City. Is whiteness invisible? Or is gayness?

What *do* people of color have to do with AIDS theater? The first attempt to include diversity in AIDS theater was Joe Pintauro's *Raft of the Medusa* (1992), a kaleidoscopic rainbow of people coping with AIDS in a therapy session. The characters were merely types, lacking psychological development. In its effort to show a diversity of experiences, including those of class, sex, and race, this play was almost tokenist in nature, even including a deaf female character with AIDS.

Only one African American play on AIDS, Cheryl L. West's *Before It Hits Home* (1992), has been staged (off-Broadway) and received critical attention.[14] The play is about a bisexual jazz musician who returns home to die. The reviews were not very favorable; the *New York Times* review by Frank Rich, entitled "A Black Family Confronts AIDS," stated that the play was crudely written, predictable in plot, full of archetypes, and melodramatic. Indeed, the play did not fulfill Rich's horizon of expectations and he frankly suggests that it should have been a docudrama on television, where its "aesthetic failings would be less apparent." However, he still concludes that "[f]or the moment, this particular slice of the AIDS story is one that the theater may be in a position to tell best, and that it may yet tell better."[15] Whose theater is Rich talking about? Who is the audience? And what does he mean by "aesthetic failings"? When Rich enters the territory of aesthetics, he falls in the trap of Eurocentric, phallocentric, and ethnocentric ways of doing, seeing, and reviewing theater. Are mainstream critics equipped to evaluate alternative theater, that is, African American, Asian American, women's, gay, AIDS, and Latino theater? What does Rich's aesthetic platform stand for, when faced with George Whitmore's statement that "AIDS is about shit and blood."[16] Indeed, AIDS is a minefield in the arts; as cultural critic Jan Zita Grover has provocatively stated, "AIDS brings an already existing social debate—*What is the purpose and value of art?*—to a crisis point. It throws into relief the irreducible fact that art work is based not simply (or romantically) on personal visions, but on social realities."[17] There is an urgency in AIDS writing, an urgency to write about AIDS that cannot wait for aesthetic distancing. As AIDS activist John Preston has mandated, "The purpose of AIDS writing now is to *get it all down*. To repeat: The purpose of the writer in the time of AIDS *is to bear witness.* . . . To live in a time of AIDS and to understand what is going on, *writing must be accompanied by action.*"[18]

The development of white, gay theater on AIDS can be outlined in three stages: (1) anger and accusation; (2) safer-sex campaigning; and (3) creativity. The first plays are educational and want to voice the gay experience. These are agitprop pieces full of terror, anger, and fury. They vociferate discrimination, compassion, frustration, pain, confusion, grief, death, loss, helplessness, and activism. As the plague sits in the theater, around the clock and all season long, a search for creative spaces begins. In this way, AIDS theater moves from propaganda to creative theatrical and poetic forms. Aesthetically diverse plays appear—musicals like *Falsettos*, which is a show about a new understanding of the family and masculinity; or plays that mediate and transfer AIDS to other illnesses (as in *Marvin's Room*), or hybrid plays combining poetic imagery, spectacle, and political issues such as *Angels in America* and *Rent*, and plays with humorous, escapist, ludic overtones like Paula Vogel's *The Baltimore Waltz*.

In 1993, AIDS theater entered a new phase when *Jeffrey* opened on the Off-Broadway stage. The message now is that AIDS has become a part of life and all that can be done is accept it, move on, and laugh at it—as exemplified in *Sharing the Delirium*. There is cynicism here, yet laughter also has its cathartic effect—that is, uncontrollable laughter releases emotional pressure. As *Jeffrey's* author, Paul Rudnick, has expressed, "Only money, rage and science can conquer AIDS, but only laughter can make the nightmare bearable."[19] With *Jeffrey*, AIDS has entered the realm of comedy, leaving behind the lugubrious phase. Also, Anglo-American AIDS theater has started to search for utopia, a longed-for-cure in the future. This is seen in two solo performance monologues by white men: Tim Miller's *My Queer Body* and David Drake's *The Night Larry Kramer Kissed Me*. Although they articulate a gay identity and a gamut of subject positions in the white gay community, these performances erase historicity and the reality of AIDS with their utopianism. Nevertheless, utopia, like nostalgia, can alleviate and help to cope with the AIDS epidemic and survival.

Given that the dominant paradigm of AIDS theater has been shaped by white, middle-class, Eurocentric standards, it is hard for other minorities and people of color to enter into this realm of representation. Do they have anything to add? Has it all been said? How can people of color keep up with the development of AIDS in the theater when they have not made it to Broadway and scarcely to Off-Broadway or regional theater?

The Facts

U.S. Latinos/as comprise almost 10.5 percent of the U.S. population, yet account for almost 20.5 percent of the total AIDS cases reported in the U.S. in 1997.[20] According to the *HIV/AIDS Surveillance Report* (December

1997), there were 115,354 AIDS cases reported among Latinos/as. Among those, 19,894 were women and 1,876 were children.[21] Latinos/as, including Puerto Ricans on the island, are one of the U.S. populations more increasingly affected by AIDS. Compared to the ten most populous cities in the U.S., San Juan, Puerto Rico presently has the second highest per capita rate of AIDS, with almost 3 percent of its population infected. San Francisco ranks number one, at 3.3 percent.[22] Indeed, the above statistics are overwhelming, the figures are shocking, and the rapid increase of the disease among Latinos/as is nothing less than dramatic and tragic. Our people are dying of AIDS. *Se nos muere nuestro pueblo.*

Latino AIDS Theater: An Inventory

In U.S. Latino communities, AIDS theater usually takes the form of workshops. There is an urgent need to educate our people, who are currently the group hardest hit by AIDS in the U.S. Among the issues at stake are prevention and education: using condoms and clean needles, protecting women and teenagers. Latino AIDS theater has a didactic intention. Teatro Pregones in New York City, and Teatro Viva in Los Angeles, for example, promote education and raise consciousness about the virus. In the skits and workshops produced by these theaters, AIDS is represented as a web with many strands. Racism, classism, sexism, homophobia, ethnocentricity, nationalism, migration, and cultural differences must be tackled. Indeed, in these webs of action, transaction, and interaction, identity is multiple and heterogeneous. The sexual revolution goes hand in hand with oppression, racism, and the need for social change. It is not conceivable to separate art and politics; nor can this theater be approached with bourgeois concepts of aesthetics, refinement, taste, and literary elitism. It is unpolished and crude.[23] It has only a social purpose for being, and a political agenda: a ritualistic performance and collective effort that allows the community to promote AIDS awareness, to learn about AIDS, to carry on condom-usage campaigns, to deliver on an activist agenda, and to cope with the devastating epidemic. Theater in this case is a matter of survival, not entertainment or leisure.

The primary goal of U.S. Latino theater on AIDS is to enhance and induce political action in order to achieve human survival and social change. This theater also considers levels of literacy in the community, and develops theatrical pieces that voice its needs and realities. For example, *telenovela*-like scripts and melodrama may be the most effective formats for reaching urban working-class and migrant audiences with nonformal education. The task of educating is performed in the languages used by Latino communities, be they Spanish, English, or "Spanglish."

Given that AIDS is affecting all U.S. Latino populations regardless of class, age, sex, or sexual preference, Latino AIDS theater is developing a growing corpus of plays with different formats, styles, languages, preoccupations, and dramatic conflicts. These plays are being written primarily by the most predominant ethnic components of the Latino population: Cuban exiles/Cuban Americans, Chicanos/as, and Puerto Ricans. Most Latino plays on AIDS are being produced for specific urban Latino communities—homosexuals, bisexuals, heterosexuals, drug users, disempowered women, teenagers, and senior citizens. AIDS is a disease affecting entire communities; nobody should be left out.

U.S. Latino AIDS theater is a vivid testimony to the pandemonium wrought by AIDS. Communal theatrical productions, as well as individual playwrights, are coping with AIDS through the staging of dramatic situations that offer ways to break the silence on AIDS—*el silencio significa la muerte,* silence equals death. In this manner, theater, like other forms of artistic expression, fulfills different functions in the war against AIDS. As political-cultural activist Max Navarre has stated on the role of art during the AIDS crisis, "Art is a lot of things: it's an educational tool, a grieving tool and a healing tool."[24] U.S. Latino theater, as an act of intervention, is primarily an act of survival based on a politics of affinity, which works through the existence of alliances and coalitions constituted by crossing racial, ethnic, class, and gender barriers. Once we all accept, respect, and tolerate our differences, theater as a part of the Latino cultural imaginary provides models of/for social action and solidarity in our fight against AIDS. In this way, theater offers social, ideological, psychological, emotional and spiritual treatment, medication, and consolation for a fatal disease.

If there is no cure for AIDS, a theatrical production has the efficacy of at least putting forth solutions for preventing AIDS, and treating the infected and affected. In these terms, Latino theater on AIDS is informational, didactic, and cathartic in its attempt to empower the Latino community in its response to the AIDS crisis. For Latinos/as, AIDS is not only a personal drama but also a communal and engaged drama, as the virus threatens to wipe out entire generations of young men, women, and children. Consequently, in order to save our community, U.S. Latino theater must not only be a *site of intervention* during the AIDS crisis, but also a *site of contestation.* As cultural critic David Román has stated, "[Performance] holds the capacity to articulate resistance and generate necessary social change."[25] For Román, U.S. Latino theater on AIDS (and queer theater) must "engage at once in the tactics of oppositional consciousness and in the coalition building available through an affinity politics."[26]

At this critical moment when Latino communities are "epicenters of AIDS," the impact of the disease has mobilized both heterosexuals and homosexuals. For example, Teatro Pregones, in New York City, develops AIDS awareness by making the audience participate in the development of the dramatic plot; in this way, it learns how to cope with AIDS and to deal with sexuality, machismo, and homophobia. The audience is expected to interrupt the play any time a case of oppression is detected. Audience members are supposed to change the course of the action: to rewrite the play by replacing the characters with their own acting and lines. This direct participation allows for a better understanding of oppression. The production is followed by a panel discussion, which provides information on AIDS. In words of Jorge B. Merced, member of the group El Abrazo, a component of Teatro Pregones, this kind of theater has its artistic and political value. "If AIDS demands that we take the bull by the horns," explains Merced, "then theater about AIDS demands that we topple the fourth wall and that we reject distancing in order to allow for dialogue by means of the theater."[27] Of course, the issue here is promoting a different politics and a different way of approaching theater that is influenced by Latin American theater of liberation, particularly Augusto Boal's philosophy and techniques of the theater of the oppressed. Another theater group in New York City that has raised consciousness on AIDS is Teatro El Puente, with its AIDS Drama Project, which stages short plays. The goal is "theater for the people." In Seattle, LUCES (Latinos Unidos Contra El SIDA/Latinos United Against AIDS) produced a play called *Joaquin's Deadly Passion,* by Jaime Gallardo and Matias Alvarez, which targets youth.

Teatro VIVA! in Los Angeles is designed to bring safer-sex information to the gay and lesbian population. Its goal is to encourage people at risk to get tested for HIV. The program humorously and frankly presents a series of theatrical short skits in bars, festivals, community centers, and colleges. These contain important information and techniques for HIV intervention and prevention. The project directors are gay and lesbian artists Luis Alfaro and Monica Palacios.[28]

There are also community agencies and dedicated leaders who work directly with Latino communities on issues of AIDS, sexism, homophobia, and discrimination, such as Hank Tavera and Felipe Barragán in San Francisco. Presently, Tavera is the director of the AIDS

Theater Festival, which takes place annually in San Francisco in conjunction with the National AIDS Update Conference. His goal is to give more exposure to local and national talent and more visibility to Latinos/as and other people of color. Felipe Barragán promotes HIV education and prevention through theatrical skits directed at teenagers in the Bay Area schools. In the East, in Washington D.C., Teatro Nuestro and Teatro LatiNegro have developed and performed AIDS theater workshop and sketches.

In charting community-based U.S. Latino theater on AIDS we cannot leave out Puerto Rico. Why? Because, as mentioned earlier, Puerto Rico has the nation's highest per capita rate of new cases—at least every tenth resident has been exposed to HIV. By the year 2000, one-third of the island's population will be HIV positive. As American citizens, Puerto Ricans can come and go freely, and given that Medicaid does not cover medical treatment and expenses in Puerto Rico as it does in the continental U.S., Puerto Ricans come to the States, starting a new pattern of migration. As gay Latinos/as, we also migrate, as I did, to escape Catholic influence and stigmatization by the family. (How can we forget Cardinal Luis Aponte Martínez's irresponsible statement of ignorance: "It is more sinful to wear a condom than to have AIDS"?) As Puerto Ricans get sick with AIDS, those in terminal stages return to die and be buried in Puerto Rico. The ultimate drama of the death-bed scene, indeed, takes place via the air; the air bus becomes a floating theater.

In Puerto Rico, the theater of Rosa Luisa Márquez, performed by Los Teatreros Ambulantes de Cayey (in collaboration with Antonio Martorell), has taken the lead in raising consciousness about AIDS. Márquez's theatrical imagery and aesthetics are in constant dialogue with Latin American theatrical expressions. Her piece on AIDS, *El sí-dá (AIDS)/It Does Happen,* is not simply a workshop; what we have here is a working philosophy of doing and seeing theater. As Márquez explains, *"El sí-dá (AIDS)* is a theater image that intervenes in classrooms to provoke a reflection about the epidemic in Puerto Rico.

We don't want to put together a melodrama or a manual of instructions. In spite of the severity of the problem, we don't want to terrify the spectators nor to assault or offend them. We want to raise consciousness by the most direct means possible and in a provocative way."[29]

Besides Márquez's theater, Teatro del Sesenta produced the play *Mete mano . . . es cuestión de bregar (Act Now, It's Time to Get Involved)* in 1992. The same year another play was staged, *El amor en los tiempos del SIDA (Love in the Time of AIDS).* The play, adapted by playwright José

Luis Ramos Escobar from a book of poetry with the same title by Eric Landrón, centers on raising consciousness among heterosexuals. It is allegorical and poetic, yet at times, it even seems like a commercial for AIDS prevention. Its structure is fragmented, its genre hybrid. In one of the fragments, there is a gay man asking for respect, but he is just a marginal voice, excluded from the play's central mission, which is to educate the heterosexual community.

Mapping Latino Theater on AIDS

As I document U.S. Latino AIDS theater, an archipelago of art forms, styles, theatrical models, and diverse audiences emerge. This mapping delineates the spectrum and diversity of Latinos/as in the U.S. and how they cope with AIDS in their communities by means of theater. Now I would like to move to a more "literary theater," a theater that without becoming explicitly apolitical has an aesthetic literary dimension. "Literary theater" does not participate in the spontaneity and direct political action that characterizes Latino community-based militant theater. The plays are rehearsed and written to be published and eventually staged. Although theater is ephemeral, published theater pretends to be ever present through the written word—the script aspires to a future production. With these publications (if their potential is realized), the U.S. Latino theater of AIDS would enter the realm of literature (drama). But in my quest for Latino AIDS theater, I found that the overwhelming majority of the plays have not been published.

In my search for manuscripts, I was surprised by the number of playwrights with plays on the subject. It dismayed me to hear from these playwrights that they were struggling to write about AIDS while their relatives and friends were dying of AIDS. In these cases, as described for example by playwrights Dolores Prida and Migdalia Cruz, there was no distance between life and drama. It was all a matter of waiting and processing the shock, pain, and losses of friends and relatives.

I found myself surrounded by a growing body of AIDS plays. Latinos/as were mailing me their work from locations nationwide, from California to Puerto Rico. Obviously, U.S. Latino theater on AIDS was alive and well in our communities, but it had yet to see the light of day in mainstream culture, theaters, or publications. I discovered and recovered plays in English, Spanish, and "Spanglish" about heterosexuality and gay issues. Plays with political and aesthetic dimensions were being written but not necessarily produced by Cubans, Chicanos/as, and Puerto Ricans. These plays are vivid testimony to the pandemonium and the spiritual struggles indigenous to Latino communities confronting AIDS. Indeed, AIDS in these works is not only at the heart of the communities, but at the heart of the family. Education, prevention, and survival are the main coordinates structuring the plots as the characters fight oppression, dismantle taboos, and search for acceptance. Truth and honesty, fear and pain force the characters to define their subject positions and their identities in relation to HIV-infected people, people with AIDS, people dying of AIDS, and others affected by its devastation. To date, I have compiled the following list of plays:

Juan Shamsul Alám, *Zookeeper*
Luis Alfaro, *Downtown*
Alberto Antonio Araiza, *H.I.Vato*
Alberto Antonio Araiza, Paul Bonin-Rodríguez and Michael Marínez, *Quinceañera/Sweet Fifteen*
Rane Arroyo, *Wet Dream With Cameo by Fidel Castro*
Janis Astor del Valle, *Fuchsia*
Migdalia Cruz, *So . . . and Mariluz and the Angels*
Louis Delgado, Jr., *A Better Life*
Daniel Fernández, *Fuerte como la muerte/Strong Like Death*
Raymond J. Flores, *Puzzle Box*
Ofelia Fox and Rose Sánchez, *Siempre Intenté Decir Algo (S.I.D.A.)/I Always Meant to Tell You Something*
Jaime Gallardo and Matías Alvarez, *Joaquin's Deadly Passion*
Michael John Garces, *Now and Then*
Chuck Gomez, *Deal*
Eric Landrón, *El amor en los tiempos del SIDA/Love in the Time of AIDS* (adapted by José Luis Ramos Escobar from Landrón's book of poetry by the same name)
Esteban López, *Paisanos/Countrymen*
María Mar, *Temple of Desire*
Pedro R. Monge Rafuls, *Noche de ronda/Cruising at Nighttime*
Carlos Morton, *At Risk*
Cherríe Moraga, *Heroes and Saints*
Elías Miguel Muñoz, *The Greatest Performance*
Manuel Pereiras, *All Hallow Even*
Alfonso Ramírez, *The Watermelon Factory*
Oscar Reconco, *Elegía para un travestí/Elegy for a Transvestite*
Guillermo Reyes, *Men on the Verge of a His-panic Breakdown* (see the section "Drag Flamenco")
Carmen Rivera, *Delia's Race*

5.1 The poster for *Paisanos*.

José Rivera, *A Tiger in Central Park*
Edwin Sánchez, *The Road*
Héctor Santiago, *Camino de ángeles/Patch of the Angels, Un dulce cafecito/
    The Sweetest Cup of Coffee, Al final del arco iris/At the End of the Rainbow,
    Toda la verdad acerca del tío Rachel/The Whole Truth About Uncle Rachel,
    Guerreros antes del apocalípsis/Warriors Before the Apocalypse,* and *¿Qué
    le pasó a la Tongolele?/Whatever Happened to Tongolele?*
Alberto Sandoval-Sánchez, *Side Effects*
Cándido Tirado, *Like the Dream*
Teatreros Ambulantes de Cayey, *El sí-da (AIDS)/It Does Happen*
Teatro VIVA, *Deep in the Crotch of My Latino Psyche*

A Close Critical Reading of Latino AIDS Plays

Of the plays above, I will analyze *Noche de ronda* and *A Better Life* as
two examples of U.S. Latino theater on AIDS in which a new paradigm
of Latino identity is in formation. I will explore how AIDS has pushed
the limits to reconfigure political and sexual identities in the theater
and in the communities at large to deal with the crisis. In these two
plays, a new Latino ethnicity is articulated within the parameters of a
politics of representation, a politics of identity, and a politics of affinity.
By a *politics of representation* I mean the deconstruction of negative stereotypes and degrading images of Latinos/as in the dominant culture,
and the need to construct new images, especially in the theater, for a
better self-representation. I define a *politics of identity* as the articulation
of subjectivity in process, both in language and discourse—the constitution of the subject position as a speaking subject in relation to all
kinds of discursive formations and power relations. I define a *politics
of affinity* as the move to break away from labels and divisive (racial,
class, ethnic, sexual, gender, ideological, political, religious, and gen-
erational) barriers in order to discard stereotypes, to decenter oppression, and to recognize difference as a fact of life. Only through equality,
mutual respect, and tolerance of difference in our democratic society
can we achieve a politics of affinity.
   Noche de ronda (Cruising at Nighttime; fig. 5.2) by the Cuban exile
Pedro R. Monge Rafuls,[30] is at first sight an updated version of Mart
Crowley's *The Boys in the Band* (1968), and like that play, takes place at
a party of gay men, this time Latinos. The protagonist, Eladio/la Chicana, has decided to celebrate his last birthday because he has convinced himself that he is HIV-positive and is going to die. He has been
tested, but is afraid to find out the results. This party is a farewell to

5.2 The poster for *Noche de ronda*.

life and friends. All ethnicities and Latin American nationalities make up his gay circle of friends: the Dominican, the Cuban, the apparently assimilated Puerto Rican who comes with his Anglo-American boyfriend, a Colombian, a "new Hispanic." There is a spectrum of gay identities and sexual preferences: *la loca* (the effeminate faggot), the closet case, the U.S. gay clone, the "straight-acting" gay man, the coming-out gay man. As the party goes on, and as they await for another guest, Juana la Cubana—who is in a hospital dying of AIDS, but they do not know it—an uninvited guest arrives. It is Eladio's father, from Mexico, a super macho who cannot believe what he sees: his son is surrounded by *locas* and a stripper—a Nuyorican bisexual—that they rented for the occasion. He is in shock to find out that his son is a loca himself.

Eladio hates his father's machismo; he had earlier left Mexico because his father had always embodied homophobia and chauvinism.[31] For this reason, as an "orphan," Eladio's main crisis in the play is his relationship with his father and patriarchy. Looking for an alternative position, he identifies with the lyrics of a *ranchera*, "La Hija de Nadie" ("Nobody's Daughter").[32] The folk song tells the story of a young woman who is a bastard. She does not carry her father's last name, nor has she ever met him. She accuses him of cruelty, and he does not deserve to be called a man, for all of his abuse to women.

Noche de ronda centers on the dismantling of machismo and how Latino gays move across national, state, and barrio borders to urban areas in search of a new identity. Eladio's group of friends forms an extended family of gay men who are cast out from their homes and family. As the play evolves, it articulates a sense of self-respect, pride, and belonging to a community.

Noche de ronda is a comedy that comes close to being a tragicomedy because of the AIDS epidemic. Given that AIDS would seem to have destroyed all hope of sexual liberation, the play must promote the prevention and education of AIDS without being propagandistic. Among other critical issues covered are promiscuous sexual behavior, incestuous relationships between *primitos* (young cousins), bisexuality, homosexual encounters with married men, and internalized homophobia. Sexual identities intersect constantly with ethnic, class, racial, and national identities. For example, Eladio is Mexican but they call him "la Chicana," as he explains he got the name from "a Latin American boyfriend I had that didn't understand the difference between a Chicano and a Mexican woman like me" (5). Miguel, who is a "Hispanic" without any national labeling, responds: "We 'Hispanics' are a big mixture which we don't even understand" (5). Eladio defines his nationality with pride: "I'm not Hispanic. I'm Mexican" (5). Of course, Eladio is

an immigrant who defines his identity in relation to Mexican paradigms of nationality rather than in relation to U.S-born Latinos/as. As
we can see, the subjectivity of each is in process as the men struggle
with labels and challenge sexual and ethnic stereotypes.

In *Noche de ronda*, gender roles and stereotypes are dismantled
through laughter, parody, and campy feminine behavior. At the same
time, the spectrum of Latino subjectivities and nationalities is staged
to the fullest. Even language is at stake with the formation of a U.S.
Latino identity, as Miguel says, "The United States is a bilingual country. We are a fast growing community. Soon we will be the majority in
this country" (21). Note that Miguel defines himself as a gay man who
is a member of the Latino community. Ethnicity and sexual identity are
not incompatible. He negotiates his political and social identity with his
sexual one, without producing further dislocation, marginalization, or
exclusion. Such a process of inclusion is further personified in Gustavo,
who is gay, Caribbean, and black. "The black beauty from the Caribbean has arrived," he says. "Cuba, Santo Domingo and Puerto Rico are
united in my beauty. . . . My love, I am international by injection" (22).
(Between the lines he exposes his promiscuity and sexual preference
for anal penetration.) What begins as a joke reveals a crossroads of gay
identity, sexual preference openly expressed, and ethnicity.

On the subject of AIDS, the play is educational, but also humorous
and nondogmatic. It is human and emotional, as the characters deal
with their terror, fear, anguish, pain, their ailing friend's agony, and the
loss of other friends. In the middle of all this catastrophe, a good joke
on the subject is always welcome to release the pain and break the
taboo:

Have you heard the story of the little asshole who was being pursued by AIDS?
(Making the appropriate gestures.) A little asshole was running and running
and AIDS was just behind him, trying to catch him. Run, little asshole, run
and puuum, he jumped into a church. And my dears, the Priest was there.
And the little asshole says, "Help me, Father, help me." And the Priest asks
"What's wrong?" "Oohh, Father! AIDS is after me. Work a miracle, Father."
And the Priest said, "Let us pray," and puuum, the miracle was performed.
The little asshole turned into a little bird. "Now go, little bird," said the Priest,
and the bird flew away. But outside, AIDS was still waiting for him. "Where
are you going? Who are you?" "I'm a little bird. Look at my wings flapping."
"Let's see, prove it to me. Sing!" AIDS said. And the little asshole began to
sing. (He makes great gestures with his mouth and puckers his lips as if he
were blowing wind.) Fffffuuuuussssss (26).

It is no coincidence that the joke takes place in the church. The de-
sacralization of the Catholic Church is an act of appropriation in order to fight back Catholic homophobia and terrorism against gays and

people with AIDS. The miracles of the church and the prayers to be heard have not worked: people are still dying. The priest has not done anything to save the bird, just as the church has been indifferent to people with AIDS. Furthermore, as for the image of the *pajarito* (little bird), it is a metaphorical, ironic, and euphemistic displacement of *pato* (duck) *tener plumas* (to have feathers). Once a gay Latino is diagnosed HIV-positive, it is said that *"se le salen las plumas"* ("his feathers fall out"). AIDS pushes his sexual identity to the extremes: he can no longer hide his *patería* (queerness).

In the play, the fact that Juana la Cubana never shows up is very significant. S(he) has always kept secret her (his) illness, and is dying alone in a hospital. The pressure of a prejudiced society causes her/his exile up to a point that s/he must die on her/his own, alone and isolated. On the other hand, instead of Juana showing up to the party, it is Eladio's father who arrives. In this way, the prejudiced society that kills Juana is exemplified in the figure of the father. He insists after his arrival that his son is straight and that Eladio will give him grandchildren. Ironically, the father says that he has come to see Eladio because his mother is worried that he may be sick. After all, *las madres siempre saben* (mothers always know). The father identifies the group of friends immediately as locas, but he denies that his son is one of them. He pretends that the behavior is part of the U.S. ways of being: "Look at you, Jairo. I really like you. It's true you're a little effeminate, but it doesn't matter. You're young and modern. I know that the people in this fucking country are different than in mine, but that's okay" (45). Once you cross the borders, tolerance is acceptable, at home it is unacceptable. Finally the father reveals the mother's fear that Eladio may have contracted AIDS, and convinces himself that his son is not gay: "Your mother told me she was worried you'd have AIDS but I told her, 'Lupe, that's a fag's disease and my son's no fag.' Right, son?" (46).

What has happened is that AIDS has pushed identities to the extreme: because of AIDS, Eladio is forced to accept his gay identity. His father must face reality: he is not going to have any grandchildren to carry on his last name. Machismo and patrilinearity come to a halt as the play highlights the oppressiveness of traditional roles and the family unit. His father's heterosexual, sexist, and homophobic dreams have totally disintegrated. At this point, Eladio comes out of the closet and defends his mother. When Gustavo joins in, the father, full of anger and hatred, expresses his racism and homophobia: "Shut up. The worst thing in the world is to be black and a fag" (59). Eladio has no other choice but to show pride, ask for respect, and defend his gay friends. When he says, "You've forgotten that this is my house and these are my friends" (60) he decides to "send his father to hell" and to unite with his friends—his community—as a family. The father faces the challenge of accepting his son's gayness rather than view it as *"castigo de Dios"* (God's punishment) (58). Unfortunately, the father's machismo is too strong to accept it. He has no language, no discourse, no room at home for his gay son. His last words are fragmented and halting: he cannot articulate the identity of a supermacho father who happens to have a gay son. "No . . . ," he says, "When he came I . . . today . . . I'm going now, when I return to México . . . to . . . No . . . your mother . . . If she knew . . . that . . . he . . ." (63). It is Gustavo, the loca, who has a voice to enunciate the crisis of the father and patriarchy: "Poor idiot. He thinks that his world has come to an end, that his life is over because he won't have grandchildren . . . Poor idiot. It doesn't matter if his son dies, just that he's been deceived. That matters. (PAUSE. WITH DIGNITY) Being a man is more complicated than just opening a woman's legs" (60). At the end, machismo and patriarchy have no discourse after Latino gays become stronger and proud of their gay identities. Eladio's party ends on a bad note, but the real party, his celebration of being honest and proud of himself and his new family, has just begun.

Noche de ronda stages a diversity of identities among the U.S. Latino gay community. It is ironic that the title refers to a song, Agustín Lara's bolero. *Noche de ronda*, a song dedicated to prostitutes, highlights sexual marginality in its lyrics. With AIDS, the song acquires a new reading, the rereading of an illness that kills people. In these terms, nightlife has once again allowed for the expression of desire and sexual satisfaction for those, who like Lara's prostitutes, live marginally in the darkness of night.[33] Gay visibility and AIDS is registered in the song because a prostitute's promiscuous sexual life and marginality can be compared to some gay men's lifestyles. AIDS puts gay men and prostitutes at risk, placing them on a course toward tragedy, and the song cautions that cruising is not good, that it can hurt you, make you cry. Outside heterosexual gender relations and outside marriage, according to conservatives and religious fanatics, gay men participate in a continuous "noche de ronda." Like prostitutes, gays symbolize a sexual threat, and a freedom from family responsibilities that the mainstream can easily associate with all the dreaded stereotypes of the "other."

Lara's song, in a way, puts in the open the marginalized identity of the prostitute, just as Monge Raful's play places gay identities at center stage. The dialogue between the song and the play has a point of contact: sexuality, sexual preference, and the eroticism associated with a "noche de ronda." Lara's song, like the play, voices an unconventional yet unconditional love, a love that dares not speak. After AIDS, the unsaid is spoken, the taboos are broken as we all hope for tolerance, mutual respect, and acceptance, not only in boleros or in the campy appropriation of those boleros but in the search for a better life after AIDS.

    A Better Life, by U.S. Puerto Rican playwright Louis Delgado, Jr., who grew up in the Bronx, is the only play about AIDS by a Latino that has achieved critical acclaim. It opened Off-Broadway in August 1993, at the Theatre Row Theatre. This play stages the interaction between macho, streetwise, heterosexual Marty, an African American intravenous drug user and pusher, and the upper-middle-class Howard, a gay Asian American dancer, as they share a room in a hospital AIDS ward. After their diagnoses, both men are abandoned by their respective lovers. Their condition of abandonment is a double one: it means the end of their love relationships as well as an exile from healthy lives to the world of opportunistic diseases. Their sharing a room leads to a better understanding of each other and mutual respect. The play looks for a key to cross-racial understanding and coalition, an image that is represented by the set of keys that the Asian American gives to the African American when he invites him to move into his apartment after he leaves the hospital. Marty has no family and may be homeless. Howard may never make it out of the hospital. They must learn how to live together, to share the key to life although they are from different worlds in terms of social status and lifestyles. As Howard says, "The point is, I don't like your lifestyle anymore than you like mine. But the fact of the matter is that I can't do anything about it right now. I've got enough things on my mind without having to listen to put-downs and your abuse. You want to kill me? Go ahead and kill me, I'm going to die anyway!" [34] In the play, AIDS erases differences and pushes the two men together, in order to dismantle homophobia, machismo, and social prejudices. With AIDS there is no time for dishonesty; Marty and Howard are there to support each other, to take care of each other, to survive together, to fight together for a better life. At the end of the play, both characters have gone though a process of transformation, as Marty tells Howard's sister, "not once did he put me down. He just listened and understood. I've never been able to do that with anyone" (160). Because of AIDS, mutual care and respect lead to social change. That new beginning is founded when Pat, Howard's sister, says to Marty, "Howard asked me to take care of something for him. He asked me to make you a set of keys to his place" (162). Utopia? Yes. But why not? A sign of hope is welcome at the end, especially since Howard has been taken away after having a coughing attack and difficulty breathing. Howard may die, but there is a new beginning: a new politics of cultural representation and difference has only just begun.

Both characters represent a new politics of affinity despite class bias, racism, homophobia, and social prejudices. In these terms, the playwright trespasses ethnic and racial boundaries by representing characters with different sexual, racial, class, and ethnic backgrounds. For example, Howard's lover is an upper-class white man who is married and in the closet. This character gives testimony to interracial relationships as well as depicting the possibility of bisexuality in heterosexual marriages. One might ask why there are no Latinos in the play. But, why should there be any? The point here is diversity: a new politics of representation articulated by a consciousness of ethnicity. New identities result from a more inclusive politics of affinity. All these articulations, definitions, and identity formations of subjectivities in process are possible because of AIDS. Once again AIDS is the factor that pushes individuals to forge new hybrid identities that are multiple, porous, and heterogeneous. Indeed, diversity and multiculturalism are possible only through the recognition and acceptance of difference. In the play, difference is ironically contained in one humorous and honest line, when Howard explains how the two men have contracted AIDS in different ways: "It's almost the same . . . We both put foreign objects into our bodies" (131). In a multicultural society, difference is the recognition of pluralism and the multiplicity of identities. As in *Noche de ronda*, the cultural politics of difference results from new representational practices, what Stuart Hall calls "the recognition of the immense diversity and differentiation of the historical and cultural experience of black subjects." This also applies to what Hall sees as a new politics of ethnicity: "The term ethnicity acknowledges the place of history, language and culture in the construction of subjectivity and identity, as well as the fact that all discourse is placed, positioned, situated, and all knowledge is contextual. Representation is possible only because enunciation is always produced within codes which have a history, a position within the discursive formations of a particular space and time."[35]

The importance of *A Better Life* is not limited to the issue of inclusiveness and representation of difference. The play is also based on personal experience; it explores marginality and gives a voice to Louis Delgado, Jr., a recovering drug user. As in the play, for him there is always hope, a better life. There will be a time and place for reconciliation and unity, emblematized in Marty's singing the lyrics to "We Gotta Get Out of This Place." He must get out, there must be a better place.[36]

Getting out means crossing boundaries, breaking grounds, dismantling machismo, debunking taboos, coming out, coming to terms, finding a home away from home, building community and coalitions. In order to reach freedom—that is social change—we must accept and understand each other for what we are, for our differences. Acceptance and toler- ance also must take place in the heart of the family (as Howard's sister Pat demonstrates in her visits to the hospital), with love, support, and care.

To conclude, U.S. Latino theater on AIDS is diverse. Playwrights stage the personal, social, and political dimensions of the crisis in a variety of forms within a theatrical spectrum from workshops, street theater, protest plays, agitprop, documentary, and popular theater to conventional models of theatrical genres and staging. Latino theater on AIDS is all about articulating a new politics of representation as it maps new ethnicities in a postmodern, global society. People of color can only intervene in this historical process, with our own cultural representations, as long as we practice a politics of affinity.

An Agenda for the Future

Ilka Tanya Payán, a Latina actress who died of AIDS in 1996, once suggested an alternative way of campaigning during the AIDS crisis. She believed that we should "start a whole campaign instead of the ribbons, instead of the quilt, for the people who are alive. Let's build a wall of support. That support can be shown in different ways. Which- ever way you think it is best."[37]

Could this campaign be centered in community-based theater? What about enacting rituals and performances that are embedded in the heart of Latino communities? A campaign for our communities must use the theater for acts of education, contestation, and interven- tion. In the AIDS crisis, theater is an act of mourning; it is also an act of solidarity. But most important, it is an act of survival and creativity for those living with and affected by AIDS. Nobody else has defined AIDS theater as well as Chicano activist and theater director Hank Tavera has, in his poem "What Is AIDS Theater?"

What Is AIDS Theater?

Let me begin by saying what it is not:
It is not victim art.
It is not about hopelessness and despair.
It is not about a faceless disease that only affects Gay men.
It is not without purpose.

It is about struggle
   and pain and suffering,
   and bigotry and AIDSphobia,
   and discrimination because of sexual orientation,
                 and race
                 and gender.

It is about drama
   and art, and music and dance and poetry and song.
It is about all our human expressions
   about not so pretty bed pans.
   about wasting syndrome and rage. . . . .
   and lovers dying in your arms,
And the shock and tears of finding out you're HIV+
And about being afraid to talk about being HIV−.
It is above all, a practiced or spontaneous art form, created by people
   who must do it.
It has its practitioners from peer educators to substance
   abuse clients—and always the people with AIDS.
It has its playwrights, directors, actors, technicians, producers
   and among them always people infected and affected by HIV;
It has its dramaturgs, its cultural critics, its journalists,
   its reviewers—and always among them people dealing with AIDS.

It is a theater of passion and politics—a festival of inclusion,
   a theater at war with an epidemic;
   a theater of hope, above all, a theater of hope. . . . and
   always people living,
   I said living,
   with AIDS.[38]

6

No More Beautiful Señoritas
Latina Playwrights' Deconstruction of Beauty Myths and Gender Stereotypes

"Men look at women. Women watch themselves being looked at. This determines not only most relations between men and women but also the relation of women to themselves. The surveyor of woman in herself is male: the surveyed female. Thus she turns herself into an object—and most particularly an object of vision: a sight."
—John Berger, *Ways of Seeing*

What is a *beautiful señorita*? It is probably unnecessary for me to answer the question, though it is not simply posed as a rhetorical one. All of us have seen or have had close encounters at one time or another with beautiful señoritas, either on television, in movies, theater, advertisements, or in a midnight drag show. We can easily recognize them, because we have internalized, in one form or another, all of those Carmen Mirandas, Chiquita Bananas, and Charos as stereotypical images of Latina femininity and gender relations, as portrayed by the hegemonic Anglo-American cultural and ideological apparatus of patriarchy.[1] Nevertheless, what processes are at work when we spot a beautiful señorita? Is it just a matter of reactivating the idealization and mythification of U.S. Latina women as objects of beauty, exoticism, passion, and desire of/for otherness? What is a beautiful señorita when staged as a dominant cultural configuration on Broadway and in Hollywood, with women-as-spectacle, and as models of/for gender identity for U.S. Latinas?

Close your eyes and you will see the theatrics of the beautiful señorita from "south of the border" as a cultural exotic construct, and as an object of entertainment and (sexual) pleasure. Picture it: Lawrence Welk, that "American institution," announcing Anacani, the lovely little Mexican girl from Escondido; "Ah One, Ah Two; here she is, our own beautiful señorita singing 'Cielito Lindo.'" Neither can we forget *West Side Story*, in which Rita Moreno played the loose woman and loud Spanish señorita, and Natalie Wood played Maria, the most pure, virginal, angelic beautiful señorita of them all, singing in front of the mirror, "I feel pretty." Neither can we disregard Linda Ronstadt, that born-again "Hispanic" señorita of the 1980s who took "America" by surprise by flaunting her Mexican roots. She toured the country with her musical show *Canciones de mi padre: A Romantic Evening in Old Mexico*, and even had a run on Broadway. There she was, putting on the show of ethnicity, cross-dressing as a sweet and lovely mestiza with *trencitas* (braids); dark, shining eyes; colorful flowers in her hair; and a brilliant multicolored sarape.

I even vaguely remember a commercial with the most eccentric beautiful señorita I have ever seen or imagined. She was wearing a Spanish flamenco dress crowned by her *peineta* (comb) and *mantilla* (veil), had a flower in her mouth, was dancing a tango, and had a Mexican accent. Indeed, she was an incredible collage of images of womanhood from Latin America to Spain, converged into a bizarre folkloric monstrosity, a queer feminine idealization in excess. Not even a drag queen would have done such a hilarious sui generis campy act in her impersonation of a beautiful señorita. But there she was, performing "alone of all her sex," staging her gender attributes and displaying her ethnic hybridity. Once a beautiful señorita, always a beautiful señorita, making a spectacle of herself and masquerading ethnicity in order to please the Anglo-American audience and to fulfill the horizon of expectations of Latina stereotypes according to the ways of seeing of an Anglo cultural imaginary. There she was, silent, without a discourse or subjectivity. This ad, for which I do not remember the product advertised, came to mind when I saw Linda Ronstadt's picture on the album she dedicated to her father. In the act of singing "las canciones de mi padre" (the songs of my father), she can only look at herself through his eyes and express herself through his words, in fact parroting her father. Ronstadt becomes "simplemente María," an image to be looked at, an object to be possessed, an other to be exoticized, a speaking "I" to echo male speech and desire. The cultural trope of the beautiful señorita, as seen above, materializes in a myriad of representations. Among these, Carmen Miranda constitutes the most flamboyant, stereotypical, and popular manifestation, as demonstrated in the first chapter of this book.[2]

Indeed, beautiful señoritas like Carmen Miranda, "Latin bombshells," and "Mexican spitfires" have long been the fabrication of voyeuristic conventions, constituted by ethnic- and gender-role misrepresentations, misperceptions, and misconceptions of U.S. Latinas in the dominant Anglo-American cultural imaginary. As time has progressed and these images have been perpetuated, Latinas with a feminist consciousness have found that they can no longer put up with nor identify with such negative stereotypes, nor remain trapped as beautiful señoritas in mainstream culture. Most important, they have had to challenge patriarchal imagery, male desire, and the perpetuation of a visual pleasure registered as a "to-be-looked-at-ness" condition in dominant representations. They have had to deconstruct discursive models of femininity that simply please the Anglo-American gaze and fulfill the Anglo desire of/for the "exotic, ethnic, racial, and sexual other."[3]

Since the 1970s, U.S. Latina playwrights, via feminist critical practice and as an act of resistance, have responded to the iconic formation and fixation of the beautiful señorita. They have started to refract, disrupt, resist, and destabilize the male gaze and dominant cultural and patriarchal conventions of female dramatic representation. They have put into question the traditional and pleasure-granting ways of looking at the ethnic, racial, and sexual other. These playwrights have stage-managed and moved to center stage the sexualized, objectified, erotic body of the Latina from a re-visionist and resisting position. Thus, their works debunk and demythify the patriarchal and imperialist fantasies and ideals of feminine stereotypes of U.S. Latinas. However, their feminist intervention and critical re-vision cannot be limited to only deconstructing stereotypes in the dominant Anglo-American cultural realm; they have also had to question and reevaluate stereotypical representations and gender roles of women in Latin American culture. Consequently, U.S. Latinas have had before them a double task: to deconstruct both Anglo and Latin American representations of gender and to create a space for self-representation and U.S. Latina experience.

The Usurpation of the Beautiful Señorita

This chapter analyzes the ways by which U.S. Latina playwrights question dominant stereotypes of Latina femininity and sexuality through their own politics of representation, discursive practices, and the construction of gender identity. I focus on the works of Cuban American playwright Dolores Prida's *Beautiful Señoritas*, and continental U.S. Puerto Rican playwright Janis Astor del Valle's *Where the Señoritas Are*, in order to show how these plays inaugurate a discursive space for ideological contestation in which U.S. Latina identity formation is in process, multiple, and always shifting according to power relations. I examine how these plays represent strategies of resistance to stereotypes, and how they question taboos of female sexuality. From this perspective, these plays aim at deconstructing essentialist notions of U.S. Latinas as beautiful señoritas and try to reconstruct a female subjectivity in its contradictions, multiplicities, and ambiguities, not only by mapping the body but by subverting official cultural constructs of U.S. Latina ethnic and sexual stereotypes. Such acts of apprehension, appropriation, and self-recognition lead to a political re-vision and reaffirmation that redefine women's roles and identities in U.S. Latino culture. From this feminist critical practice and political agenda, their goals are to stage the questioning of sexual taboos, the reversal of stereotypes, the dismantling of machismo, the destabilization of gender roles, and the recognition of the female body and sexuality as a body politic.

In these plays, U.S. Latinas explore their own personal experience in introspective monologues and testimonial tableaux: they stage their phases of life as rites of passage; they do not hesitate to enunciate their erotic desires and experiences; they negotiate identity and permutations of self, not only in a woman's life, but across generations of women; and they denunciate male dominance, exploitation, sexism, and chauvinism. In the denunciation of male domination, U.S. Latinas redefine their cultural roles as part of a process of self-examination. They claim control of their bodies and advocate self-determination in social and gender relations both in Anglo and Latino cultures.[4]

Whatever Happened to Those Beautiful Señoritas?

When Teatro Duo produced Dolores Prida's *Beautiful Señoritas* in 1977, the Latino/a audience was confronted for the first time in U.S. Latino/a theater with issues of gender and feminism. The play constituted a conscious response to the absence of positive female characters on the stage, as well as to the invisibility of U.S. Latina playwrights.[5] Prida's musical play was an act of intervention undertaken to debunk dominant images of femininity and deconstruct stereotypes of Latinas in the U.S. and Latin America. In her own words, *Beautiful Señoritas* "is a feminist play, [a] very early feminist play. It [deals] with stereotypes about Latin women. What I do is I use all these characters, the Carmen Miranda types with bananas on her head, the Latin bombshell, *la madre sufrida* [the suffering mother], and all of them go through a process where they take away all this superficiality and dig inside themselves, to find who they are. It's a *búsqueda*, a search."[6] Indeed, *Beautiful Señoritas* focuses on the process of being born a woman, of being trapped in gender roles in a patriarchal world, of being Latina in the U.S.

The musical opens with the birth of a young girl whose future life as a woman is projected in a series of vignettes. The girl learns about what it means "to be a woman" by going through the experience of a beauty contest. As the contestants parade in front of the girl, the participants provide her with the necessary props, adornments, and cosmetics to express her femininity in a patriarchal world. The beauty contest also functions as the medium that brings to the stage all the stereotypes that limit Latina women from being themselves: the Carmen Mirandas, the Latin bombshells, las madres sufridas, prostitutes, beauty queens, Chiquita Bananas, *las guerilleras* (fighters), and so on. As the contest unfolds, these stereotypes are attacked, as are patriarchy, machismo, and the exploitation of women. Through comedy, satire, parody, irony, cynicism, and sarcasm, Prida denunciates a patriarchal world where women are victims of machismo, misogyny, and compulsory heterosexuality.[7] By doing so, Prida challenges all patriarchal institutions that oppress, exploit, marginalize, and silence women, such as Catholicism, the family, the media, beauty myths, and the like. While the girl is processing and assimilating all the images of what she is supposed to be or could be, at the same time she and the audience are exposed to and engaged in a process of questioning, dismantling, and demythifying images of Latinas in Latin American and Anglo-American culture.

The process of deconstruction starts with the opening scene, when the audience is put face-to-face with male chauvinism. Without any delay, machismo is promptly attacked in the portrayal of an expectant father who is hoping his wife will bear him a son. As he awaits for the birth, he becomes a caricature of machismo: "Come on, woman. Hurry up. I have waited long enough for this child. Come on, a son. Give me a son . . . I will start training him right away. To ride horses. To shoot. To drink. As soon as he is old enough I'll take him to La Casa de Luisa. There they'll teach him what to do to women . . . My name will never die. My son will see to that . . ."[8] His masculinity is undermined when the midwife informs him that it is a girl. His reaction is total disillusionment and disappointment: "A girl! ¡No puede ser! ¡Imposible! What do you mean a girl! ¿Cómo puede pasarme esto a mí? The first child that will bear my name and it is a . . . girl! ¡Una chancleta! ¡Carajo!" (20). This sexist response positions the spectators vis-à-vis rampant machismo and misogyny in Latino culture. As the father is ridiculed, patriarchy, patrilinearity, and primogeniture are put into question in order to devalue male chauvinism and sexism.

After mocking the father's behavior and value system, this opening scene stages a feminist agenda, when the midwife becomes the bearer of a feminist consciousness: "He's off to drown his disappointment in rum, because another woman is born into this world. The same woman another man's son will covet and pursue and try to rape at the first opportunity. The same woman whose virginity he will protect with a gun. Another woman is born into this world. In Managua, in San Juan, in an Andes mountain town. She'll be put on a pedestal and trampled upon at the same time. She will be made a saint and a whore, crowned queen and exploited and adored" (20–21). Consequently, the midwife's role is to deauthorize the male figure and to introduce the feminist agenda of the play. The message is clear and direct: women are oppressed and exploited in dominant cultural representations and patriarchal discourse.

In the following scene, the midwife is interrupted by the voices of beautiful señoritas who sing a rumba and perform for the young girl:

> WE BEAUTIFUL SEÑORITAS
> WITH MARACAS IN OUR SOULS
> MIRA PAPI AY CARIÑO
> ALWAYS READY FOR AMOR (21)

These women, who are dressed as Carmen Miranda, Iris Chacón, Charo, and María la O, embody the stereotypes of women in Latin American and Anglo-American culture; moreover, these are precisely the role models that the girl has to emulate and idealize. These images offer the girl a series of gender-specific roles and a construct of femininity that perpetuate the representation of women-as-spectacle and the disposition to please the male gaze and sexual desires. In these images, women are objectivized and denied a subjectivity to the extent that they internalize negative stereotypes of women:

> WE BEAUTIFUL SEÑORITAS
> MUCHA SALSA AND SABOR
> CUCHI CUCHI LATIN BOMBAS
> ALWAYS READY FOR AMOR (21)

In order to deconstruct these images, the girl is taken to a beauty contest where women parade their bodily assets and contribute to the perpetuation of sexism. The beauty contest, moreover, is employed as a device for parodying dominant representations of women in order to raise the girl's feminist consciousness. The ultimate spectator is not the girl but the audience itself, which is being entertained by and educated about women's issues.

If the father is a chauvinist pig, so is the emcee of the beauty contest, who propagates the stereotypes of Latinas as beauty objects:

You will have the opportunity to see the most exquisite, sexy, exotic, sandun-
gueras, jacarandosas and most beautiful señoritas of all. You will be the judge
of the contest, where beauty will compete with belleza; where women of the
tropical Caribbean will battle the señoritas of South America. Ladies and gen-
tlemen, the poets have said it. The composers of boleros have said it. Latin
women are the most beautiful, the most passionate, the most virtuous, the best
housewives and cooks. And they all know how to dance to salsa, and do the
hustle, the mambo, the guaguancó . . . And they are always ready for amor,
señores! (24–25)

At work here is not only a battle of the sexes, but a battle of stereotypes in both Anglo-American and Latin American cultures. Latinas
start to parade in order to display their stereotypes and to enact their
"to-be-looked-at-ness," as predetermined in gender conventions. As
they walk on the ramp, they become a parody of gender roles and
femininity. In this way, stereotypes are dynamited in a humorous and
ironic manner: Ms. Little Havana's only assets are her body measure-
ments (36–28–42); Miss Chile Tamale is an illegal alien who wants
to marry an American; Ms. Commonwealth from Puerto Rico only
wishes to be a mother and a housewife; and Conchita Banana brings
to life the commercial cartoon that stereotypes and degrades all Latinas in Anglo-American culture. These stereotypes are juxtaposed to
a choir of women's voices that instigates feminist consciousness about
women's silence, oppression, and objectification. This spectacle is performed solely for the new girl, who finds herself within a process of
assimilation and imitation. In her effort to imitate the contestants, she
applies an exaggerated amount of makeup that results in "her face
made up like a clown" (24). This grotesque image of a mask is a distancing technique that serves to constantly make the audience aware
of women's dependence on beauty myths, and of their complicity in
making a spectacle of themselves in order to please men.[9] In this sense,
women's pressure to look "feminine" and the desire to make themselves the objects of the male gaze are unveiled as patriarchal constructions that women must decenter and resist.

Unquestionably, the purpose of having the girl participate in a
beauty contest is to challenge and undermine dominant representations of femininity. In many scenes, the ultimate goal is to break away
from sexual and cultural taboos. In one, for example, the señorita's
open confession of her sexual desires and sexuality serves to present
an attack on the Church for restricting women's sexuality. The priest
condemns them: "No, not in a beautiful señorita's mouth! Such evil
words, Señor, oh Lord!" (31). This satirical assault on Catholicism helps
to liberate women from guilt, and empowers them to control their own

bodies and sexuality. Throughout the play, the girl and the audience are engaged in questioning traditional ways of seeing that limit sexual expression to the confines of male desire. The señoritas' disciplined and tortured bodies must do away with patriarchal control and submission to the Church. Most important, women must challenge positions of obedience and chastity so that patriarchal dominance is destabilized. As a result, the girl and the audience locate themselves in a critical perspective in which gender attributes and behavior imposed by the Church are questioned. In these circumstances, the audience also acquires the tools necessary to dismantle traditional roles assigned to women by the Church and society at large.

Act 2 centers mainly on demythifying male-female relationships in which women are passive and submissive. Wives, mothers, and martyrs are portrayed as the stereotypes of women who internalize abuse and domesticity. The sacrificed, abused, pregnant, and abandoned women must wake up to domestic violence and victimization:

Martyr 1: Cry my child. Las mujeres nacimos para sufrir. There's no other way but to cry. One is born awake and crying. That's the way God meant it. And who are we to question the ways of the Lord?
Martyr 2: I don't live for myself. I live for my husband and my children . . .
Martyr 3: We women were born to suffer. I sacrifice myself for my children. (35)

Between the lines, the audience can read that women who do not live for themselves and who are there just to please men must become independent, self-assured, and self-reliant. It is the guerrillera who mobilizes the community of women, saying, "We can change the world and then our lot will improve! . . . We, as third world women . . . Are triply oppressed, so we have to fight three times as hard! . . . Have your consciousness raised! . . . Come with me and help make the revolution!" (36). As a matter of fact, the guerrillera does not escape stereotyping when the women think of her as a lesbian. Also, irony runs rampant: although the guerrillera has been successful in raising consciousness, once the women hear the voice of a man asking "Is dinner ready?" they all run to comply with their domestic duties and to show obedience to their husbands:

Woman 1: ¡Ay, se me quema el arroz!
Woman 2: ¡Bendito, las habichuelas!
Woman 3: ¡Ay Virgen de Guadalupe, las enchiladas! (39)

The women leave the guerrillera as they rush to resume their daily household tasks at home. "Wait!" she says, "Wait!" What about the revolution?" (39). For now, women's liberation will have to wait, at least until after dinner.

The following scene centers on demythifying the popular belief that women's work at home does not compare to a man's job. Although women work all day, their work is meaningless for men: "Of course, she doesn't work. I told you, she stays home!" (40). By accentuating men's unfairness and lack of consideration, the stereotype that women belong at home is challenged. The message is that if women stay home, they still do all the work: cleaning, cooking, raising the children, pleasing a husband. Also in this scene, the man is condemned when he harasses a social worker and asks for a date after his wife goes to bed: "Hey, psst, señorita . . . my wife goes to bed at ten o'clock. I can answer more questions for you later" (21). His behavior is not only indecent, but clearly disrespectful of his wife and women in general. The same can be said of the new father of the baby girl and the emcee of the beauty contest, earlier in the play.

In a dramatic and serious scene that contrasts with all the humor and parody in the play, a group of women—who really are a choir of consciousness-raising—appear to condemn the suffering of women. They vociferate the crimes: women are abused, victimized, raped, killed:

Woman 1: Sometimes, while I dance, I hear—behind the rhythmically shuffling feet—the roar of the water cascading down the mountain, thrown against the cliffs by an enraged ocean.

Woman 2: . . . I hear the sound of water in a shower, splattering against the tiles where a woman lies dead. I hear noises beyond the water, and sometimes they frighten me.

Woman 3: Behind the beat of the drums I hear the thud of a young woman's body thrown from a roof. I hear the screeching of wheels from a speeding car and the stifled cries of a young girl lying on the street.

Women 4: Muffled by the brass section I sometimes hear in the distance desperate cries of help from elevators, parking lots and apartment buildings. I hear the echoes in a forest: "Please . . . no . . . don't . . ." of a child whimpering.

Woman 1: I think I hear my sister cry while we dance.

Woman 2: I hear screams. I hear the terrorized sounds of a young girl running naked along the highway.

Woman 3: The string section seems to murmur names . . .

Woman 4: To remind me that the woman, the girl who at this very moment is being beaten . . .

Women 1: raped . . .

Woman 2: murdered . . .

Woman 3: is my sister . . .

Woman 4: my daughter . . .

Woman 1: my mother . . .
All: myself . . . (41–42)

These acts of denunciation and solidarity that condemn crimes committed against women and their bodies are followed by the emcee's announcement that a winner has been chosen. The new beauty queen is Miss Señorita Mañana: "Ladies and gentleman, the choice has been made, the votes have been counted, the results are in . . . and the winner is . . . señoras y señores: the queen of queens, Miss Señorita Mañana! There she is . . ." (42). Obviously, patriarchy is indifferent to women's oppression and exploitation; the emcee must go on with the show.

To everyone's surprise, the new beauty queen is a disaster, wearing the various items she has picked up while encountering all the stereotypes and images of woman: the tinsel crown, the flowers, a mantilla, and so on. The choir surrounds her, the women realizing that they have confused the girl: "I think we goofed. She's a mess" (43). Yet the only one to blame is the emcee, and his beauty contest. Ironically, this confusion leads to the final scene in which the women clean the girl's face, removing the excessive makeup, and give the girl this final advice:

Woman 2: Honey, this is not what it is about . . .
Woman 3: I'm not sure yet what it is about . . .
Woman 4: It is about what really makes you a woman.
Woman 1: It is not the clothes.
Woman 2: Or the hair.
Woman 3: Or the lipstick.
Woman 4: Or the cooking.
Woman 3: But . . . What is it about?
Woman 4: Well . . . I was 13 when the blood first arrived. My mother locked herself in the bathroom with me, and recited the facts of life, and right then and there, very solemnly, she declared me a woman.
Woman 1: I was 18 when, amid pain and pleasure, my virginity floated away in a sea of blood. He held me tight and said: "now I have made you a woman."
Woman 2: Then from my insides a child burst forth . . . crying, bathed in blood and other personal substances. And then someone whispered in my ear: "Now you are a real woman." (43)

The choir of women starts to articulate a subjectivity in process at the moment that they recognize their own bodies and experiences based on menstruation, the loss of virginity, pregnancy, and childbirth. In this way, the women's act of intervention is a definite feminist praxis that foments consciousness-raising. Given that the play is a conscious effort to explore female identity, the final message is that women must articulate their own subjectivity and enunciate their own experiences.

In these terms, there is a reminder that all stereotypes must be debunked in order to construct a new U.S. Latina identity. This objective is summarized by saying, "In their songs they have given me the body of a mermaid, of a palm tree, of an ample-hipped guitar. In the movies I see myself as a whore, a nymphomaniac, a dumb servant or a third-rate dancer. I look for myself and I can't find me. I only find someone else's idea of me" (43).

Undoubtedly, *Beautiful Señoritas* is a musical play that embarks on a search, a self-examination, and a critical inquiry of stereotypes that culminates in Latinas celebrating their bodies and subjectivity as they "look at each other as images on a mirror, discovering themselves in each other" (44). The final act of resistance is looking at themselves face-to-face, diverting and displacing the patriarchal gaze. "Mirror, mirror on the wall" (44), like other patriarchal stories and discourses of power that manipulate women and rob them of their agency, becomes obsolete once women start telling their own stories. Thus, the male gaze is bounced back; the woman will no longer view themselves through patriarchal imagery. Enunciating their independence and freedom, the women look at themselves and refuse to make a spectacle of themselves. They are ready to celebrate their own lives, their bodies, their stories. At this point, and only at this point, male sexist ways of looking are totally reversed: women are the ones who look at men looking at them, in the process of subverting men's self-flirtation, as they sing, "Mira Mami, psst, cosa linda / Look at me looking at you."[10] Now, woman has the final look and the final word. She is free at last to articulate her U.S. Latina identity.

The new girl (as well as the audience) will be able to see women in a new way. Indeed, before the play closes, the girl, who never before had said a word, pronounces her first words in the play as she realizes that "there are possibilities. That women that go crazy in the night, that women that die alone and frustrated, that women that exist only in the mind, are only half of the story, because a woman is . . ." (44). The notion of what it means to be a woman is left uncompleted by the new girl. The other women complete it for her:

Woman 1: A fountain of fire!
Woman 2: A river of love!
Woman 3: An ocean of strength! (44)

With these women, the girl starts a process of self-definition and self-realization that is concretized in the action of looking at other women face-to-face in order to discover what a woman is. The girl's new (feminist) identity is articulated in a song; she has found her own speech, becoming the subject, and decentering woman-as-spectacle and as object of visual pleasure in patriarchal discourse. In a song, the women, who are no longer typical beautiful señoritas, proclaim their independence and affirm their self-esteem and liberation:

WOMAN IS A FOUNTAIN OF FIRE
WOMAN IS A RIVER OF LOVE
A LATIN WOMAN IS JUST A WOMAN
WITH THE MUSIC INSIDE . . .
I AM JUST A WOMAN BREAKING
THE LINKS OF A CHAIN
I AM JUST A WOMAN
WITH THE MUSIC INSIDE. (44)

The girl represents a new generation of U.S. Latina women who are liberated and empowered after breaking the patriarchal mirrors and shattering the myths that imprisoned them.

Even though *Beautiful Señoritas* unveils sexual and cultural taboos as the protagonists' cultural critiques debunk myths and deconstruct stereotypes of Latinas, lesbianism still remains a taboo. In U.S. Latina theater, a first attempt at breaking the silence on rape, incest, violence against women, and lesbian desire is Cherríe Moraga's *Giving Up the Ghost* (1984). Chicana critic Yvonne Yarbro-Bejarano has lucidly stated, in relation to the politics of representation in Moraga's play, that "[the protagonists] Marisa and Corky do not conform to the codified gender representation of 'woman' on stage, neither in their appearance (hair cut short, clothes, etc.) nor in the way they move. . . . The text explores the ways in which Chicanas, both lesbian and heterosexual, have internalized their culture's concepts of sexuality."[11] This process of exploration, and the construction of a lesbian subjectivity, was fully accomplished in 1995, with Janis Astor del Valle's lesbian romantic comedy *Where the Señoritas Are.* Because the action of the play centers on lesbian desire and identity, it represents the ultimate effort to give up the ghosts of beautiful señoritas and compulsory heterosexuality in U.S. Latina culture.

Where the Señoritas Are was produced at the Nuyorican Poet's Cafe in New York in September 1994. In 1995, it received an award at the eleventh annual Mixed Blood Versus America contest sponsored by Mixed Blood Theatre Company of Minneapolis. The action takes place in Cherry Grove Beach, Fire Island, where two Puerto Rican friends spend a "women's weekend" together. Luli, a lesbian feminist, has invited her best friend Maxie, a flaming heterosexual and homophobe, without informing her that the Grove has a predominantly gay and lesbian population. Their friendship, which goes back to adolescence, takes a new turn when they experience their first mutual sexual encounter that weekend. The play portrays the vicissitudes of coming out through the exploration of lesbian sexuality and the experiences of lesbian relations. Focusing on lesbian desire, the play calls into question internalized heterosexism and homophobia in an effort to break the taboo of lesbian sexuality within U.S. Latina communities. By exposing lesbian sexuality, the protagonists disrupt patriarchal discourses and horizons of expectation that employ femininity to secure and perpetuate the male power relations that Teresa de Lauretis has described in her "Sexual Indifference and Lesbian Representation": "The construction and appropriation of femininity in Western erotic ethos has also had the effect of securing the heterosexual social contract by which all sexualities, all bodies, and all 'others' are bonded to an ideal/ideological hierarchy of males."[12]

The title of Astor del Valle's play, *Where the Señoritas Are*, contains an ironic intention with the purpose of deconstructing dominant stereotypes of Latinas. The "señoritas" here are not traditional representations of heterosexual Latinas who flaunt their femininity and disposition to attract men. These señoritas are proud Latina lesbians who are no longer in the closet. Where are the señoritas? Where they are is unimaginable in Latino culture: they are spending a weekend in a lesbian and gay environment. What are they doing in that space? These lesbian señoritas are coming out and coming to terms with their lesbian desire and identity. In this context, the horizon of expectations of a heterosexual audience is subverted, but what is most important is that the play opens up an alternative space where lesbians and gays interact while displaying their sexuality and erotic desires. Given that the action takes place in a location frequented and appropriated by lesbians and gays, the audience is forced to recognize the existence of such an alternative space as well as the existence of both Latina lesbian and gay male identities.

The opening scene introduces the audience to Maxie's problematic and abusive relationship with her boyfriend, who has told her that he needs his space. Her friend Luli responds with an attack on male mistreatment and manipulation: "You're a *pendeja* [which translates roughly as "asshole"], Maxie, letting these guys live with you, rent-free, cleaning up after them while they don't lift a finger around the house or anywhere else."[13] Luli's response reveals her feminist consciousness as well as a critique of male sexist abusive behavior. Ironically, Luli is also a pendeja ("And you call me a pendeja—Look at you, you're a mess!" [4])—for allowing her ex-girlfriend Maria to confuse her. In this direct mode, and without any apologies, Luli's sexuality is exposed. Her lesbian relationship with Maria has come to an end because Maria is now supposedly bisexual and having an affair with a man. Furthermore, both Maxie's and Luli's relationships mirror each other's dysfunctionality, regardless of sexual orientation. That is to say, once the butch-femme roles reproduce the heterosexual model, they also replicate its dysfunctionalities based in the uneven power relations imposed by the patriarchal (Latino) model.

As they board the ferry to go to Cherry Grove, Maxie notices that the sexes are divided in two lines: "Luli, why do they have separate lines for men and women?" (5). Maxie's homophobia is reactivated once she realizes that Luli has tricked her: "The only single people here are gay! Luli, when you invited me to Fire Island, you did not say the gay part of it!" (7). In these terms, Maxie enters an alternative space of lesbian and gay sexual relationships where her heterosexuality is not the norm. Luli promptly reminds Maxie that "whenever we go out, it's always to a straight place!" (8) Luli wants to introduce Maxie to gay and lesbian life, and in doing so in this alternative space, heterosexual relationships are put aside while lesbian and gay sexual relationships take center stage. In this space, lesbian existence is neither denied nor invisible; indeed, lesbian representation is a feasible task once heterosexuality is displaced, especially once the male gaze is interrupted and dislocated.

Maxie's panic arises from the possibility of becoming an object of desire for women. Although she accepts Luli as her best friend, women desiring women, women seducing women, women having sex with women is repulsive to Maxie: "I accept you, I just can't—the physical part . . . it grosses me out . . ." (9). In spite of the fact that Luli reassures Maxie that no one is "cruising" her, Maxie's homophobia progresses as she fears that people may think that they are a couple. After they come to terms with their differences, Luli hugs Maxie who, not feeling comfortable, rejects her immediately: "Okay, don't hold me so long, people will think we're—" (13). Maxie is so homophobic that she cannot even utter the word *lesbian*. In this sense, she has not only internalized homophobia, she is also an accomplice to Latino sexual taboos that erase lesbians, making them invisible and silent.

At the beach, Luli runs into Maria, who still wants her. But Maria is not the only one after her; there are two *bailadoras* (dancers) who regularly appear in Luli's imagination. These bailadoras embody the stereotypical Anglo-American image of Latinas as beautiful señoritas dressed in flamenco regalia, performing a seductive tango. Given that the beautiful señoritas are two lesbians, these apparitions contribute to the demythification of femininity and women-as-spectacle or objects of desire for men. Their function is to seduce Luli that weekend, a seduction that is doubled in Luli and Maxie's sexual attraction. These bailadoras—who provide lesbian role models—allegorize Luli's relationship with Maxie; they appear specifically when the two women are bodily close. For example, when Luli applies some suntan gel to Maxie's back, the bailadoras seduce her, inciting sexual desire. Such a seduction is emblematized by one of the dancers saying "take me": "Toma, mami, toma" (34). Whatever she is giving and offering is not clear, but what is indisputable is that lesbian desire, pleasure, and sexuality are incarnated in the bailadoras and their seductive tango. In any case, if anything is being offered at all, it is the dancers' lesbian bodies. These visions occur more regularly and with growing intensity until Luli and Maxie become the dancers themselves.

At the end of act 1, Maxie and Luli miss the ferry to return home, and this time it is Maxie who wants to stay and have fun. Act 1 closes with Luli and Maxie dancing to disco music while Juanita and Maria feel jealous. In a disco scene, Maxie and Luli on the dance floor become literally the seductive dancers of Luli's visions. Such duplication demonstrates how Astor del Valle has refocused the male gaze in order to validate and authorize lesbian existence: *women* now look at women. Once lesbian existence enters representation as an act of resistance to male voyeurism, the outcome is an act of subversion that gives visibility to lesbians and their ways of seeing and being.[14] This transgressive act also allows for a lesbian subject position in U.S. Latino culture and the expression of erotic attraction and desire between women.

At the beginning of act 2, Maxie and Luli are spending the night at a gay friend's beachfront cottage; Jesus has offered them his place to stay after they miss the ferry. Their sexual encounter is predestined by the fact that there is only one bed. In addition, the bailadoras make their appearance, performing for Luli once more. As before, Luli is the only one to see them and to be seduced. While the bailadoras surround Luli, she responds with the desire to possess them. However, her efforts are in vain; as the stage direction tells us: "Luli may even reach out to Bailadora, but every time she does this, the dancer should move away from her. Bailadora #1 is seductive, taking the lingerie from Luli, teasing her and trying to bring Luli out of herself, to let loose her true, innermost desires and identity" (70). While Luli's lesbian imaginary is exposed through the fantasy of seductive dancers, her desire becomes a reality when Maxie emerges from the bathroom in lingerie. What is at stake here is a process of substitutions and transactions in which fantasies may become reality, while at the same time those fantasies

embody Luli's ultimate desire to become a "femme" seducer and possess Maxie. Through her fantasies, Luli also deals with how she projects herself in a lesbian relationship. She wants to play femme, not
butch.[15] When Maxie asks her to wear lingerie—which, ironically, belongs to Jesus—Luli realizes that Maxie perceives her as butch. If lingerie inscribes gender roles and images of femininity in a heterosexual
world, these gender attributes are subverted with a butch-femme relationship that distorts the heterosexual model.[16] In these terms, when
traditional gender conventions are appropriated by lesbians, such an
appropriation becomes a gender performance, a campy act of excessive femininity/masculinity that parodies, like camp and drag, heterosexual gender roles. Ultimately, the butch-femme couple constitutes an
act of subversion by the mere fact that it questions and denaturalizes
traditional gender-specific conventions and categories. Judith Butler's theorization on gender identity, when parodied in the cultural
practices of drag, cross-dressing, and the sexual stylization of butch-
femme identities, applies to Luli's and Maxie's negotiations with butch-
femme categories:

[G]ender practices within gay and lesbian cultures often thematize "the natural" in parodic contexts that bring into relief the performative construction of
an original and the true sex.

*In imitating gender, drag implicitly reveals the imitative structure of gender itself—
as well as its contingency.* Indeed, part of the pleasure, the giddiness of the performance is in the recognition of a radical contingency in the relation between
sex and gender in the face of cultural configurations of causal unities that
are regularly assumed to be natural and necessary. In the place of the law of
heterosexual coherence, we see sex and gender denaturalized by means of a
performance which avows their distinctness and dramatizes the cultural mech-
anism of their fabricated unity.[17]

Luli is very conscious of butch-femme roles when she challenges
Maxie with her own politics of representation. "A piece of clothing ain't
what makes somebody butch or femme," she says. "Being butch or
femme is more of a state of mind—something so deep, it's rooted in
the heart and soul; it's a spirit, an attitude—an aura!" (72). For Luli,
butch-femme roles do not mean gender performance and/or gender-
specific behavior that registers visual markers of masculinity or femininity; rather, for her, butch-femme is the process of articulation and
constitution of a given lesbian identity. This subjectivity in process appropriates heterosexual gender behavior in order to construct a lesbian
identity that continually destabilizes traditional gender roles and behavior. In doing so, butch-femme couples carryout in their imitation
an act of resistance and appropriation that permits the formation of

lesbian identity and validates lesbian sexual relationships. On this matter, Teresa de Lauretis has theorized that

> butch-femme role-playing is exciting not because it represents heterosexual
> desire, but because it doesn't; that is to say, in mimicking it, it shows the
> uncanny distance, like an effect of ghosting, between desire (heterosexuality
> represented as it is) and the representation; and because the representation
> doesn't fit the actors who perform it, it only points to their investment in a
> fantasy—a fantasy that can never fully represent them or their desire, for the
> latter remains in excess of its setting, the fantasy that grounds it and that con-
> tinues to ground it even as it is deconstructed and destabilized by the mise en
> scène of lesbian camp.[18]

In these terms, if Luli's notion of being butch or femme is a "state
of mind," clearly being butch or femme implies an ontological outlook
that comprises the impossibility of linguistic representation. Consequently, for Luli, lesbian identity, sexuality, and desire demand a subject position and lesbian agency in which butch-femme representation
is a matter of desire, fantasy, and subjectivity: "it's a spirit, an attitude—an aura!" Luli's definition does not limit gender to a performative act that is readable on the surface of the body; gender performance
also depends on unspoken, the unrepresented, of a given interiority
that strives for its representation without achieving it.[19]

Luli and Maxie's preparation for their inevitable sexual encounter is
introduced in two ways: through the bailadoras and through Maxie's
curiosity to know in detail about lesbian sexuality. About sexual acts,
Luli explains to Maxie that "the mouth is a whole sexual organ unto
itself" (74); "Dental dams go between the chocha and the tongue. Or
the culito and the—" (75). After such a sexual and erotic preamble that
even puts into practice safer sex, the inevitable sexual scene takes place
when they start a pillow fight. At that moment, a statuette of the Virgin
hanging on the wall above the bed crashes to the floor and breaks. This
breaking is a campy act of transgression that signifies the shattering of
the myths of virginity imposed by both the Church and patriarchal
order. The breaking of the Virgin is a sign of liberation from idealized
purity and motherhood in the patriarchal world. Although the ideal
lesbian model proposes sex without guilt, Luli is terrified because she
sees the breaking of the statuette as an omen of bad luck. As they kiss,
Maxie does not hesitate. "Forget about la virgen tonight," she says (83).
The bailadoras reappear, dancing a tango that validates lesbian sexuality. Their dance not only projects Maxie and Luli's sexual act but it
also concretizes the possibility of lesbian desire and sexuality. At this
point, the beautiful señoritas are no longer objects of pleasure and

desire for males. Moreover, the protagonists are equipped to see themselves as the subjects of desire, refusing to be men's objects of desire and sexuality.

At the end, Luli breaks up definitively with Maria and starts a relationship with Maxie. Maxie's coming-out experience and her sexual relationship with Luli empower her: "Luli, no one has ever touched me the way you have—and I'm not just talking sexually—you've always been there for me, the one person I could always count on, the most positive force in my crazy, mixed up life . . ." (90). Their relationship is not limited to sexual pleasure; it is more than that. The relationship evidences what Adrienne Rich has called the *lesbian continuum*, which as she explains it includes

a range—through each woman's life and throughout history—of woman-identified experience, not simply the fact that a woman has had or consciously desired genital sexual experience with another woman. If we expand it to embrace many more forms of primary intensity between and among women, including the sharing of a rich inner life, the bonding against male tyranny, the giving and receiving of practical and political support, if we can also hear it in such associations as marriage resistance . . . we begin to grasp breadths of female history and psychology which have lain out of reach as a consequence of limited, mostly clinical, definitions of lesbianism.[20]

Maxie and Luli's sexual act has contributed to the solidification and strengthening of their love and true friendship.

Yet Maxie and Luli are not alone. There is a gay community that supports them. Indeed, it is from their friend Jesus that they learn the most as he advises them to put aside their fear, that fear is like a "parasite, feeding on the dark side of your mind, staying with you like a deep sickness, eating away at your heart, blinding your soul, until you no longer see what is good, you can't remember what's pure—" (94). The AIDS crisis has taught Jesus to be strong and has given him the tools to be confident, to be proud of being gay, and to live with dignity:

Mija, I spent the last ten years watchin' all my friends die. That's scary. One by one, they just started getting sick, and never getting better . . . People we grew up with, people younger than us . . . funny, how when you are little, you think death is only something that happens to old people; you expect to see all your friends forever and ever . . . but it don't work like that, mija. And I was the only one who wasn't gettin' sick. I started to feel un pocito guilty, tu sabes? Like, "Why me?" I told myself, "Jesus, si Dios quiere, you just got to be strong for them." I didn't think about bein' strong for myself . . . And that part of my life seemed to pass como un blur . . . going from hospital to hospital, breakfast for Carlos—he used to love my harina de arroz—lunch for Victor, dinner for Lydia, changing sheets and cleaning bedpans for all of them . . . they all started to look the same to me; sometimes I couldn't remember if I was in Manhattan or the Bronx. . . . Nights were my saving grace; I'd do my shows and rush home to Joaquin . . . in his arms, I could feel like everything was gonna' be all right. Until he got sick. Then I felt everything inside of me just fall apart . . . he was the only man I ever really loved, tu sabes . . . and within six months, he was gone . . . taken away from me, just like that . . . pue, we had seven previous years together; I only wish to Dios we could have had more . . . Mija, I'm tellin' you this, because I seen the way you look at Maxie and I seen the way she looks at you—it's the same way Joaquin and me looked at each other . . . and that kind of love only happens once in a lifetime. (94–95)

Primarily at work here is a politics of affinity resulting from the tragedy of AIDS in the gay and lesbian community. AIDS has pushed men and women out of the closet, forcing them to recognize the power of true friendship and the meaning of love. Nothing can stop them, not even fear—as we have seen in Pedro Monge Raful's *Noche de ronda*, in the previous chapter. Jesus's advice bears witness to his courage and survival in the age of AIDS. "But you girls have got to get over it, pafuera el miedo, and get your shit together because love is the most precious thing on this Earth!" he says (95). Luli echoes Jesus's words after coming to terms with having a relationship with Maxie: "Si, pafuera el miedo!" (106); "exile all fear!" Finally, Luli and Maxie are able to articulate a subject position that validates their lesbian existence. Furthermore, their lesbian agency provides them with a series of positions in which class, ethnicity, and even AIDS intersect. In this sense, lesbian identity is de-essentialized as the two women inhabit multiple subject positions and take control of their sexuality and desires. Luli and Maxie are mapping a new U.S. Latina identity that allows for diversity and difference among Latinas; it also proposes an alternative way of building community. Once Latina lesbians and Latino gays come out, their act of resistance empowers them to intervene politically in all kinds of cultural practices, through cultural critique and transgressive strategies of lesbian and gay representation. Doing so, lesbian and gay invisibility in U.S. Latino culture is vanquished: Latinas/os are willing to stage their own self-representations in order to dismantle homophobia, disrupt compulsory heterosexuality, and, in solidarity, fight AIDS.

There is no doubt that the newly assumed U.S. Latina subjectivity in process, and growing feminist and/or lesbian-feminist consciousness, mobilize a theatrical agenda, a system of expectations for developing strategies, new visions, and new options that will engender Latinas' bodies and embody diversity and plurality from female experiences and points of view. In this way, these plays give evidence of a U.S.

Latina agency based on negotiations, difference, and conflicting subject positions. By no longer portraying women as beautiful señoritas,
the theatrical space will be opened to a new U.S. Latina subjectivity.
As Gloria Anzaldúa dramatically explains, "The new *mestiza* copes by
developing a tolerance for contradictions, a tolerance for ambiguity.
She learns to be an Indian in Mexican culture, to be Mexican from an
Anglo point of view. She learns to juggle cultures. She has a plural
personality, she operates in a pluralistic mode—nothing is thrust out,
the good the bad and the ugly, nothing rejected, nothing abandoned.
Not only does she sustain contradictions, she turns the ambivalence
into something else."[21]

U.S. Latina theater since the 1980s has become an accomplished and
fruitful enterprise that embodies a heterogeneity of voices, a plurality
of discourses, and a diversity of experiences. Latinas in the theater
have come a long way; playwrights such as Dolores Prida and Janis
Astor del Valle have opened the doors to a new way of approaching theater, both in subject matter and dramatic structure. In addition
to playwrights, Latina performers such as Marga Gómez, Carmelita
Tropicana, and Monica Palacios have broken the lesbian silence.[22] As a
result, they are mapping their female bodies, voicing their experiences,
dismantling sexual and cultural taboos, exploring difference and diversity, and constructing multiple subject positions at the center stage
of the theaters of the Americas. And the rest, as they say, is *her*story.

7

"There's No Place Like Home"
Is It Just a Matter of Clicking Your Heels Together in U.S. Latino Theater?

I had to leave that space I called home to move beyond
boundaries, yet I needed also to return there.
—bell hooks, *Yearning: Race, Gender, and Cultural Politics*

U.S. Latino theater offers a privileged cultural space for displaying and
putting to test models of/for identity formation. Since its inception in
the 1960s, it is evident that Latino theater has centered on a politics of
identity and location. The stage has functioned as a crossroads where
previous and emergent ethnic, cultural, racial, class, gendered, and
sexual identities intersect, overlap, and clash. Having as its historical
foundations migrancy and exile, U.S. Latino theatrical productions
constantly unfold the crisis of the family unit. This is so because after
migration and exile, the institution of the family and the "Hispanic"
household face a series of structural and ideological transformations.
During this process of instability, adaptation, and transition, it is a perfect historical and critical moment of cultural dynamics to analyze
how national and ethnic identities are dialectically related to a politics
of location. While parents may embrace nostalgia after displacement
from their homeland, a second generation must find a way *to feel at
home*. Under these circumstances, Latino theater not only represents
the struggle and survival of the family, its true protagonist, but also
the agonizing ontological condition of the individual, a second generation trapped between two worlds, two languages, past and present,
here and there. For this generation, constructing a new U.S. Latino/a
identity requires not only reconnecting to a distant geography and a

national past, but also constructing a subjectivity in process as determined by geographic, local, political, social, and cultural spaces in the U.S. *Be(long)ing*—read as belonging, being, and longing—encapsulates the dramatic crisis of the Latino family as represented in theater: the parents belong to their homeland and they long for their past; the children struggle to belong to the U.S. as they accommodate and negotiate their parents' worldviews. For this second generation, being is searching for a place of belonging, but where?

In this final chapter I will exercise a critical reading of U.S. Latino/a playwrights whose works propose new ways of seeing, being, and knowing as the protagonists act, interact, and transact within a cluster of notions that composes a new politics of representation, identity, and location. These notions are migrancy; exile; nostalgia and amnesia; myth of the eternal return; dysfunctionality of the family; crisis of patriarchy; empowerment of women; formal college education; a Protestant ethic promoting individualism; hybrid, bilingual, and bicultural identities; social mobility; and—last but not least—the whole conceptualization of *home*. Continental U.S. Puerto Rican playwright José Rivera's *The House of Ramon Iglesia* and *Marisol*, Dolores Prida's (Cuban American) *Botánica*, and Roy Conboy's (Chicano/Irish) *When El Cucui Walks* articulate crises of identity as children contemplate breaking away from family, community ties, and home. Formal college education provides these children with the passport to enter Anglo-American society, as well as equipping them with a new system of values and beliefs to the extent that the children will feel out of place at home. Each play presents an array of alternative models of identity formations for the protagonists as they strive to negotiate with the concept of home. Rivera's plays bring to the stage the protagonists' crises of identity in their decisions to break away from home as a result of their assimilation. On the other hand, Prida's play attests to how the crisis of finding a Latino/a identity after college can be overcome as long as the protagonist juggles languages and cultures, recognizing a new hybrid, bilingual, and bicultural identity, with all of its contradictions and fluidity. As for Conboy's play, the protagonist learns that she does not have to throw away her culture and ethnic past as long as she is able to accommodate into her life past and present, mythical and quotidian, emotional and rational, oral and literary ways of seeing and being.

If the children of a second generation must erase their Hispanic heritage after attending college, there is *no place called home* for them, no family and community to return to, no feeling of homesickness. Once they assimilate, they are homeless, wanderers. No one better captures the story of assimilation and upper-class mobility than Richard Rodriguez, in his autobiography *Hunger of Memory*. "Once upon a time," he explains, "I was a 'socially disadvantaged child'.... Thirty years later I write this book as a middle-class American man. Assimilated."[1] Having lost all sense of home, of family ties, of belonging Rodriguez explains that his surname is "[t]he name I carry from my parents—who are no longer my parents, in a cultural sense." He adds that "[i]t is education that has altered my life. Carried me far." Yet, later in the book, he also adds, "... I think, however, that education has divided the family ..."[2] U.S. Latino/a children who come from a second generation, like Rodriguez, are forced to make a choice between self-acceptance and self-denial, affirmation and ambiguity, authenticity and pretension, assurance and alienation, displacement and relocation, discontinuity and tradition. The crisis of identity fully arises when these children take for granted that their Hispanic heritage, Spanish language, and U.S. Latino culture is not sufficient, relevant, or functional enough to achieve social mobility, to succeed in their pursuit of happiness and the "American dream." For them, "making it" means erasing their ethnic identity, their history, their cultural heritage.

Going to college guarantees a second generation of U.S. Latinos/as a one-way "yellow brick road" to assimilation. Once the children return home, there is often little communication with their parents, relatives, and the community at large. Family interaction is difficult, problematic, confrontational, or nonexistent. At worst there is silence, a total lack of communication and understanding, as in the case of Richard Rodriguez, whose book closes with such silence. As the children depart from home after a family reunion on Christmas, only then does he realize that he has not talked to his father: "He asks if I am going home now too. It is, I realize, the only thing he has said to me all evening."[3] It is clear that Rodriguez has crossed over, that there is no attachment to his Hispanic household. Home is not home any longer. Can an individual have a sense of place and a sense of be(long)ing without the notion of *home*? What does *home* really mean?

Home Sweet Home/Dios Bendiga Nuestro Hogar

By staging *home*, U.S. Latino/a playwrights dissect the composition of the institution known as *family*. Their theatrical works exhibit how home as a sociocultural construct locates them in given symbolic and imaginary interrelational and interactive spaces. Home operates as a discursive site where social and power relations depend on the socio-symbolic and geopolitical signification and interpretation of migrant mobility and identity. If before migration home did not require questioning, after migration home becomes a site of conflict that loses its aura as a sacred locus for shelter, comfort, security, and nourishment. The diasporic experience disrupts and dismantles the conceptualization of home as a place of/for stable and homogeneous identities. Home becomes problematic: it is an unattainable place of origin, always framed by longing and desire for an identity believed to be fixed in that memorial/memorable space of a place left behind. So many boundaries have been crossed, so many displacements and dislocations have taken place, that home will not always be what it was believed to be. Identity removed from home is multiple and provisional, always manifesting the impossibility of a fixed subjectivity.

If home, after arrival in the U.S., has multiple meanings and is always in a constant process of transmutation and redefinition, Latino theater is a cultural imaginary space that offers a cornucopia of conceptualizations, notions, and metaphors of home according to specific individual, familial, and collective experiences.[4] Home functions as a sociocultural space, a site where identity exists in relation to what was left behind, constructing a new *home away from home*, or an instance of *not feeling at home* at all. Any definition of home relies on how the family and its constituents bargain with relocation, distantiation, abandonment, and/or appropriation of space. There are fundamental questions in the process of constituting hybrid subjectivities after migration. How can previous concepts of home, family, and community be transplanted, accommodated? Can home as place or as household anchor displaced immigrants? How does the space of home, articulated within a network of discursive formations and practices, function as a site for identity articulation for a second generation?

In U.S. Latino theater, the concept of home sustains the interdependence and negotiations between past and present, the public and the private, experience and imagination, the political and the emotional, nostalgia and amnesia. For parents, home in the U.S. is a symbolic construct of a home lost. For Mexican Americans, the lost home came with the annexation and the creation of a modern U.S. imperial nation-state in 1848, with the Treaty of Guadalupe Hidalgo enacted after the Mexican-American War. For Puerto Ricans, the lost home became a colony after the U.S. invasion in 1898, when Puerto Rico became a booty of the Spanish-American War. For Cubans who despised Fidel Castro and Communism, home was lost with the Cuban Revolution in 1959. It is precisely because of the location of home in the realm of nostalgia that it is always situated on the verge of erasure and amnesia. In this chapter, I will focus on the plays of migration where parents left a homeland behind, a place where they started from, and where a second generation cannot remember/recollect their parents' concepts of home, nor can they *make themselves at home*. After migration, home as a base for the domestic and public social construction of reality has become provisional, mobile, and portable. In this sense, the children of immigrants feel out of place: their identities are fractured, porous, multiple, hybrid. The house of memory converts into a house of difference. Somewhere in between, home is a floating signifier lost in space, where subjectivities are always positioned at the border, at the margin, in the liminal space of hybridity. Consequently, subject positioning constitutes identity as process, always transitory, conflictual, fragmented; so is home.

The subject formation intersects with a politics of location when that space, home, locates the subject at an intersection of discursive formations and practices, and multiple geopolitical and sociocultural sites. At that significant juncture, "Where am I?" cannot be separated from "Who am I?" Within a politics of location and identity, that particular personal experience makes room for a speaking position where the subject can claim his/her agency. By doing so, mapping one's identity requires the identification of a history of locations where migration, exile, deterritorialization and reterritorialization, dislocation and relocation determine identity in all its plurality and liminal condition of betwixt and between. In these terms, where one comes from is not the sole marker of identity. Rather, identity is determined by where one is *at*. It is at this site of subject position that I locate the conceptualization of home as represented in U.S. Latino theater: a home in situ, in given social and power relations, positioned at the intersection of discursive formations and practices and cultural dynamics here and now in the U.S.

Knock, Knock. Anybody Home?

José Rivera's *The House of Ramon Iglesia* centers on a Puerto Rican immigrant family and its endless dilemma of whether to return to the island or not. Through the years, the parents have dreamed about their return, but when the time comes—after nineteen years—one of their sons decides to stay in the U.S. The oldest son, Javier, who is college educated, assimilated, and willing to cross over, faces an identity crisis while trying to break away from home, family values, and Hispanic cultural traditions. His alienation is accentuated by his refusal to speak Spanish, and by his embarrassment of his ethnic parents. He sees his father, an alcoholic with a critical case of diabetes, as a loser.

Javier's father came to the U.S. in search of a better life and economic gratification, but his dream has been shattered. The restaurant he worked at went bankrupt; the house he bought is decrepit: the furnace breaks down constantly, the water pump does not work, and the septic tank in the back may overflow at any time. If this were not enough, his family is collapsing. In order to escape his own sense of failure, he turns to alcohol, as he sourly laments, "It's right for a man to drink a drop of rum for every drop of water he has cried. . . . This shot's for success! For Ramon Iglesia! Cook! Janitor! Manager of a failed, greasy diner!"[5] The truth is that Ramon Iglesia was never able to "make it" in the U.S. He has never been in control, though he is the patriarch. It is his wife pointing to the crisis of patriarchy that reminds him and accuses him of his own failure and lack of authority at home: "You're afraid of him [Javier] and he's ashamed of you" (225).

Above all, *The House of Ramon Iglesia* puts the crisis of the father figure in motion. As a result of migration, Ramon Iglesia has lost power at home and in society at large.[6] His tragic situation has become more aggravated because of unemployment and a concomitant lack of self-esteem. As an alcoholic, his financial problems are endless, to the point that he can no longer keep his position as breadwinner. Such a state of uselessness and alienation leaves this father figure powerless; full of anger, frustration, and despair; and violent. He is lost, demoralized, and castrated. He has abandoned all sense of pride, and cannot provide a positive image as a role model for his children, who do not respect him anymore. His crowning humiliation is having to sell his house.

On the other hand, the mother has been waiting for nineteen years to return to Puerto Rico. In the first place, she never wanted to migrate but she had to follow her husband. Her life has been nothing but misery, pain, and loneliness in the U.S. Her name, Dolores, translates as "pain" in Spanish. After the death of her daughter Felicia, she can only blame her husband, the house, the winter. If Ramon Iglesia cannot function as head of the household because of his failed dreams, nostalgia paralyzes Dolores's life: she longs for the island and she mourns the death of her daughter. Nostalgia has frozen her in time, literally; she is immobilized after Felicia's death: "I . . . stood by that window for a whole day facing Puerto Rico" (228). Trapped in homesickness; she is obsessed with her journey back home. She is convinced that winter in their cold home, with its broken furnace, has killed her daughter. For her, *home*—Puerto Rico—is the space of memory, desire, and felicity. Home there meant shelter, nation, utopia, an idyllic peasant way of life, tropical weather, Spanish, and most important, the place where her daughter would never have died. Indeed, the play opens with Dolores's determination to return home, as she addresses her daughter's picture, saying, "Don't worry, Felicia, we're going home" (197). This imaginary conversation with her daughter, for whom she has erected an altar, shows how, through the ritual of remembrance, nostalgia is activated. For Dolores, the house of Ramon Iglesia has never been, nor could ever be, her home, as she confesses to her son Javier:

Javier: Hasn't this house ever been home?
Dolores: Never. This place has never been good to any of us . . . This "home"
    took away my little girl . . . this cold house killed her! (228)

Not only does the house incarnate a space of loss and death, but it also constitutes a prison, as her son Charlie accurately explains, "This place is worse than San Quentin to her" (209). Dolores's desire to return to Puerto Rico registers how migration has made her aware that home is a place from which one has left, and to which one must return. For years Dolores has not only been homeless, but *house*less, inhabiting home solely in negative terms: nonattachment, cold indifference, and neglect.

The irony is that nostalgia in a certain way empowers Dolores; it works not merely as a sentimental yearning for the place of origin and the past. As anthropologist Debbora Battaglia suggests, "Nostalgia for a sense of future—for an experience, however imaginary, of possessing the means of controlling the future—may function as a powerful force for social reconnection.[7] Yet Dolores's geographic, cultural, and linguistic nostalgia, no matter how it empowers her vision of the future, is detrimental to the second generation. The parents' nostalgia, which closes in upon itself and refuses to negotiate between cultures, erases any possibility of accepting that home is in the U.S. With determination, and in control of her future, Dolores confronts and threatens her husband with departure and abandonment:

I swear on the spirit of my Felicia, if you keep me here another year, it'll be our last year together. Every year you promise me we'll go back and every year you break your promise. No more, Ramon! I let you do what you want to do for nineteen years, now I do what I want. If you don't, I'll leave you. I'll go home by myself. (225)

Javier, who is ashamed of his father, cannot escape Dolores's authority when she is forced to play the gender role of the traditional father figure, reprimanding, "Don't yell at your father! Respect your father!" (227).

Of the Iglesias's three sons, Javier is the major protagonist given his state of assimilation. His brothers make life decisions: Julio is joining the marines, and Charlie is moving back to Puerto Rico with his parents. Charlie's move to the island is mainly motivated by the excitement of the tropics and the beaches; in this sense, he will visit his parents' homeland as a tourist. (The honeymoon will soon be over, however.) Javier is the most conflictive and problematic son because he feels ashamed of his parents and all Puerto Ricans. He detests the poverty of migrant Puerto Ricans, and he condemns his parents' ambivalence and incapacity toward establishing a permanent residency and rooting in the U.S.

Javier's identity crisis, according to all family members, results from his college education; they blame it for his behavior, detachment, and rejection of "all things Puerto Rican." His brother Julio belittles it, saying, "Hey, at least I didn't waste four years in some obscure little college, learning political science, just so I can come home and hang my brain on the loading dock of a warehouse!" (219); "You're mixed up. That school really made you confused" (210). Dolores condemns college for changing her son, claiming that "when he came home from school he was a stranger" (223). Obviously Javier has been unable to reconcile his formal education with his nonformal education. His only way out of the Iglesia's house is to walk away. "I want out," he proclaims. "I want my freedom. Freedom from . . . fatalism . . . superstition . . . docility . . . from thinking like a peasant" (227). At this point Javier's identity crisis results from his inferiority complex, internalized racism, and self-hatred. According to him, Puerto Rico is great for those who love "polyester, food stamps, babies, mosquitos, radios . . ." (239). As he tells Charlie, the best thing about Puerto Rico is that he does not live there.

Javier's negative visualization and stereotyping of Puerto Ricans clashes with the views of his family because he can only see Puerto Rico as an underdeveloped country with tropical jungles, full of peasants and wild fauna. He constantly undermines his parents' idealization of their homeland with his derogative attitude toward Puerto Rico: "They can go to Puerto Rico and eat green bananas all day" (207). At work here are not only assimilation and disidentification from Hispanic roots, but a classist point of view that underestimates Puerto Rican people and their culture.

Javier is convinced that his future is secure as long as he is capable of distancing himself from his family and his parents' homeland. This process of separation started in college, and will reach its peak at the end of the play, when he decides to stay in the U.S. By gradually refusing to be a part of the home, Javier becomes homeless as his process of separation becomes a process of alienation. Indeed, homelessness is a recurring theme in the play. At one point, Javier must ask his ex-girlfriend to give him some money to survive for a few days. If she is not willing to do so, he will be out in the streets. As he explains, "My options are simple: the Y on 92nd street, a Central Park bench . . ." (240). On another occasion, it is Calla, the neighbor buying the Iglesia's house, who not only threatens Javier with eviction, but also makes a death threat against him should the deal fail, warning, "you may be living in the bottom of the Long Island Sound" (238).

At the end of the play, Javier is trapped in his own dreams, and by the individualism promoted in the U.S. ideology of the self-made man. It is his own brother Julio who has predicted Javier's state of estrangement and homelessness: "*Your* dreams are killing you" (220). Because of his assimilation, Javier only wants to run away. He tells his father, "I just want to be allowed to forget the old world, *your* old world. Because that world has forgotten you and the new world doesn't want you. And I won't let that happen to me" (232).

In order to get rid of his parents, Javier flies to Puerto Rico to get family signatures to close the sale of the Iglesia's house with the neighbor, Calla. Although Calla is tangential to the dramatic action, his role is crucial in the future return of the family to Puerto Rico. Ironically, during the negotiations, it is Javier who stands in the place of the father. It is precisely Calla who incites Javier to exercise his masculinity and to prove that he is not, like his father and all Puerto Ricans, a bunch of losers. "Like father, like son; losers breed losers," he says. "It's like some assembly line in Heaven got stuck one day and turned out a whole island of you: these little Spanish people who don't know shit about the world. There is this *smell* coming from you people, Javier, the smell of fear, it's all over you, don't tell me it ain't. You just don't know how things get done in the world" (238). No matter how racist and ethnocentric Calla's portrayal of Puerto Ricans is, Javier must prove, and convince himself, that he is not one of them. By finalizing the sale of the house, Javier asserts his agency. He makes the final decision to stay in the U.S. without his family, both houseless and homeless.

In the play's final scene, the Iglesias are on their way to their ancestral homeland. Javier is alone in the empty house; he turns on the tape recorder and plays salsa music. He starts dancing, then stops and pronounces the last lines of the play: "Dance for us, Javier. Salsa for us . . . Javier" (242). These are the same words that his father had spoken earlier when accusing him of blatant assimilation and selling out: "You've made them so important! You eat their food, wear their clothes, love their women, talk their language but you're still their little Puerto Rican. You're their entertainment, their fun. Something new. Dance for us, Javier! Salsa for us, Javier! Wear the clothes, Javier! Fool yourself, Javier! Keep fooling yourself, Javier! You're a little Puerto Rican, Javier!" (232–33).

The play closes with this tragic and ironic note of self-hatred. Javier realizes that his ethnicity will be stereotyped in Anglo-American society, and that he will always be a token. Nevertheless, he decides to stay because that is where he belongs.

Javier's alienation and loneliness is the result of not having been able to reconcile the process of his assimilation with the nonformal education received at home. Not able to negotiate nor cope with hybridity, Javier totally separates himself from his past, his family, and his culture. He is left *a la intemperie*, unsheltered, to struggle with his own identity crisis and confusion after assimilation. Javier is trying to find a place but he is always *out of place*. Expressed by his homelessness, his real struggle with *total* displacement—emotional, psychological, linguistic, social, and cultural—has just begun. At this point Javier does not fit in anywhere. His separation marks the total fragmentation and disintegration of the family and all sense of home.[8] He cannot return to Puerto Rico because he is an American—the U.S. is his homeland. Yet at home in the U.S., as long as he is perceived as a minority token, he will be homeless. He is searching but he cannot find a solution to his identity crisis, not only because of his rejection of his family and people, but also because he lacks any sense of community and affinity with other U.S. Latinos/as. He does not identify with people of color, nor does he desire to be labeled an ethnic minority. This had surfaced earlier in an interaction with his brother Charlie, when Javier had explained that he doesn't speak Spanish because ". . . I don't know. Got out of the habit. But I've been starting to think. About our people, you know? And I don't even know what those words mean, "our people." Chicanos in California? Dominicans? Cubans in Florida? Puerto Ricans in New York who still go back to the island and never made a commitment here? I don't know, I look around. I know what our people feel and need and want—and I want to help them someday—and I know I will someday—but, something pushes me away . . ." (210). Clearly, Javier misunderstands the colonial, historical, and political condition of the islanders, who as a people have been American citizens since 1917, a factor that facilitates the Puerto Rican constant circuit of migration.[9] Furthermore, the Iglesias have no connection or alliance with the Puerto Rican migrant community. Their insularism has erased any possibility of inventing a home within a collective migrant experience. Neither Javier nor his family have a place to go to create a home within the foundations of a collective memory.

Can Javier "get his act together," affirm his multiple identities, and survive in the U.S.? The play ends with this question, this lack of closure. With a note of irony signaling self-hatred and victimization, Javier performs a somber monologue that registers his own solitude and lack of any family and community attachment—that is, to Puerto Ricans, U.S. Latinos/as, or Anglo-Americans. Javier is left alone without any possibility of redemption. There is *no place here called home.* An empty house is not home.

When taken into consideration that Rivera modeled Javier after himself, the play acquires a significant historical dimension since it bears witness to the psychological, mental, emotional, and ontological complexities of children of migrants and their identity crises. In a certain way, the play allegorizes Rivera's own crisis:

It is based on my life right after I graduated from college. I was living at home but wanted to be on my own. . . . I was hung up on success, I'd gone to this preppy school. I couldn't accept the world I was in, I yearned for this other world where people were successful. . . . Now I wince at some of the things Javier says, at the self-hatred evident in him. [Javier embodies] my own anger at the time and how unresolved it was. I once felt that in order to transcend my culture I had to escape it, to run away from it.[10]

For Rivera and his protagonist Javier, crossing over means exploding all notions of home. In this setting of deterritorialization and reterritorialization, second-generation U.S. Latinos/as must learn how to adopt, and adapt to, Hispanic and Anglo-American ways of being and seeing. After their college education, there are several options: (1) to disidentify totally from Latino culture through assimilation; (2) to negotiate assimilation and ethnic values, to cross over without losing one's "Latinidad"; (3) to accept one's family for what it is and to learn to interact in different social and ethnic environments; and (4) to learn to juggle the nonformal education with the acquired/imposed dominant formal education. In this difficult process of identity formation and articulation, the children face a serious crisis of identity, as do their parents. As a result of education, a generation gap and an ethnic gap occur. Furthermore, the parents' fear of losing their children undermines their achievements. For them, assimilation can only be understood as betrayal. It also signals the parents' failure to transmit their values, traditions, language, and culture to a second generation. The interaction can become critical when the parents suspect that they are an embarrassment to their children, or when the children feel ashamed of their culture. The total process can be visualized in the following way: at home the children receive a nonformal education that consists of Spanish language (or bilingualism) and a nationalist and ethnic model of Latino/Latin American culture. Once they receive a formal education, English will be imposed as the primary language, and Anglo-American dominant culture will be enforced as the only channel to assimilation and success; at this point, children can totally break away from the notion of home. If not, a new process of nonformal education could start: they must reeducate themselves and educate their parents in order to configure and construct their new hybrid identity. Such a new identity formation is always a subjectivity in process; it always oscillates between past and present, here and there, Latino and Anglo-American social constructions of reality. For many, after they leave home to receive an education, they must find a way to come back home. The process is a painful one.

No Place Called Home

In a 1983 *New York Times* review of *The House of Ramon Iglesia,* Frank Rich curiously wondered where Rivera's dramaturgical practice would be heading: "[A]fter seeing how much Mr. Rivera makes out of family materials, one keenly looks forward to watching how he'll progress as he ventures further from home."[11] Two observations cannot be dismissed: the expectation that Rivera "will break new ground" and that his playwriting will "venture further from home." Does this mean that he must leave behind his ethnic roots, family ties, and Hispanic culture? Does breaking new ground imply starting anew in a sociocultural space that is not home, a space where bilingual and bicultural identities are silenced after assimilation? With his play *Marisol* (1992), Rivera does venture away from home (fig. 7.1). In this well-acclaimed play, he picks up where Javier was left at the end of *The House of Ramon Iglesia:* without a family, in limbo, home alone, homeless.

Marisol is a Puerto Rican "yuppie" working in publishing whose life becomes a nightmare when her guardian angel deserts her. In a dream, the angel informs her that she will abandon her to fight a revolution against a senile old white god. "I called a meeting," the angel says. "And I urged the heavenly hierarchies—the seraphim, the cherubim, thrones, dominions, principalities, powers, virtues, archangels, and angels—to vote to stop the universal ruin . . . by slaughtering our senile God. And they did. Listen well, Marisol: angels are going to kill the King and restore the vitality of the universe with His blood. And I'm going to lead them."[12] Once the guardian angel leaves, Marisol is

7.1 José Rivera's *Marisol* at Hartford Stage. (Photograph © by T. Charles Erickson.)

on her own, confused and with no family, no community, no home to go to. She wanders homeless though the apocalyptic and chaotic streets of the Bronx, a world of natural and human cataclysm, pollution, crime, racism, and hatred. In the streets she meets all kind of strange characters: characters who are displaced, alienated, bizarre, psychotic, dead; she meets a man who lost his skin, neo-Nazi skinheads, homeless people, a pregnant man, a pyromaniac. To exist is to live in perpetual warfare and paranoia: no one is safe—not even children, since the whole "universal body is sick. . . . Constellations are wasting away, the nauseous stars are full of blisters and sores, the infected earth is running a temperature, common sense has deserted the planet, and everywhere the universal mind is wracked with amnesia, boredom, and neurotic obssessions" (30). Once Marisol's angel leaves her, it is impossible to keep her home safe.

Given that such a nightmare can only take place in the realm of dreaming, Rivera erases the boundaries between imagination and reality, between the world of the dead and the world of the living. It is never clear as to whether it is all a dream, or whether after the angel appears in a dream, Marisol awakens to a living nightmare. What matters is that Marisol inhabits the world of the living dead, and, in this nightmare, she is believed to be dead. When she shows up to work in the morning, she realizes that the media has aired and published her tragic death the night before, when a man killed her with a golf club. (Earlier, in the play's opening scene, a man attacks her in the subway with a golf club and announces that her guardian angel is going to leave her.)

Marisol's whole life is in ruins, in shambles. Her world is fragmented and disconnected. The more she tries to find her way home, the more she gets lost. There is no sense of direction, no possibility of a homecoming. Her effort to return to the Bronx can be read as her search for a place of belonging. Being a Puerto Rican, the Bronx is marked by ethnicity; as Marisol tells one of the characters, "There's supposed to be a bodega right *here*" (37). That bodega functions synecdochically: it represents *el barrio y su gente*, the barrio and its people. Marisol is lost because she has left the barrio behind and suffers from familial, ancestral, communal, cultural, and geographic amnesia to the extent that she has forgotten her home address. "I was born in the Bronx," she explains. "But—but—I can't name the street!" (38). Her assimilation has caused her trauma: "I commuted light-years to this other planet called . . . called—Manhattan! And I learned new vocabularies . . . wore weird native dresses . . . mastered arcane rituals . . . and amputated neat sections of my psyche, my cultural heritage . . . yeah,

clean, easy amputations ... with no pain expressed at all—none!—
but so much pain kept inside I almost choked on it. ... so far deep
inside my Manhattan bosses and Manhattan friends and my broken
Bronx never even suspected ..." (38). Marisol's ethnic, cultural, and
familial separation have turned into a painful amputation. Assimilation has disconnected her from home and turned her into a nomad.

If *Marisol* is read as an allegory of Javier's future life in the U.S.,
there is no hope. Marisol's odyssey is an urban nightmare in which
anarchy and loss accelerate her journey into loneliness and misery. The
whole experience is poetically described as a "celestial Vietnam": a
place where coffee and apples are extinct, where exceeding credit limits justifies torture, where natural resources have turned into salt,
where the moon has left its orbit and the children are stillborn. Loneliness, desolation, despair, rage, agony, fear, terror, and violence rule
Marisol's future life. Such a hellish, apocalyptic nightmare dominated
by displacement and deterritorialization serves to project Marisol's
identity crisis as if saying that her life can only be staged in an excessive manner. Only excess and extravagance can deliver the epic spectacle of doomsday.

At the end of this epic piece, Marisol has a revelation and narrates
the war of the angels. When it ends, Marisol briefly foresees a new
world order, a new millennium: "New ideas rip the Heavens. New
powers are created. New miracles are signed into law. It's the first day
of the new history. ... Oh God. What light. What possibilities. What
hope" (44). And that's it. The action stops there, without bringing Marisol back home or to a future home. She is suspended ad infinitum
without solving her identity crisis, without finding a place where she
belongs. She takes residency in the black holes of the universe.

What did losing her guardian angel mean to Marisol? Losing her
identity? Losing her culture? Losing her Hispanic ethnicity? Losing
her faith and hope? Did Javier, like Marisol, lose his guardian angel
when he decided to stay in the U.S.? To what degree does Marisol
reflect Rivera's abandonment by his own guardian angel? I believe that
the key to finding an answer to these questions is tackling the issue of
assimilation. In an article in the *New York Times*, Rivera confessed the
following: "Marisol is, like me, a consummate assimilationist. I live
with a constant sense of melancholy for what I have denied."[13] In another article he goes further in his assessment of Marisol's assimilation:
"Marisol has been so successfully assimilated that she has lost touch
with her roots and her humanity."[14] It is clear that Rivera's characters
have not created a new cultural space in which to articulate their hybridity and accommodate their difference. What is at stake is that they

cannot accommodate their Hispanic heritage and belief system after Anglo-American assimilation. Although Rivera is conscious that his protagonists—like himself—belong to a new generation, there is no articulation of a discourse through which hybrid speaking subjects assume their agency. "This is the first play I've written with an eye on the next generation," he tells us. "We need to find new heroes and new myths for our society—the old ones just aren't working. The God we know now is a right wing, white male, corporate God, in whose world racism, sexism and political injustice are rampant. As the millennium nears, I am amazed these things are still valid."[15] For both Marisol and Javier, their identity crisis remains unresolved. They know that something must be done, but assimilation has stripped the possibility of "fixing" their identities in space and time. They know that subjectivity is always in process—in short, migratory. They want to find a place in the world, however, by discarding and rejecting previous cultural spaces and ways of seeing, they constantly feel *out of place* and are incapable of constructing something positive out of their bilingual and bicultural condition.

Homecoming

If Rivera's protagonists are characterized by existential dilemmas and homeless conditions after assimilation, Dolores Prida's theatrical works offer a model of/for the construction of bilingual and bicultural identities. Prida successfully represents in her work how, through continuous negotiations and accommodations, her protagonists can function in both Latino and Anglo-American cultures. Her plays, like *Coser y Cantar* and *Beautiful Señoritas*, showcase, within a pedagogical framework, how her protagonists' hybrid identities are constructed in all their heterogeneity, difference, and multiplicity. In *Botánica*, once again making her didactic message clear, Prida demonstrates the ability and feasibility of her protagonist, Millie/Milagros, to claim her agency and to oscillate between Anglo-American and Latino worldviews. By learning how to juggle cultures and by straddling Anglo and Latino ways of seeing, Millie, unlike Marisol and Javier, is capable of reaffirming her Hispanic heritage. Once positioned at the crossroads of assimilation and resistance, Millie's hybrid cultural identity makes it possible for her to redefine where she stands and where home is. She remaps the boundaries of what constitutes home, and by doing so, she positions herself at that point where her politics of identity fuse with her politics of location. She becomes a survivor, always taking into consideration that her identity is determined by antagonisms, binary oppositions, oscillations, vacillations, discontinuities, plurality, ambivalence, and constant negotiations as she formulates a new, hybrid, second-generation U.S. Latina identity.

In *Botánica*, Millie struggles between values acquired at an Ivy League college in New Hampshire and those learned at home. The process of assimilation started when she changed her name from Milagros to Millie. When her long-time friend Ruben calls her Milagros, she explains, "I don't like to be called Milagros. . . . It's just that in college . . . every time I'd have to explain my name, they'd laugh: Miracles, what kind of a name is that. . . . I had to deal with a lot of things. The name thing was one of the easiest. Milagros in El Barrio may be an everyday thing, but, Miracles in New Hampshire . . . no way!"[16] Millie's relocation demands a new subject positioning and new ways of seeing. Taking into consideration the changes that she has had to go through, renaming herself was not as traumatic when one reads between the lines that going to college meant confronting class discrimination and racist prejudices. Both family and spectators have witnessed how extreme Millie's assimilation was in order to be accepted in a white society and achieve success.

The dramatic action starts with Millie's unexpected return home. She has decided to lie to her family, saying that her unanticipated arrival is due to the fact that graduation took place earlier than expected; the truth is that she intentionally did not invite her relatives to her graduation because of cultural and ethnic shame. In fact, she would have been terribly embarrassed if they had shown up in New Hampshire with a cargo of *pasteles* (the Puerto Rican version of tamales) to celebrate her triumph.

Millie's reentry into her family is not easy. First of all, her grandmother is a powerful matriarch who controls and protects her family clan from any threat from the outside, including assimilation. Second, the grandmother's authority is omnipresent, since men are absent in her territory (Millie has no father, nor any brothers). Third, the crisis of patriarchy experienced by Latinos after migration has empowered Latinas enough to affirm their agency and to resolve any family crisis. And fourth, the matriarch has planned Millie's future: she will manage the family business, her grandmother's botánica, and she will live at home. Clashes start as a result of her family's expectations and manipulation of Millie's future.

In contrast, Millie has other plans. She majored in business administration and has an offer from a bank to be vice president of its international department. She is also looking forward to being independent, moving away from home, breaking away from her family. As she tells Ruben, "As soon as I start working, I'm moving downtown. I want my own place" (12). There is no doubt that a college education is Millie's passport to upward social mobility and economic independence. By remarking later that she is not willing to stay in the "ghetto," her statement is loaded with classist and racist prejudices:

Ruben, I don't want to live here. I won't live here. I have my own plans. I want something different. I want to leave all this behind. I want to forget the smell of fried plantains, and Florida water. I hate this business. I've always wanted to escape from the incense, the camphor, the cleansing rituals, the spirits and the saints, for people looking for an easy way out [of] life's problems, from my grandmother, ruling over everybody's life, like a queen in her palace of cholesterol and patchouli. I may have been born in the ghetto, but I don't have to live here. (13)

Her education has resulted in the total devaluation of her roots. All she wants is to get rid of her family and get out of the "ghetto." Her desire for independence has a strong dose of selfishness, blatant individualism, self-sufficiency, and aggressivity, virtues that promote the "self-made man's" value system of Anglo-Protestant ethics.

As the play progresses, Millie rejects her grandmother's future plans for her. Their confrontations are the result of Millie's education and rational thinking. College has made her despise and be irreverent toward her family's beliefs. As she tells her grandmother, "We're almost in the 21st century and you still pretend to solve people's problems with herbs, essence and mumbo jumbo" (24). In response, her grandmother credits her "mumbo jumbo" as the means for making possible her education: "Thanks to that mambo jambo you went to college!" How do you think you won your scholarship?" (24)[17] answering, "Because I studied," Millie defiantly challenges her, because I fried my brains to get good grades, because I was the token spic for that scholarship. I don't fool myself, grandma. I deal with reality" (34). In Latino culture, Millie's disrespect for the elderly is an act of arrogance and insolence. Millie's attitude and behavior cause her grandmother to collapse at the end of act 1. In the following act, it is apparent that her grandmother's illness functions as the catalyst that ignites Millie's recovery from assimilation.

One of Millie's critical confrontations with her family takes place in this second act, when she tells her grandmother about her agonizing experience and excruciating abuses in college for being a Latina. In a monologue she educates her family about racist and elitist practices at school:

I got there ready to conquer the world, to learn it all. But immediately the small cruelties began—jokes about my clothes, about my accent, about the

music I liked . . . about my name . . ."Miracles, what kind of name is that?" . . .
I did not want to be different. I wanted to be like the others. And I changed
my name to Millie, and hid my salsa records. And I hid the amulets and beads
you sent me—your "survival kits." One day my roommate found the box
where I had hidden it all in the back of the closet. She didn't say anything to
me, but told the whole school: "Miracles Castillo from El Barrio is a witch.
Guess what I found in the closet?" . . . She asked to be transferred to another
room . . . Earlier on I had applied to one of the sororities. And I had been
accepted. The day of the initiation they decided to play a trick on me. They
took me to the forest, and tied me to a pine tree. At my feet they put a bunch
of red tissue paper. It looked like a bonfire. They lit up candles and poured a
bottle of rum all over my body. One of them beat a little toy drum. The others
danced around me a sort of Indian dance, and . . . and . . . I know it was an
accident, but . . . one of them dropped her candle . . . and that tissue paper
bonfire became a real blaze. In the confusion . . . by the time they untied me,
my rum-soaked feet . . . They burned my feet, grandma! . . . But I didn't quit.
Because that's what they want, that we give up. But I won. And I graduated.
Summa Cum Laude." (38)[18]

Millie's horrific and racist experience ultimately shows how ignorant
and barbaric people can be when they do not respect difference. With
this chilling account, Millie has saved herself in the eyes of the family
and the audience: her assimilation was a survival skill. Now at home,
Millie, with this confession, has started her process of healing.

Eventually, Millie must come to terms with her formal education
and her present situation. She must reeducate herself, and educate her
mother and grandmother. It is a painful process through which she
gradually recognizes her denial of her Hispanic culture. In the end,
Millie decides to stay home, and she succeeds in blending her college
experience with her Latino cultural reality. She modernizes the botánica, renaming it Ceiba Tree Herbs and Candles Boutique. The new
name inscribes her grandmother's powerful presence in the image of
the ceiba—throughout the play she is emblematized as a ceiba, a tree
that is known for its strength and leafiness. She also computerizes her
grandmother's systems of folklore and religious belief. After Millie
takes over the family business, she is able to create a new home at the
heart of the family and her community. Furthermore, she refuses to
sell the building for profit as gentrification threatens her people with
eviction. When a real estate dealer, who has been trying to buy the
building, calls Millie at the end of the play, she informs him, with self-
assurance, "I've changed my mind . . . it's not the money . . . it's that
the buffaloes are not for sale!!" (46). This proverbial line, continually
uttered throughout the play by the character Pepe El Indio, encapsulates the moral of the drama. Pepe, who is homeless, dispossessed,

and disfranchised, voices the terrible experience of Native Americans after losing their land and their freedom: "Young lady, you have to protect your little buffalo. Without them we are nothing. They've killed all of mine, and you see, I'm nothing. . . . the white men came killed them all and we were left with nothing . . ." (17). It is Millie's friend Ruben who decodes for her the meaning of Pepe's proverb. "Believe it or not, Pepe El Indio is a well-read man," he explains. "He read that Native Americans lost not only their land but also their culture and identity when the white man killed their buffalo" (28). Ruben's role in the play is to help Millie in her homecoming.

Millie takes the road to recovery when she negotiates with San Lázaro, the patron saint of the ill. In this hilarious but instructive scene, she puts into use her religious faith by praying to him for her grandmother's healthy recovery. In this way Millie engages in a process of negotiations. Yet she does not give in easily: instead of a promise, she makes a deal. What is significant in this scene is that Millie starts a process of recollecting communal memories. Her cultural amnesia, as a result of her assimilation, begins to break apart, to disintegrate as her cultural collective memory intermittently resurfaces.

With the intercession of San Lázaro, and with Ruben's advice and guidance, Millie learns that her social construction of reality is anchored in the U.S. and that with her bilingual/bicultural identity seen as an empowering advantage and privilege she has a solid foundation. Unlike José Rivera's Javier and Marisol, her identity is firmly consolidated in biculturalism, as her response to the real estate man—that her "buffaloes are not for sale"—signifies.

With the popular wisdom of her grandmother and her community, Millie succeeds in accommodating her past and her present without selling out. She will keep her family business, her family home, and save her people from homelessness and dispossession. Millie's act of *conscientización* (consciousness) crystallizes the possibility of a new U.S. Latina identity that can put into action what was learned in college with the knowledge and experiences of her grandmother and her people. She proves wrong her family's assumption that college education, like Javier's in *The House of Ramon Iglesia*, has distanced and divorced her from her culture and her family. Her grandmother, like Javier's mother, has feared that education would change Millie; early in the play she tells Millie's mother, "What happens is that you can't accept that Milagritos has changed a lot since she's been up there in that lily-white college" (7). Later, she says directly to Millie, "I don't know what they did to you in the university, Milagritos, but you're changed" (38). Even Millie's best friend Ruben condemns her behavior: "You've changed a lot, Milagros" (11). Indeed, it is Ruben who, at the end of the play, will make her proud of her heritage and help her to deal with her identity crisis. Ruben's speech exemplifies the consciousness of a new U.S. Latino generation in its effort to articulate identity in the borderlands. The gist of it is that it is not where one comes from, but where one is at now:

What does it mean "to be from here"? Well, for me, to be from here is, well . . . mangoes and strawberries . . . alcapurrias and pretzels . . . Yemayá and the Yankees. . . . What's the difference? What's the big deal? That's what we are: brunch and *burundanga*, quiche and rice and beans, Chase Manhattan and the numbers game. . . . It all depends on how you pack your suitcase. But it's all part of your baggage. It's all the same. You see, I decide what it means to be from here, because out there, a lot of people think that even if you are born here and you change your name to Joe or Millie, they think you are not from here anyway. And there on the island . . . they think we are not from there, either. From here, from there . . . what do I know? There's no reason to leave it all behind . . . no reason to let them kill our buffalo. (28)

With such a philosophy of life and understanding of a bicultural/bilingual identity, Millie will construct her new U.S. Latina identity at home and locate herself in a new social and cultural arena. Millie, unlike Javier and Marisol, who are homeless, has found her way back home, found home with her family, even moved to the apartment upstairs. For her, *there is no place like home*, a bilingual and bicultural home in the borderlands, in the barrio. After college, Millie's construction of home will never be over; home will always be in the making. And there will always be homework to accomplish.

Homemaking

Usually children of a second generation are expected to find their way home on their own; it is up to them to make themselves at home again. Given that they were the ones who went away, it is taken for granted that they are the ones who have changed. However, to what extent are parents and relatives responsible for *making them feel at home*? Why should a homecoming not be a place where both parents and children negotiate and accommodate their experiences, worldviews, and differences? In order to tackle these issues I will analyze Chicano/Irish playwright Roy Conboy's *When El Cucui Walks*, a play that brings to center stage the transformation and restructuring of home in U.S. Latino theater.

When El Cucui Walks presents the devotion of a great-grandfather, Papi-Tres, in his effort to bring his great-granddaughter Camila back home.[19] Being a storyteller, he uses the mythical tale of El Cucui, the Mexican bogeyman, to awaken her desire to come back home. El Cucui is a trickster of death: once he gets his victims to dance with him, they fall prey. Alternating dreams, myth, folklore, and storytelling, Papi-Tres weaves El Cucui's story with the sole purpose of getting Camila to return to her culture, her roots, and her ancestral home before he dies. His strategy is to make Brian, a young Irish American man, the protagonist with whom his granddaughter will become emotionally involved. Brian functions as the mediator who facilitates Camila's re-entry into the domain of a mythical world that constitutes the Chicano/Latino cultural, communal and collective imaginary.

Camila is the only family member who takes care of her great-grandfather. Life is not easy, since she has to care for him at home, work long hours to survive economically, and struggle to get a college education. In the opening of the play, Papi-Tres wants her to remember the story he tells, but she refuses to do so. As he recites the lines throughout the play, the story gradually develops. In the first scenes the only information given is that it takes place in the woods in a dark night: "The forest was very dark that night, And the dark was alive with sounds."[20] While Camila refuses to listen, Papi-Tres has as an admirer, Brian, who is willing to listen and learn from his stories. Brian has been spiritually attracted to Papi-Tres; somehow, Papi-Tres has touched Brian's soul. Brian, like Papi-Tres, has the ability to cross boundaries, to move between the world of dreams and myths—a world that Camila has disowned. Yet Brian and Papi-Tres are not alone: the audience also joins in to assemble the development of the story. In these terms, the play constitutes a performance of storytelling. Brian and Camila, as well the audience, must put all the pieces of the story together. Brian and Camila are both the protagonists and addressees in Papi-Tres's story. Whatever they do has the potential to change Papi-Tres's story (and the plot of the play).

By centering on the oral transmission of storytelling as performed by Papi-Tres, the younger generation recovers its past, collective memory, cultural heritage, and value system. Indeed, the whole process constitutes a ritual in which collective memory is recycled, reactivated, and mobilized between generations. In order to transmit effectively the cultural knowledge, Camila experiences a rite of passage through which her Latina identity is rearticulated. In the process of listening and internalizing the story, she enters a state of liminality as she inhabits a world of dreams—the subconscious—and myths. In a dream, narrated by Papi-Tres, a young girl is running in the darkness of the woods. This darkness symbolizes Camila's lack of vision, and lost eth-

nic and cultural roots. Both in the story and in her dream, animals—
the owl, the snake, and the wolves—are out there menacing her. At
this point she remembers her parents' advice: "Don't go into the woods
at night, *mija*.... You might get lost. You might lose your way" (5).
Only by remembering the story will she be able to survive. The story
itself functions as an allegorical pilgrimage of Camila's way back home.
Her journey into her culture is her journey home.

Camila's incapacity to recite the story allows El Cucui to make his
presence certain and interfere in the development of the story. As a
trickster who personifies death, El Cucui is willing to stay until one of
the protagonists succumb to his power, until he convinces Camila that
he does exist. Her statement, "I don't believe in El Cucui" (5), shows
Camila's distance from, and denial of, her culture. Realizing her state
of assimilation and disbelief, her grandfather intervenes in the story in
order to guide her to where she started from—home.

Papi-Tres's perseverance to "save" Camila contributes to the formation of a new protagonist in U.S. Latino theater: Camila, like Millie in
Botánica, must negotiate both her past and her present. Although Papi-
Tres guides her in finding the way home, he takes his time. His teaching is far from being indoctrination in or nostalgia for his own cultural
past. He allows Camila to exercise her own agency; instead of con-
demning her behavior, he uses cultural memory to allow her to perform in a place called home. Her cultural position will depend on how
she regains her agency and reclaims her Latino culture through the art
of remembering. Why does she *not* remember? First, she is too busy to
listen to Papi-Tres's stories. Second, he does not realize that her cultural
memory is not the same as his. It is El Cucui who reminds Papi-Tres
that Camila lives in an urban world where his stories are an anachronism and do not have any relevance to her present reality. She has lost
all attachment to family ties and discarded any responsibility of caring
for the elderly as dictated by the model of the extended family. El
Cucui tortures Papi-Tres, saying, "[I]t looks like the nursing home for
you, old man" (7). On another occasion, when Camila finds Papi-Tres
dancing with Brian, she reacts in an aggressive and inhuman way,
threatening to put him away. "And you make me carry you," she says.
"You make me your walker. You make me your slave. And then I find
you dancing.... You'll dance everyday when I'll put you in a nursing
home ... And I'll dance too.... I'll dance on your grave!" (15).

As El Cucui plots Papi-Tres's death, there is more interaction between the two. At the beginning of the play, El Cucui has mortified
Papi-Tres with his conviction that Camila will never remember. Now
emphasizing how the setting of the story has changed—"There's no

forest here. There's no snakes or owls or wolves here" (7)—El Cucui exposes how identity, culture, and location are interrelated and interdependent. His declaration definitely registers that Camila's recovery of her memory is a failed attempt because her social construction of reality and her position in the world have been removed from Papi-Tres's mythical, folkloric, social, and cultural world. With cruelty, El Cucui constantly undermines Papi-Tres's efforts.

Despite El Cucui's wishful thinking that Camila will never find her way home, Papi-Tres manages to get Brian to intercede for him. Brian, unlike Camila, likes to listen to his stories. Given that Camila does not have time for these stories because of her busy life, Brian enters into her dreams in order to deliver Papi-Tres's mythical world. It is for Brian that Papi-Tres narrates the story about his encounter as a young man with El Cucui. In the story, he asked El Cucui to teach him how to dance, and as they danced all through the night, Edilberto (Papi-Tres's real name) delayed his own death. When El Cucui ran out of dances and time, Edilberto gave El Cucui a mirror. Being a vain person, El Cucui admired himself, while Papi-Tres escaped from his fate. He fooled death; the trickster was tricked.

Once again Papi-Tres is not willing to give up: he will not rest until his great-granddaughter remembers. For him, Brian is a last resort. Brian is the only one who can touch the soul of Camila, who refuses to dream, to believe in magic, to believe in anything. Before it is too late, Brian explains what a person like Papi-Tres should mean to her, that she is "lucky to have someone like him around. I never had anyone like that. In my family all that got lost a long time ago. They never even talked. They just faded out in silence. Now I wonder if they ever existed. So yeah, I think you're lucky. You're lucky that he makes noise. At least you've got some magic in your life" (18). Brian tells her that if she does not remember Papi-Tres's stories, her past will be lost, her future will have no history, her life will be amputated. Camila responds incredulously because she cannot make sense of his stories; she has neither inhabited nor experienced the places Papi-Tres speaks of. "But what do his stories mean now?" she asks. "Where is that forest? Where is El Cucui? Where are the snakes and the owls and the wolves? The only wolves I meet are at the tables I wait on. And the only fight I have with them is with their hands. Their hands on my butt. (18). She has lost all faith, and Papi-Tres has become but a financial burden for her.

As the plot develops, Camila cannot figure out who Brian is. All he says is that he came to be in an old man's dream, and that that dream was "a dream of an old man . . . a dream of a story" (25–26). Here dreaming and storytelling intersect, positioning Camila and Brian in the mythical world. It is because of Brian that Camila enters into Papi-Tres's story; she will be totally involved when Brian becomes a bait to the animals in the darkness of the forest. In a dream, Camila desperately searches for Brian crossing over into Papi-Tres's mythical realm. In the morning she tells her dream to Papi-Tres. At this point he has succeeded: Camila has begun to wander in the liminal zone of the subconscious in his story, which manifests itself to her as a dream. Papi-Tres confesses that he brought Brian over because only he could make Camila remember his stories. "You think my stories mean nothing to you," he explains. "You think that your life is a car, a TV, a mall, a job, a phone, a man, a credit card. You think there is nothing more. But there is, *mija*. There is" (30). Papi-Tres's role is to educate Camila, to make her aware of the banal and worthless world of materialism and consumerism. He wants only to teach her some values, some myths left behind in a rural world where nature and human interaction were "a memory, a dream, a beast, a darkness" (30).

Without Brian, and with El Cucui now threatening to take Papi-Tres away, Camila is forced to enter the story. This time she is the girl running lost in the woods. Her errant wandering causes El Cucui to speculate as to why she has been running. Obviously she was lost; yet El Cucui goes further, asking, "was she running away from home?" (32). It is here that the meaning of the whole play crystallizes: Camila has left *home* behind. The only way to find her way home is to tell Papi-Tres's story. To recite his story is to recover memory, to find her place in history: *memory* is *home*. El Cucui repeatedly urges Camila to tell the story. "Open your mouth and let it pour out, like blood, like a song," he says (33), but Camila is stubborn and keeps her mouth shut.

Ultimately, El Cucui makes Camila tell the story; his trick is to change the location: instead of the forest, the story takes place in the city. "The city was very dark that night," he says. "And the streets were alive with sounds." Papi-Tres joins in, echoing, "The city was very dark that night" (33). Finally, Camila can tell the story. "Wind blew through the fences and the parking lots," she recites. "Snakes hissed from the offices and shopping malls ... Owls hooted in the doorways and the telephone lines ... Wolves cried out from the alleys, and the rooftops, and the vacant lots ..." (33–34). From now on, the girl running is Camila herself; she is running away from sexual harassment from her boss, running from an eviction from her house, running from the responsibility of taking care of Papi-Tres. In short, she has been running away from home; but now there *is* no home anymore. As El Cucui tells her, "Your home, his home, home sweet home, or home on the range, it don't mean shit because it's gone now" (35). Like home, Papi-Tres will soon vanish. El Cucui tortures Camila with his new version of the story; by modernizing and urbanizing the setting, he gets Camila to listen, to react, to intervene:

And when the owl [Papi-Tres] was gone they had no home, they had no roof, and they had no fire. They were lost in the city, without food, or warmth, or shelter. Without friend, or prayer, or purpose. The young woman and the old man. And the noise of that city pressed closer and closer around them. And they thought they heard the wind, but it was only the hollow ache of their empty stomachs. And they thought they heard the snakes, but it was only the poison in their brains. And they thought they heard the owls, but it was only the honk and hoot of the traffic on the streets. And they thought they heard the wolves. . . . (36).

As Camila is surrounded by wolves, her fear increases. El Cucui reminds her that it was her choice to be homeless in the streets: "Why should [the wolf] stay away? This is the streets, no? This is the nameless streets. And you have to fight here. You have to slug and slice and psych here" (36).

Bringing the story to its end, El Cucui corners Camila. She can now only save one person—Papi-Tres or Brian. "Who will it be?" El Cucui asks. "The wolves are dancing, mujer. Which one will you save?" (37). She must tell the story, and bring it to its close. In her version, Camila becomes the sole protagonist of the story, finding herself mired in affliction and desolation: "She began to cry and cry and cry," Camila recites. "Because there in her darkness she saw how alone she was. And how alone her Papi-Tres was. And how alone Brian was. And how alone each of them would always be . . . Like old age, their loneliness was a disease for which there is no cure" (38–39). The story comes to its end with Papi-Tres's death. Camila is left with Brian, and with the story. As long as she remembers the story, she will always remember Papi-Tres. As she tells Brian, "I was just remembering. One of the first stories I can remember Papi-Tres ever told me" (39). The act of remembering takes place in a new context and location, that of the city. At the play's end, Camila and Brian are the protagonists of the new urban and interracial/interethnic version of Papi-Tres' story, but this time as they run, they remember. Papi-Tres has left his legacy, his myths, his dreams, and his stories to a new generation. Happily, he dances away with death.

When El Cucui Walks succeeds in locating myth in an urban environment. Most important, it registers the urbanization of Chicano theater. Cultural survival is possible as long as the cultural past is accommodated to the present realities of a younger, urban generation. Without stories, dreams, and myths, Camila would have been forever stripped from her ethnic identity and evicted from home. For her, adapting and retelling Papi-Tres's stories means finding a site for be(long)ing within the cultural imaginary. Her remembering and recovery of home illustrate how identity is always shifting and being shaped by location. Camila succeeds because she is able to translocate, and *translate*, Papi-Tres's stories. By *translation*, I mean she crosses over, slides into other discursive sites where she can juggle identities and claim her agency, where she can intervene, appropriate, and discard fragments of her cultural past. In this sense, *translation* can be understood as Salman Rushdie has defined it: "The word 'translation' comes, etymologically, from the Latin for 'bearing across.' Having been borne across the world, we are translated men. It is normally supposed that something always gets lost in translation; I cling, obstinately, to the notion that something can also be gained."[21] Although there are gaps, intervals, interstices, and silences in any act of translation, any sense of loss can be supplanted by a new sense of place in which memory and desire position identity in a dialectical relationship with *home*. No matter how migratory the notions of *home* are, *home* is always a place of negotiation for translations and resistance.

Mobile Homes

If the protagonists of *The House of Ramon Iglesia* and *Marisol* wander, homeless, in *Botánica* and *When El Cucui Walks* they find their way home. The rupture and failure of homecoming do not incapacitate Millie and Camila to position themselves at the crossroads of bilingual and bicultural identities. Their oscillations between the Latino and Anglo-American worlds forge a sense of identity always defined by the question of position. Although there are dislocations and translations, they revise the notion of place in order to *house* their own subjectivities in process. Finding and belonging to a place is a constant negotiation, through which these protagonists assert their agency by remapping territories, crossing borders, redefining identities.

As these characters find a voice, a new mode of representation emerges in U.S. Latino theater. Theater operates as a practice of memory, a performative site where cultural collective memory is preserved, reinterpreted, and reinvented; a site where there is a regeneration of beliefs, values, and traditions, and an alternative definition of *home*. U.S. Latino theater, indeed, is *a place called home* when it functions as a location of/for retracing, recovering, recollecting, recycling, reconnecting, envisioning, negotiating, and reconciling the cultural, ethnic, familial, communal, and national past. Finding the way back home represents a political act of resistance and intervention. Such resistance is not anchored in a fixed location, since identity is always fluid, transitional, provisional, mobile, problematic, and conflictive. From this perspective, identity inhabits a *mobile home*, one that is portable and provisional; one that is imagined in liminal and alternative locations; one in which the only survival kit is comprised of memory and desire.[22]

No one has better conceptualized the notion of *home*—in a postmodern world—where migrancy, exile, diaspora, deportations, social and geographic mobility, disruption, and displacement determine the boundaries of hybrid and plural identities—than bell hooks, who writes that

the very meaning of "home" changes with the experience of decolonization, of radicalization. At times home is nowhere. At times, one knows only extreme estrangement and alienation. Then home is no longer just one place. It is locations. Home is that place which enables and promotes varied and everchanging perspectives, a place where one discovers new ways of seeing reality, frontiers of difference. One confronts and accepts dispersal and fragmentation as part of the construction of a new world order that reveals more fully where we are, who we can become, an order that does not demand forgetting.[23]

In other words, for a new generation of Latinos/as, U.S. Latino theater represents *a place called home;* a place for subject positioning in multiple discursive locations; a place where an identity politics of location reproduces at given historical intersections new ethnicities in the borderlands, in the margins of previous, partial, residual, present, and emergent conceptualizations of *home.*

Notes

Bibliography

Index

Notes

Overture

1. Ngugi wa Thiong'o, *Decolonising the Mind: The Politics of Language in African Culture* (London: James Currey, 1987).

2. Adrienne Rich, *On Lies, Secrets, and Silence: Selected Prose 1966–1978* (New York: W. W. Norton, 1979), 35.

3. Judith Fetterley, preface to *The Resisting Reader: A Feminist Approach to American Fiction* (Bloomington: Indiana University Press, 1981), viii.

4. Roland Barthes, *Mythologies*, trans. Annette Lavers (New York: Hill and Wang, 1979); John Berger, *Ways Of Seeing* (New York: British Broadcasting Corporation/Penguin, 1981).

5. Catherine Belsey, "Disrupting Sexual Difference: Meaning and Gender in the Comedies," in *Alternative Shakespeares*, ed. John Drakakis (London: Methuen, 1985), 167.

6. I am using Louis Althusser's definition of "interpellation," through which individuals in given social practices, ideologies, and discursive positions are constituted as subjects. In this process of social construction, ideology is not only a system of values and beliefs taken for granted, but also contains a dimension of false consciousness. Jeremy Hawthorn interprets the process of interpellation as follows: "individuals come to 'live' a given set of ideological assumptions and beliefs, and to identify these with their own selves, by means of a process whereby they are persuaded that that which is presented to them actually represents their *own* inner identity or self. For Althusser, then, the SUBJECT is the *concrete individual* after interpellation." Jeremy Hawthorn, *A Concise Glossary of Contemporary Literary Theory*, 2d ed. (London: Edward Arnold Press, 1994), 97; emphasis in the original.

7. bell hooks, preface to *Feminist Theory: From Margin to Center* (Boston: South End Press, 1984), ix.

8. I am adopting Benedict Anderson's term "imagined communities": "It is *imagined* because the members of even the smallest nation will never know most of their fellow-members, meet them, or even hear of them, yet in the minds of each lives the image of their communion." Benedict Anderson, *Imagined Communities* (London: Verso, 1991), 6; emphasis in the original.

9. Frederic Jameson defines "ideologeme" as follows: "the ideologeme is an amphibious formation, whose essential structural characteristic may be described as its possibility to manifest itself either as a pseudoidea—a conceptual or belief system, an abstract value, an opinion or prejudice—or as a protonarrative, a kind of ultimate class fantasy about the 'collective characters' which are the classes in opposition." Frederic Jameson, *The Political Unconscious: Narrative as a Socially Symbolic Act* (Ithaca, N.Y.: Cornell University Press, 1982), 87.

10. I am borrowing the phrase "model of/for"—and, more broadly, the concept of something being "of/for" something else—from Clifford Geertz, *The Interpretation of Cultures* (New York: Basic Books, 1973), 93–94.

11. The debate on which term to use to identify U.S. Latinos/as is extensive. Among the many studies, I highly recommend Suzanne Oboler's *Ethnic Labels, Latino Lives: Identity and the Politics of (Re)Presentation in the United States* (Minneapolis: University of Minnesota Press, 1995). See also Candace Nelson, and Marta Tienda, "The Structuring of Hispanic Ethnicity: Historical and Contemporary Perspectives," *Ethnic and Racial Studies* 8, no. 1 (1985): 49–74; David E. Hayes-Bautista, "Identifying 'Hispanic' Populations: The Influence of Research Methodology Upon Public Policy," *American Journal of Public Health* 70, no. 4 (1980): 353–56; Hayes-Bautista and Jorge Chapa, "Latino Terminology: Conceptual Bases for Standardized Terminology," *American Journal of Public Health* 77, no. 1 (1987): 61–62; Martha E. Gimenez, "'Latino'/'Hispanic'—Who Needs a Name?: The Case Against Standardized Terminology," *International Journal of Health Services* 19, no. 3 (1989): 557–71; Alfred Yankauer, "Hispanic/ Latino—What's in a Name?," *American Journal of Public Health* 77, no. 1 (1987): 15–17; and Fernando M. Treviño, "Standardized Terminology for Hispanic Populations," *American Journal of Public Health* 77, no. 1 (1987): 69–72. See also the works of Candace Nelson cited in this volume's bibliography.

12. See J. Harvey M. Choldin, "Statistics and Politics: The 'Hispanic' Issue in the 1980 Census," *Demography* 23, no. 3 (1986): 403–18; and Marta Tienda and Vilma Ortiz, "'Hispanicity' and the 1980 Census," *Social Science Quarterly* 67, no. 1 (1986): 3–20.

13. See Oboler, *Ethnic Labels*, chapter 1: "Hispanics? That's What They Call Us," 1–16.

14. I am specifically referring to Oscar Lewis's introduction to *La Vida: A Puerto Rican Family in the Culture of Poverty* (New York: Random House, 1965), xi–lii.

15. In the age of global communication, Miami, Los Angeles, and New York have become epicenters of cultural productions, entertainment, and music exported to Latin America. Latin American entertainers who flocked to these cities have become artistic migrants who have put into circulation the term "Latino." They have relocated their identities in a border zone where "Latino/a" encompasses migrancy; they have jettisoned the term "Latin American" and the reductionist concept of national identity. They are speaking from a new position: Miami, Los Angeles, and New York signal the constitution of a collective new identity. That new positioning relegates national identities to

the margin and embraces a more continental term: "Latino." In an effort to sell their talent, "Latino" registers a new state of being that speaks from a new location. As a result, "Latino" bridges the U.S. Latino and Latin American audiences. Unfortunately, for many, their usage of the term excludes U.S. Latinos/as who were not born and raised in their parents' country of origin and who are bicultural and bilingual but speak only English. "Latino" in Spanish does not translate literally into "Latino" in English.

16. As if there were not enough puzzlement in the usage of terms, some people refuse the term "Latino" because it registers an origin in the (Latin) Mediterranean and Roman colonies. It is reductionist to limit "Latino/Latin" to its philological roots. It is important to bear in mind that the meanings of words *do* change through time, in given social, ideological, political, and historical formations; such is the case with the term "Latino." In the United States, "Latino" no longer refers to the Mediterranean, but refers instead to the people coming from Latin America. In its present and immediate usage, the term has lost all its connection to the original Latin linguistic referent.

17. The most classic example of Latinization is the *Time* special issue ¡*Magnífico!: Hispanic Culture Breaks Out of the Barrio*, 11 June 1988.

18. Frances R. Aparicio and Susana Chávez-Silverman, introduction to *Tropicalizations: Transcultural Representations of Latinidad*, ed. Aparicio and Chávez-Silverman (Hanover, N.H.: Dartmouth College Press, 1997, 3.

19. For the theorization of transculturation and its genealogy, see Silvia Spitta, "Transculturation, the Caribbean, and the Cuban-American Imaginary," in Aparicio and Chávez-Silverman, eds., *Tropicalizations*, 160–80.

20. Coco Fusco, *English is Broken Here: Notes on Cultural Fusion in the Americas* (New York: The New Press, 1995), 70–71; emphasis in the original. See also Richard Fung, "Working through Cultural Appropriation," *Fuse* 16, nos. 5–6 (1993): 16–24; Fung states that the "critique of cultural appropriation is therefore first and foremost a strategy to redress historically established inequities by raising questions about who controls and benefits from cultural resources" (18).

21. On "Latinidad," see Juan Flores's "The Latino Imaginary: Dimensions of Community and Identity," in Aparicio and Chávez-Silverman, eds., *Tropicalizations*, 183–93; Felix M. Padilla, "On the Nature of Latino Ethnicity," *Social Science Quarterly* 65, no. 2 (1984): 651–64; and Padilla, "Latin America: The Historical Base of Latino Unity," *Latino Studies Journal* 1 (1990): 7–27.

22. See Laurie Sommers's articles on the creation of "Latinismo." Her reading of cultural performance as a medium to invent ethnic identity is a great contribution to the understanding of social processes, coalitions, and the utilization of strategies for political and cultural expressions. Laurie Kay Sommers, "Latinismo and Ethnic Nationalism in Cultural Performance," *Studies in Latin American Popular Culture* 10 (1991): 75–86; "Inventing Latinismo: The Creation of 'Hispanic' Panethnicity in the United States," *Journal of American Folklore* 104, no. 411 (1991): 32–53; and "Symbol and Style in *Cinco de Mayo*," *Journal of American Folklore* 98, no. 390 (1985): 476–82.

23. Puerto Ricans, like Chicanos/as and blacks, constitute an internal colo-

nial population within the U.S. Their exploitation and poverty, based on social discrimination or blatant racism, can be seen as a product of imperialism. Indeed, third world ghettos in the U.S. function as a form of internal neocolonialism, according to J. M. Blaut: "[Neo-colonialism] leads to the poverty, social immobility, and physical permanence of the Third World ghetto." J. M. Blaut, "The Ghetto as an Internal Neo-Colony," *Antipode* 6, no. 1 (1974): 39. See also his "Assimilation versus Ghettoization," *Antipode* 15, no. 1 (1983): 35–41.

24. Kobena Mercer, *Welcome to the Jungle: New Positions in Black Cultural Studies* (New York: Routledge, 1994), 91; emphasis in the original.

25. Ibid., 92.

26. Ibid., 214.

Chapter One

1. I have adopted Edward Said's terminology "imaginative geography" from chapter 2, "Imaginative Geography and Its Representations: Orientalizing the Oriental," of his *Orientalism* (New York: Vintage, 1979), 49. *The American Heritage Dictionary of the English Language,* 3d ed. (Boston: Houghton Mifflin, 1992), 1889, gives the following definition of "topography": "1. Detailed, precise description of a place or region; 2. Graphic representation of the surface features of a place or region on a map, indicating their relative positions and elevations. 3. A description or an analysis of a structured entity, showing the relations among its components. . . . 4. a. The surface features of a place or region. b. The surface features of an object. . . . 5. The surveying of the features of a place or region. 6. The study or description of an anatomical region or part."

2. For example, Columbus reads the New World as a woman's body: "I find that [the world] is not round. . . . and on one part of it is placed something like a woman's nipple." "The Third Voyage of Columbus," in *The Four Voyages of Columbus,* vol. 2, ed. Cecil Jane, (New York: Dover, 1988), 30. Among the scholars who have worked on the imagery of womanhood when used to materialize the conquering and colonization of a "virginal space" and to express colonial relations of power, see Rebecca Scott, "The Dark Continent: Africa as Female Body in Haggard's Adventure Fiction," *Feminist Review* 32 (1989): 69–89; Chandra Mohanty, "Under Western Eyes: Feminist Scholarship and Colonial Discourses," *Feminist Review* 30 (1988): 61–88; Joanna De Groot, "'Sex and Race': The Construction of Language and Image in the Nineteenth Century," in *Sexuality and Subordination: Interdisciplinary Studies of Gender in the Nineteenth Century,* ed. Susan Mendus and Jane Rendall (New York: Routledge, 1989), 89–128; and Louis Montrose, "The Work of Gender in the Discourse of the Discovery," *representations* 33 (1991): 1–41.

3. Sykes[?], "My How You Have Grown," *Philadelphia Evening Public Ledger* 1923, reproduced in John J. Johnson, *Latin America in Caricature* (Austin: University of Texas Press, 1993), 103.

4. Eduardo Galeano, *Memory of Fire: Century of the Wind,* trans. Cedric Belfrage (New York: Pantheon, 1985), 131.

5.   Nelson A. Rockefeller, "The Fruits of the Good Neighbor Policy," *New York Times Magazine*, 14 May 1944, 30.

6.   "William Ireland [?], "I'll Give You One Teaspoonful, Cuby. More of it Might Make You Sick," *Columbus (Ohio) Dispatch* 1902, reproduced in Johnson, *Latin America in Caricature*, 123.

7.   See Allen L. Woll, *The Latin Image in American Film* (Los Angeles: UCLA Latin American Publications, 1997) and Arthur G. Pettit, *Images of the Mexican American in Fiction and Film* (College Station: University of Texas Press, 1980).

8.   For the issue of Latino surplus as extras, see Luis Reyes and Peter Rubie, *Hispanics in Hollywood: An Encyclopedia of Film and Television* (New York: Garland, 1994), 8.

9.   For an excellent inventory of "Hispanic" types of characters and themes in film, see Gary D. Keller, *Hispanics and United States Films* (Tempe, Ariz.: Bilingual Review/Press, 1994).

10.   For a critical reading of "social problem films" see Chon A. Noriega, "Internal Others: Hollywood Narratives 'about' Mexican-Americans," in *Mediating Two Worlds: Cinematic Encounters in the Americas*, ed. John King, Ana M. López, and Manuel Alvarado (London: British Film Institute, 1993), 52–66.

11.   Reyes and Rubie, *Hispanics in Hollywood*, 2.

12.   See Charles Ramírez Berg, "Immigrants, Aliens, and Extraterrestrials," *CineAction!*, Fall 1989, 3–17, for an insightful article in which he reads aliens in science fiction films as a metaphorical representation of Latino/a illegal aliens in the U.S. Berg's provocative critical reading unmasks science fiction fantasies in order to demythify how the dominant culture represents the "other," and how issues of migration are embedded in science fiction films. This alternative reading opens the door to a new topo(s)graphy, one that is interplanetary and located in outer space, the *locus sidereus*, whose inhabitants are horrific alien creatures and monsters. Indeed, I have noticed how these films take place in the Southwest and California, locations whose populations have a large number of Latinos/as—for example, *Starman*, *Close Encounters of the Third Kind*, and *E.T.* More recently, *Jurassic Park* and *The Lost World* represent Central America as a *locus primitivus*. Indeed, in *The Lost World* the dinosaur brought to San Diego constitutes a threat when it crosses the border illegally, while the film shows illegal migrants being detained at the border headquarters.

13.   In order to achieve recognition and fame, many U.S. Latinas had to deny their Hispanic roots and change their names; for example: Margarita Carmen Cansino morphed into Rita Hayworth. This practice continues: Raquel Tejada changed her name to Raquel Welch, Florencia Bicenta de Casillas Martinez Cardona to Vicki Carr, Dolores Conchita del Rivero to Chita Rivera.

14.   Now, how are we to think about women who display their bodies as spectacle, as Carmen Miranda did, and which Charo perpetuates in her exhibitionism? Given that roles for Latinas are limited and require the incarnation of negative stereotypes, can Latinas use these stereotypes as a tactic of/for agency and assume the position of a speaking subject? Are Latina performers conscious of the imprisonment of their bodies and subjectivities as desired

objects in the cultural imaginary as "Latin foreign other," "Latin domestic ethnic and racial other," and/or "sexual other"? When nonstereotypical roles are not available and sex and race are visual markers of identity, Latina actresses must perform within the limited stereotypes available; such is the case of Rita Moreno in *West Side Story*, and Lupe Vélez in the film series *The Mexican Spitfires*, and as a lascivious jungle native in *Kongo* (1932). Vélez had to portray "Chinese, Eskimos, Japs, Squaws, Hindus, Swedes, Malays and Javanese." See Woll, *The Latin Image in American Film*, 38. Moreno had to impersonate other ethnic and racial groups, including "half-breeds," native Americans, and even an "oriental" in *The King and I*; María Montez is well-known for her exotic roles, including that of *Cobra Woman* (1944), and her impersonations of Arab women, such as Scheherezade in *Arabian Nights* (1942).

15. I am using Laura Mulvey's theorization of women as visual pleasure: "In a world ordered by sexual imbalance, pleasure in looking has been split between active/male and passive/female. The determining male gaze projects its fantasy onto the female figure, which is styled accordingly. In their traditional exhibitionist role women are simultaneously looked at and displayed, with their appearance coded for strong visual and erotic impact so that they can be said to connote *to-be-looked-at-ness*. Woman displayed as sexual object is the *leitmotif* of erotic spectacle: from pin-ups to strip-tease, from Ziegfeld to Busby Berkeley, she holds the look, and plays to and signifies male desire." Laura Mulvey, *Visual and Other Pleasures* (Bloomington: Indiana University Press, 1989), 19; emphasis in the original.

16. "Chiquita Banana (I'm Chiquita Banana)," words and music by Len Mackenzie, Garth Montgomery, and William Wirges, 1946; in *Great Songs of Madison Avenue*, ed. Peter and Craig Norback (New York: Quadrangle, 1976), 87–89.

17. Paul W. Drake summarizes briefly the U.S. military interventions in Latin America in "From Good Men to Good Neighbors," in *Exporting Democracy*, ed. Abraham F. Lowenthal (Baltimore: Johns Hopkins University Press, 1991), 3–40.

18. For an excellent outline of the political framework of the Good Neighbor policy, see Harold Molineu, *U.S. Policy Toward Latin America: From Regionalism to Globalism* (Boulder, Colo.: Westview Press, 1986), 11.

19. Rockefeller published two "manifestos" that sum up the philosophy and political platform of the Good Neighbor policy. In one he stated, "I believe the Good Neighbor Policy expresses the will of the people of the United States. It proclaimed complete forbearance from interference by any one republic in the domestic affairs of any other. It inspired greater confidence and trust. It developed the inter-American system as a realistic laboratory for the form and type of world organization which may lie ahead . . . The New World has been, is today and always will be, a land of opportunity. Together we hold the resources, the mutual confidence and the experience which, with courageous leadership, can translate our common aspirations into reality." Rockefeller, "The Fruits of the Good Neighbor Policy," 15, 31. He also proclaimed, "the opportunities are there. An atmosphere of mutual confidence has been built

up by many years of political, commercial, technical and cultural contacts. The partners—the United States and the twenty other American republics—are already co-operating in a dozen practical fields, including long-range plans for the postwar period. Why should we not succeed? The problems are great, but they are not insurmountable. . . . Improving food supplies in all parts of the hemisphere and establishing rising standards of health and sanitation are basic necessities. Better transportation by land, sea and air, and a marked advance in industrial organization are the other factors on which we count to transform this hemisphere, raise its living standards, and immeasurably strengthen its world position." Nelson A. Rockefeller, "Will We Remain Good Neighbors After the War?" *Saturday Evening Post*, 6 November 1943, 16.

20.   These projects included many sectors: the appointment of cultural attachés; radio broadcasting; journalistic propaganda; the study of Spanish; visiting scholars; translations; Latin American studies projects; exchanges of intellectuals, writers, faculty and graduate students; the establishment of libraries; the presentation of lectures; the financing of research; art exhibitions; the Rockefeller Foundation and Guggenheim fellowship awards; and many other activities and programs. I highly recommend the Bureau of Educational and Cultural Affairs' *Cultural Relations Programs of the U.S. Department of State*, Historical Studies 2 (Washington, D.C.: U.S. Department of State, 1976) for a detailed description of all the programs and cultural exchanges available during the time of the Good Neighbor policy.

21.   Latin America was finally on the map. Proof of this is in the many movie titles with actual geographical references to countries with a surplus of material goods, commercial ports, and militarily strategic locations: *The Cuban Love Song* (1931); *Flying Down to Rio* (1933); *Under the Pampas Moon* (1935); *Down Argentine Way* and *Girl from Havana* (1940); *Down Mexico Way, That Night in Rio, Havana Rose*, and *Weekend in Havana* (1941); *Panama Hattie* and *Moonlight in Havana* (1942); *Holiday in Mexico* and *Club Havana* (1946); and *Mexican Hayride* (1948). For those films without a specific geographic referent, there was always an imaginary topo(s)graphy of exotic and stereotypical locales that had cropped up since the 1920s: "Bargravia, San Mañana, Santa Maria, Costa Blanca, Costa Casaba, Centralia." Keller, *Hispanics and United States Film*, 116.

22.   Franklin D. Roosevelt, "The Year of Crisis: 1933" in *The Public Papers and Addresses of Franklin Delano Roosevelt*, vol. 2, comp. and collated by Samuel I. Roseman (New York: Random House, 1958), 14.

23.   "The son is perhaps the oldest and certainly the classic Afro-Cuban form, an almost perfect balance of African and Hispanic elements. Originating in Oriente province, it surfaced in Havana around World War I and became a popular urban music played by string-and-percussion quartets and septetos. Almost all the numbers Americans called rumbas were, in fact, sones. 'El Manicero' ('The Peanut Vendor') was a form of son derived from the street cries of Havana and called a pregon. The rhythm of the son is strongly syncopated, with a basic chicka-CHUNG pulse." John S. Roberts, *The Latin Tinge* (New York: Oxford University Press, 1979), 231.

24.   Cugat appeared in the following films: *Go West, Young Man* (1936); *The*

Heat's On (1943); *Bathing Beauty* and *Two Girls and a Sailor* (1944); *Weekend at the Waldorf* (1945); *Holiday in Mexico* and *No Leave, No Love* (1946); *This Time for Keeps* (1947); *Luxury Liner, Date with Judy,* and *On an Island with You* (1948); *Neptune's Daughter* (1949); and *Chicago Syndicate* (1955).

25. Within the Anglo-American cultural worldview, "Latinization" often implies a cultural appropriation that exoticizes or commodifies the "racial and ethnic other."

26. After talkies appeared, "Latins" were always represented in exotic locales, performing romantic or spicy musical numbers. Evidently, "Latin" actors and actresses could work as long as they had exotic looks and pronounced accents. Gary D. Keller has stated that "the production of Hispanic-focused musicals immediately followed the advent of the sound era. In fact, the stereotype of the "Latin world" as lively and musical, characterized by fiestas (when not siestas) and even music and dancing in the cantinas carried such sway that beginning with sound, it became commonplace for music to enter Hispanic-focused films even if they were not musicals per se." Keller, *Hispanics and United States Film,* 121.

27. In addition, Technicolor (full-color cinematography) opened the doors to exotic and colorful locales "south of the border."

28. José Morand, "The Rumba is Here To Stay," *Song Hits* 5, no. 7 (1941): 13.

29. Many songs had as the main theme Latin America or the peoples of Latin America. I have categorized these songs in the following manner: (a) romanticizing Latin America as paradise: "Havana," "A Weekend in Havana," "South of the Border," "Down Argentina Way," "They Met in Rio," "In Copacabana," and "Romance and Rhumba"; (b) exoticizing Latin America as sexual paradise: "With my Concertina," "I, Yi, Yi, Yi, Yi (I Like You Very Much)," "Sing to Your Señorita," "Tropical Magic," "South American Way," "Rio Rhythm," and "Thank You South America"; (c) exoticizing Latin American women: "Conchita, Marcheta, Lolita, Pepita, Rosita, Juanita Lopez," "Pepita," "Lily—Hot from Chile," "Carmenita McCoy," and "Nenita"; (d) stereotyping Latin American men: "Cuban Pete," "The Gaucho Serenade," and "The Gaucho with the Black Mustache"; (e) racist: "Rhumbaboogie," "Macumba," "Chica Chica Boom Chic," "Spic and Spanish," "Shake Your Maracas," and "South America, Take It Away."

30. "U.S. Film Stars the Best Good Will Ambassadors, Say Latin Americans," *Variety,* 19 February 1941, 1.

31. "Films' Latin-American Cycle Finds Congarhumba Displacing Swing Style," *Variety,* 6 November 1940, 22.

32. Desi Arnaz, *A Book* (New York: William Morrow, 1976), 133–35.

33. "Films' Latin-American Cycle," 22.

34. Reyes and Rubie, *Hispanics in Hollywood,* 17.

35. "South American Way," Words and music by Al Dubin and Jimmy McHugh, 1939.

36. Interestingly, Miranda is not the only "other" here: there is a song-and-dance number performed in Spanish by the Nicholas Brothers, "negro hoofers" from the U.S. whose participation puts race at the center stage. "Celluloid

Hemispheric Bid," *Newsweek*, 28 October 1940, 59. Miranda's and the Nicholas Brothers' performative acts speak from the margin, as pure entertainment and exoticism. In the film, the presence and participation of people of color is limited to a stereotypical representation as comic characters, joyful entertainers, and fiery dancers. This ethnic and racial rainbow is magnified and intensified with Miranda's sambas and the Nicholas Brothers' tap dancing and acrobatic moves, all seen in Technicolor.

37. "Twentieth-Fox erred on "Down Argentine Way". . . . in picturing the Argentinos as operating a phoney race track, while the gents from the U.S. were the good folk. (There has also been some criticism on the casting of Carmen Miranda as an Argentine. She's a native of Brazil.)" "Films' Latin American Cycle," 22.

38. In the reconstruction of Miranda's life and professional work on Broadway and Hollywood, I am indebted to the following books: James Robert Parish, *The Fox Girls* (New Rochelle, N.Y.: Arlington House, 1971) and Martha Gil-Montero, *Brazilian Bombshell: The Biography of Carmen Miranda* (New York: Donald I. Fine, 1989).

39. Joyce Dana, "Carmen, Rio Style: This One Has a Last Name (It's Miranda) And She's the Good Neighbor Policy Itself." Clipping from Carmen Miranda file, Lincoln Center Library for the Performing Arts, New York; no sources available.

40. Wilella Waldorf, "'The Streets of Paris' Opens at the Broadhurst Theater," *New York Post*, 20 June 1939, 10.

41. John Anderson, "*The Streets of Paris* Opens As Summer Revue," *New York Journal and American*, 20 June 1939, 10.

42. Arthur Pollock, "Carmen Miranda Tops *The Streets of Paris*," *Brooklyn Daily Eagle*, 20 June 1939, 7.

43. Brooks Atkinson, "*The Streets of Paris* Moves to Broadway," *New York Times*, 20 June 1939, L 25.

44. Burns Mantle, "There's Hellzapoppin' in This *Streets of Paris* Revue, Too," *New York Daily News*, 20 June 1939, 33.

45. Peter Kihss, "Gestures Put It Over for Miranda," *New York World-Telegram*, 8 July 1939, 6.

46. "New Shows in Manhattan," *Time*, 3 July 1939, 42–43.

47. Pollock, "Carmen Miranda Tops 'Streets,'" 7.

48. Waldorf, "'The Streets of Paris' Opens," 9.

49. Richard Lockridge, "The New Play: 'The Streets of Paris,' a Bright Revue Opens at the Broadhurst," *New York Sun*, 20 June 1939, 13.

50. Robert Sullivan, "Carmen Miranda Loaves America and Vice Versa," Clipping from Carmen Miranda file, Lincoln Center Library for the Performing Arts, New York; no sources available.

51. Clipping from Carmen Miranda file, Lincoln Center Library for the Performing Arts, New York; no sources available.

52. Ida Zeitlin, "Sous American Sizzler," Clipping from Carmen Miranda file, Lincoln Center Library for the Performing Arts, New York; no sources available.

53. John Kobal, *Gotta Sing, Gotta Dance: A History of American Musicals* (New York: Exeter, 1971), 193.

54. Chon Noriega has observed that [w]hen the characters speak Spanish [in films] . . . it functions as an empty code for ethnicity. In short, there is no need for subtitles, because nothing is said." Noriega, "Internal Others," 61.

55. Ana M. López, "Are All Latins from Manhattan? Hollywood, Ethnography, and Cultural Colonialism," in *Unspeakable Images: Ethnicity and the American Cinema*, ed. Lester D. Friedman (Urbana: University of Illinois Press, 1991), 419.

56. Shari Roberts, "'The Lady in the Tutti-Frutti Hat': Carmen Miranda, A Spectacle of Ethnicity," *Cinema Journal* 32, no. 3 (1993): 14–15.

57. On the subject of exoticism and otherness in films, see Ella Shohat, "Gender and Culture of Empire: Toward a Feminist Ethnography of the Cinema," *Quarterly Review of Film and Video* 13 nos. 1–3 (1991): 45–84.

58. López, "Are All Latins from Manhattan?" 418–19.

59. Kobal, *Gotta Sing*, 193. Miranda's impersonators include Imogene Coca, Betty Garrett, Mickey Rooney, Ethel Bennett, Joan Bennett, Jo Ann Marlow, Esther Williams, Eddie Bracken, Denis Quilley, Cass Daley, Jerry Lewis, Milton Berle, Bob Hope, Carol Burnett, *Today Show* weatherman Willard Scott, Bette Midler, and animated characters Bugs Bunny and Donald Duck.

60. *Carmen Miranda: Bananas Is My Business*, prod. David Meyer and Helena Solberg, dir. Helena Solberg, 91 min, Fox-Lorber Home Video, 1994, videocassette.

61. In the 1990s, Miranda's popularity has been resurrected with *Bananas Is My Business*, and also with *Biography: Carmen Miranda*, prod. Kerry Jensen-Izsak, dir. Elizabeth Bronstein, 50 min., Arts and Entertainment Television Network, 1996, videocassette.

62. Sara J. Welch, "The Mirandification of America," *Samba* 2, no. 19 (1995): 4.

63. Miranda performed in the following movies: *Weekend in Havana* (1941), *That Night in Rio* (1941), *Springtime in The Rockies* (1942), *The Gang's All Here* (1943), *Four Jills in a Jeep* (1944), *Greenwich Village* (1944), *Something for the Boys* (1944), *Doll Face* (1945), *If I'm Lucky* (1946), *Copacabana* (1947), *A Date with Judy* (1948), *Nancy Goes to Rio* (1950), and *Scared Stiff* (1953). By 1945 she was making over $200,000 yearly, becoming the highest paid actress in Hollywood. See Parish, *The Fox Girls*, 514.

64. "Carmen Miranda Is Dead at 41: Movie Comedienne and Dancer," obituary, *New York Times*, 6 August 1955, 15.

65. "South America, Take It Away," words and music by Harold Rome, 1946.

66. Desi Arnaz, in *A Tribute to Lucy*, prod. Film Shows, Inc., 93 min., Goodtimes Video, 1989, videocassette.

67. John S. Roberts had reservations about Arnaz's talent, saying, "Like Cugat, Arnaz was an important popularizer. Unlike Cugat, he knew relatively little about the music he was hybridizing. But he had looks, charm, chutzpah,

and the great advantage over most important "Latin musicians" of being both upperclass (the son of a former mayor of Santiago de Cuba) and pure white. He also had a talent for meeting useful people, encountering Bing Crosby while he was with Cugat, and Sonja Henie and Joe E. Smith in Miami. In reality, Arnaz was not a musician but an entertainer." Roberts, *Latin Tinge*, 82.

68. Arnaz also appeared in the following films: *Father Takes a Wife* (1941), *The Navy Comes Through* (1942), *Bataan* (1943), *Cuban Pete* (1946). *Holiday in Havana* (1949), *The Long, Long Trailer* (1954), and *Forever Darling* (1936).

69. Kathleen Brady, *Lucille: The Life of Lucille Ball* (New York: Hyperion, 1994), 96.

70. Review of *Too Many Girls*, *Time*, 11 November 1940, 76.

71. Brooks Atkinson, "Too Many Girls Opens with a Score by Rodgers & Hart Under George Abbott's Direction," *New York Times*, 18 September 1940, 19.

72. Bosley Crowther, "The Screen in Review," *New York Times*, 21 November 1940, 43.

73. Brady, *Lucille*, 96.

74. Will Friedwald, liner notes for *The Best of Desi Arnaz the Mambo King*, RCA/BMG compact disk CD 07863–66031–2.

75. The Native American presence is registered as another exotic token in the scene in which Consuelo is on her way to the college. After she writes a letter addressed to Beverly Waverly Esq., her secret boyfriend, she asks the bus driver to stop at an Indian trading post. She gives the letter to a Native American woman who hands it to a Native American man, who is wearing an Indian outfit and sitting with his legs crossed. This scene represents the Southwest as the land of the "other" and, by doing so, the film pretends to incorporate a touch of authenticity.

76. Arnaz relates the following anecdote about a trip to Taos, New Mexico, where Lucille Ball was filming *Valley of the Sun*: "There were a lot of Indians in the movie and, having nothing else to do, I took one of their drums and showed them the conga beat. Soon I had the whole Indian tribe doing the conga all over their village"; Arnaz, *A Book*, 127. This shows how easily Afro-Cuban culture can replace Indian culture, since both cultures are marked by difference. The drum is the medium that facilitates such a transition; in other words, the iconic image of a drum—associated with otherness—can speak a thousand words.

77. Gustavo Pérez Firmat, *Life on the Hyphen: The Cuban-American Way* (Austin: University of Texas Press, 1994), 54.

78. I am assuming that Arnaz did a rendition of "Babalú" on Broadway. In the film he only performed a conga. However, in the recording *The Best of Desi Arnaz the Mambo King* he starts with "Babalú" and metamorphoses it into a conga. I suggest that both "Babalú" and the conga constitute a single unit. Arnaz's racialized act does not acquire its full significance until he performs, in blackface, the same conga in *I Love Lucy* ("Lucy Goes to the Hospital"). *The "I Love Lucy" Collection* vol. 4., prod. CBS Entertainment, CBS/FOX Video 1989, videocassette.

79. "Babalú", Spanish words and music by Margarita Lecuona, 1939.

80. For definitions and descriptions of the African roots of conga, samba, and rumba, see the glossary included in Roberts, *Latin Tinge,* 220–33.

81. Xavier Cugat, in an unnamed interview quoted in Roberts, *Latin Tinge,* 87.

82. Pérez Firmat, *Life on the Hyphen,* 29.

83. Bosley Crowther, review of *If I'm Lucky, New York Times,* 20 September 1946, 41.

84. Arnaz, *A Book,* 77.

85. Lucille Ball, *Love Lucy* (New York: Putnam, 1996), 189.

86. Desi Arnaz and Al Stump, "America Has Been Good to Me," *American Magazine,* February 1955, 84.

87. Desi Arnaz, in *A Tribute to Lucy.*

88. Keller, *Hispanics and U.S. Film,* 98.

89. According to Lucille Ball, Thunderbird in Palm Springs was not only one of the most beautiful golf courses, but also "one of the most prejudiced. Not only did it refuse to admit Jews, but, celebrity and property owner or not, Desi was not invited to join either," Ball, *Love Lucy,* 245.

90. Desi Arnaz, in *A Tribute to Lucy.*

91. "She Could Shake Her Maracas," music by Richard Rodgers, words by Lorenz Hart, 1939.

92. "Cuban Pete," words and music by José Norman, 1936.

93. The episode, which centered around the character Lucy's giving birth, was enormously popular: "That night 44 million Americans (more than one fifth of the population—and 30,000 of them sent personal congratulations) tuned in to watch." Brady, *Lucille,* 213.

94. Michael McClay, *I Love Lucy: The Complete Picture History of the Most Popular TV Show Ever* (New York: Warner Books, 1995), 165.

95. Eric Lott, "Love and Theft: The Racial Unconscious of Blackface Minstrelsy," *representations* 39 (1992): 28; emphasis in the original.

96. Michael Rogin, *Blackface, White Noise: Jewish Immigrant in the Hollywood Melting Pot* (Berkeley: University of California Press, 1996), 9.

97. Xavier Cugat, in an unnamed interview quoted in Roberts, *Latin Tinge,* 87.

98. Miranda dressed as a bahiana, with "a silk turban, golden earrings, a starched skirt, trimmed sandals, golden bracelets and *balangandás* . . . an ornamental silver buckle, with amulets and trinkets attached, worn on feast days by the slaves. . . . The long, broad skirt was suitable for Carnival; indeed men who dressed like Bahian women had always participated in Carnival parades. Moreover, outside the markets and doorsteps of Bahia where the true Bahianas sat, turbans and the *balangandás* were considered leftovers from slavery days." Gil-Montero, *Brazilian Bombshell,* 54, 56.

99. Heitor Villa-Lobos, quoted in *Bananas Is My Business.*

100. A friend once told me the story of how her mother dressed her as Carmen Miranda and darkened her face for Halloween.

101. Bart Andrews, *The "I Love Lucy" Book* (New York: Doubleday, 1985), 231.

102. It is interesting to notice that Ball asked Miranda for permission to imitate her. Ibid.

103. Pérez Firmat, *Life on the Hyphen*, 40.

104. Cited in ibid., 38.

105. Pérez Firmat, *Life on the Hyphen*, 41.

106. According to the *American Heritage Dictionary*, 1303, "palimpsest" means "1. A manuscript, typically of papyrus or parchment, that has been written on more than once, with the earlier writing incompletely erased and often legible. 2. An object, a place, or an area that reflects its history. Latin *palimpsestum*, from Greek *palimpseston*, neuter of *palimpsestos*, scraped again: *palin*, again."

Chapter Two

1. Norris Houghton, ed., *Romeo and Juliet/West Side Story* (New York: Dell, 1965), 167. All citations refer to the above edition of *West Side Story*, and are hereafter cited parenthetically in the text. When, however, there is no page number next to the citation, I am directly citing the movie: *West Side Story*, prod. Robert Wise, dir. Robert Wise and Jerome Robbins, 152 mins., CBS/Fox Video, 1984, videocassette.

2. The term "Nuyorican" applies to Puerto Ricans born and raised in New York City. It was mainly used by literary writers to denominate their literary and artistic movement in the late 1960s as "Nuyorican poetry." This label of/ for identity expresses a consciousness about ethnic pride and difference, cultural and linguistic hybridity. For a definition of Nuyorican literature, see *Nuyorican Poetry: An Anthology of Puerto Rican Words and Feelings*, ed. Miguel Algarín and Miguel Piñero, (New York: William Morrow, 1975); and Sandra María Esteves, "Ambivalencia o activismo desde la perspectiva poética de los Nuyoricans," in *Imágenes e identidades: El puertorriqueño en la literatura*, ed. Asela Rodríguez de Laguna, (Río Piedras, P.R.: Huracán, 1985), 195–201. See also Soledad Santiago, "Notes on the Nuyoricans," *Village Voice*, 19 February 1979, 12–15; *Herejes y mitificadores: Muestra de poesía puertorriqueña en los Estados Unidos*, ed. Efraín Barradas and Rafael Rodríguez, (Río Piedras, P.R.: Huracán, 1980); and Alberto Sandoval-Sánchez, "La identidad especular del allá y del acá: Nuestra propia imagen puertorriqueña en cuestión," *Centro de Estudios Puertorriqueños Bulletin* 4 no. 2 (1992): 28–43; Sandoval-Sánchez, "Puerto Rican Identity: Air Migration, Its Cultural Representations, and Me 'Cruzando el Charco'," in *Puerto Rican Jam: Essays on Culture and Politics*, ed. Frances Negrón-Muntaner and Ramón Grosfoguel (Minneapolis: University of Minnesota Press, 1997); and Sandoval-Sánchez, ¡Mira, que vienen los Nuyoricans!: El temor de la otredad en la literatura nacionalista puertorriqueña," *Revista de Crítica Literaria Latinoamericana* 45 (1997): 307–25.

3. There were only a handful of Latino actors in the original Broadway production, as in the film.

4. Louise Sweeney, "West Side Story—The Second Time Around," *Christian Science Monitor,* 18 September 1985, 25.

5. Arthur Laurents, quoted in Terrence McNally, "West Side Story," a running discussion between McNally and the musical's production team, in *Broadway Song and Story,* ed. Otis L. Guernsey, Jr. (New York: Dodd, Mead, 1985), 42.

6. Leonard Bernstein, quoted in Craig Zadan, *Sondheim & Co.,* 2nd ed. (New York: Harper and Row, 1989) 15.

7. Arthur Laurents, quoted in Joan Peyser, *Bernstein: A Biography* (New York: Beech Tree Books/William Morrow, 1987), 257.

8. The Jets certainly concentrate on juvenile delinquency when they sing "Gee, Officer Krupke," a humorous song that narrates their social and familial crises, and defines juvenile delinquency as a social disease. (Ironically they do not identify racism as a social disease.) They sing, in their self-defense, that they are not delinquents, only misunderstood.

9. It is interesting to point out how a critic can perpetuate such stereotypes: "[T]he influx of Puerto Ricans onto the New York scene offered a group given to high passion and violence, the very meat of Shakespeare's story. Their gang wars suggested a likely substitute for family feuds." Gerald Bordman, *American Musical Theatre: A Chronicle* (New York: Oxford University Press, 1986), 604. Also, it must be considered that Puerto Ricans were conceived in the 1940s as potential criminals; see Charles E. Hewitt, Jr., "Welcome: Paupers and Crime—Porto Rico's Shocking Gift to the United States," *Scribner's Commentator,* March 1940, 11–17.

10. Keith Garebian, *The Making of West Side Story* (Toronto: ECW Press, 1995), 147.

11. Even in their dancing, the Sharks move with passion while the Jets are disciplined, self-controlled, and athletic. In the song "America," the choreography for the Puerto Rican Sharks is loud, energetic, and aggressive. They imitate guns with their hands, and scream like exotic, wild animals. Comparatively, the Anglo-Americans try to control themselves and their emotions, remaining rational and sublimating their aggressive and passionate instincts as they get "cool" and keep "cool." About the choreographic movements, Gerald Mast has observed that "Jerome Robbins found a style for slum kids to dance to that street music. His choreographic leitmotif—soaring arms opening wide, one arm spreading toward the earth and the other toward the sky, as dancers rise onto the ball of one foot—becomes an unforgettable image of reaching for sky and longing for space. The movement reveals that these kids are not fancy free but fancy that one day they might fly free from the social tangle of these very streets." Gerald Mast, *Can't Help Singin': The American Musical on Stage and Screen* (New York: Overlook Press, 1987), 301.

12. Gerald Mast justifies ethnic stereotyping, saying that "Sondheim's ethnic stereotyping is acceptable in dramatic context, for members of an ethnic group have earned the right to poke fun at their own culture"; Mast, *Can't Help*

Singin', 302. This justification fails to acknowledge, however, that the representations of Puerto Ricans are not in this case constructed by Puerto Ricans.

13. At work here is the Hays Code, which prohibited miscegenation.

14. Gerald Mast recognizes that there is no utopia: "The 'Somewhere' ballet thoroughly destroys the illusion that things might get better elsewhere. There is nowhere else. America (as that song makes clear) is as good as it gets." Mast, *Can't Help Singin'*, 302.

15. A stage direction reads, at the end of the play, "The adults—Doc, Schrank, Krupke, Glad Hand—are left bowed, alone, useless" (224). Given that Schrank arrests Chino in this final scene, he is an agent of power who exercises legal action and restores order. In this sense, he is not "useless" at all.

16. Concerning the image of women in the text, the extent to which Maria's body functions in a metonymical relationship to the Puerto Rican geographic and cultural territory, which the Anglo-American aims to possess, control, and subdue, should be analyzed. From this perspective, Tony violates the Puerto Rican patriarchial space by penetrating Maria's room and usurping and displacing the power of the father, the brother, and the family in general. The female body is the corporeal territory that the Anglo-American wants to possess and subject, either for reasons of love, as in Maria's case, or by rape, as in Anita's case. The attempted rape of Anita occurs symbolically when the Jets throw her on top of Baby John's body at the candy store.

17. There is a scene in which the Jets blatantly expel the Puerto Ricans from the U.S.:

Action: Who asked you to move here?
Pepe: Who asked you?
Snowboy: Move where you're wanted!
A-rab: Back where ya came from!
Action: Spics! (175–76)

18. It is important to notice that in the final scene Maria is left mourning Tony's death, not Bernardo's. It is also his body, and not Bernardo's, that is carried away in a solemn funeral procession.

19. Stanley Kauffmann, "The Asphalt Romeo and Juliet," *New Republic*, 23 October 1961, 28.

20. Sidney Mintz, in his introduction to a book of photographs of Puerto Rico by Jack Delano, who has lived on the island, made this observation about the song "America": "[T]he colonialism of the ruling nation goes further, for it colors the attitudes of nearly everyone who must deal with Puerto Rico. Even in its literature, art, and aesthetics, Puerto Rico is commonly misunderstood. The musical *West Side Story* is relevant here. In the words of its most popular song, the United States is referred to as 'America.' But no one in Puerto Rico ever refers to the United States as 'America' and no Puerto Rican ever did. All Latin peoples in the Southern Hemisphere believe that they are Americans, too. (Since they reached the New World and settled the Antilles more than a century before the first English colony was established in North America, they

have a fair case.) And the melodies of Bernstein, for all their beauty, could only have been composed by someone for whom Mexican and Puerto Rican music are essentially the same—that is, 'Latin.' The rich and distinctive musical tradition of Puerto Rico is almost entirely absent from *West Side Story*." Mintz, introduction to Jack Delano, *Puerto Rico Mío: Four Decades of Change* (Washington, D.C.: Smithsonian Institution Press, 1990), 4.

21.   It is important to point out that Anglo-American critics saw this scene as a humorous, jokey interplay. David Ewen notes, "In 'America' the Shark girls speak of the joyous life encountered by Puerto Ricans in this country." Ewen, *Complete Book of the American Musical Theater* (New York: Holt, Rinehart, and Winston, 1959), 64. Leonard Bernstein, in his liner notes to the original Broadway cast recording, mentions that "a playful argument develops between Anita and a homesick Puerto Rican girl over the relative merits of life back home and in Manhattan." Bernstein, *Bernstein: West Side Story*, CBS Masterworks LP, 1957, cited in David Patrick Stearns, "'West Side Story': Between Broadway and the Opera House," 7, in a booklet included in *Leonard Bernstein Conducts West Side Story*, Deutsche Grammophon 415 253–4, audiocassette.

22.   A similar situation occurs when Bernardo says to the Jets before the rumble starts, "More gracious living? Look: I don't go for that pretend crap you all go for in this country. Every one of you hates every one of us, and we hate you right back. I don't drink with nobody I hate, I don't shake hands with nobody I hate" (190). It is evident that the ethnic minority defines itself in terms of hatred and violence while the Anglo-Americans never verbalize their hatred, or rather, their racism. The system of power allows for the minority to speak on its own behalf; in this way, it takes no responsibility for discrimination and racial oppression.

23.   Stanley Kauffmann, "The Asphalt Romeo and Juliet," 29.

24.   This team was composed of Arthur Laurents, who wrote the book; Leonard Bernstein, who composed the music; Sondheim, who wrote the lyrics; and Jerome Robbins, who choreographed and directed.

25.   Stephen Sondheim and Leonard Bernstein, quoted in Guernsey, ed., *Broadway Song and Story*, 53. *The New York Times* published an article by a doctor who criticized the lyrics of "America" and defended the public health achievements in Puerto Rico: "The Puerto Ricans who have cried 'foul' have a point. The lyrics of this and the other songs created by Mr. Stephen Sondheim are clever and effective, but the reference to 'island of tropical diseases' is a blow below the belt. This is not based on fact. . . . It is not serious, but, it hits Puerto Rico in a sensitive spot. The Commonwealth of Puerto Rico by great effort has made tremendous strides forward in public health as well as education, transportation, communication, and economic development in their 'Operation Bootstrap.' They are especially proud of their public health achievements." Howard A. Rusk, M. D., "The Facts Don't Rhyme: An Analysis of Irony in Lyrics Linking Puerto Rico's Breezes to Tropic Diseases," *New York Times*, 29 September 1957, L 83.

26.   Bernstein, *Bernstein: West Side Story*, cited in Stearns, "'West Side Story,'" 7. See also Bernstein, *Bernstein Conducts West Side Story*, prod. Hum-

phrey Burton and Thomas P. Skinner, dir. Christopher Swann; BBC, Unitel/ Munich, and V.M.P., 1985, videocassette, in which it is interesting to observe that Tony was played by Spanish tenor José Carreras. The critics found this odd and disturbing, because Carreras's accent ruined the Anglo-American portrayal of Tony. While the system allows Anglo-Americans to pass as "Hispanic others," it would seem unacceptable to have a Spaniard (or any other Latino/a, in that case) play roles that will be always be seen as "white." It is fascinating to realize how discrimination perpetuates the marginalization of the other in dominant discourses and representations. In 1996, another recording was released as a tribute to Bernstein. This rendition is an updated musical interpretation that incorporates new rhythms and musical styles like rap, jazz, country pop, and modern doo-wop, and includes among its intrepreters the well-known Latina artist Selena. It also includes a hilarious, queer, and campy rendition of "I Feel Pretty" by Little Richard. Various artists, *The Songs of West Side Story*, RCA Victor/BMG, 09026–62707–2.

27. Stephen Sondheim, quoted in Zadan, *Sondheim & Co.*, 14; emphasis in the original.

28. Arturo Parrilla, "'West Side Story' sigue triunfando en Broadway," *El Mundo*, 27 August 1960, 10; translation for this volume by Alberto Sandoval-Sánchez.

29. The original review is dated 19 August, 1961. See Nilita Vientós Gastón, "West Side Story," in *Apuntes sobre teatro: 1955–1961* (San Juan: Instituto de Cultura Puertorriqueña, 1989), 90.

30. For a critical analysis of the Puerto Rican family after migration, see Alberto Sandoval-Sánchez "La puesta en escena de la familia inmigrante puertorriqueña," *Revista Iberoamericana*, 162/163 (1993): 345–59.

31. Luis Rafael Sánchez, "En busca del tiempo bailado," *El Nuevo Día*, 26 November 1989, 11; translation for this volume by Alberto Sandoval-Sánchez. I would like to indicate that a shorter version of this article was published in a Latino review in the U.S.A., *Más* 1, no. 1 (1989): 86. Although Sánchez exalts the influence of Latin rhythm in Robbins's choreography, in a picture with this article, only the Jets appear. What an irony! Why were the Jets, who were never identified with Latin rhythms or dancing, selected instead of the Sharks? What is Sánchez referring to? According to my reading, the Latino dancing is not a marker for identity, as Sánchez suggests, but rather a racial and ethnic stereotype of Puerto Ricans and Latinos/as in general in the U.S.

32. Harold Prince, quoted in Zadan, *Sondheim & Co.*, 19.

33. Nan Robertson, "Maria and Anita in *West Side Story*," *New York Times*, 22 February 1980, C 4.

34. Nicholasa Mohr, "The Journey Toward a Common Ground: Struggle and Identity of Hispanics in the U.S.A.," *The Americas Review* 18, no. 1 (1990): 83.

35. Judith Ortiz Cofer, "The Myth of the Latin Woman: I Just Met a Girl Named Maria," in *The Latin Deli* (Athens; Ga.: University of Georgia Press, 1993), 148.

36. Ibid., 153–54.

37. Ibid., 154.

38. Joseph Berger, "Old Film Mirrors New Immigrant Life," *New York Times*, 18 September 1991, B 2.

Chapter Three

The title of this chapter is drawn from the song "One," the finale to (and probably the most famous number from) *A Chorus Line*, in which the entire ensemble sings "One singular sensation / ev'ry little step he takes."

1. Conrado Morales was born 22 November 1941 in Spanish Harlem, New York City, to Puerto Rican immigrants. His father was a Metropolitan Transit Authority employee. When he quit Cardinal Hayes High School to go onto the stage as a dancer, Morales changed his name to Nicholas Dante. As a dancer he joined Broadway road shows, and in New York, he danced in the choruses of *Applause, Smith, Ambassador, I'm Solomon* and other stage and television productions. Dante, a Nicheren Shoshu Buddhist, cowrote *A Chorus Line*, his first professional effort as a writer, he later completed a screenplay, *Fake Lady*, which was based on the character Paul's story in *A Chorus Line*; it was never produced. He also wrote the book for another musical show, *Jolson Tonight*. In 1991, at the time of his death from AIDS at age 49, Dante was writing a new play, *A Suite Letting Go*.

This short biography has been compiled with information from the following sources: "Nick Dante," in *The Best Plays of 1974–1975* ed. Otis L. Guernsey, Jr. (New York: Dodd, Mead, 1975), 243; "Nick Dante," *Playbill*, September 1979, 43; "Nick Dante," *Playbill*, June 1983, 59; and Eleanor Blau, "Nicholas Dante, 49; Dancer and a Writer Of 'A Chorus Line'," obituary, *New York Times*, 22 May 1991, D 25.

2. For biographical information on López, see Robert Viagas, Baayork Lee, and Thommie Walsh, *On the Line: The Creation of* A Chorus Line (New York: William Morrow, 1990).

3. For a summary of the plot and pictorial documentation of the Broadway production, see "The Ten Best Plays," in Guernsey, ed., *The Best Plays of 1974–1975*, 242–44. For the book and lyrics, see James Kirkwood, Michael Bennett, and Nicholas Dante, *A Chorus Line: The Book of the Musical* (New York: Applause, 1995); hereafter, all quotations are from this edition and cited parenthetically in the text unless otherwise noted. The film version was released in 1985 by Polygram Pictures.

4. According to Martin Gottfried, "'line' refers to a) the chorus line, b) the line of the tape on the stage floor, and c) sticking one's neck out." Martin Gottfried, *Broadway Musicals* (New York: Abradale Press/Harry N. Abrams, 1979), 35.

5. Bennett's skills for manipulation have been openly addressed in the writings about the making of *A Chorus Line*, and Dante spoke directly of it on a few occasions: "Now Michael was the great manipulator of all time. . . ."; "Michael believed he had to manipulate you to get the work out of you, and he romanced everybody. . . . It's one thing to manipulate your talent; it's a whole other thing to manipulate your personal emotions to get your talent."

Dante, quoted in Ken Mandelbaum, *A Chorus Line and the Musicals of Michael Bennett* (New York: St. Martin's Press, 1989), 125, 274. James Kirkwood declared that Bennet was "a master of manipulation, and Jesus Christ, sometimes it was so humiliating and damned sick." James Kirkwood, quoted in Kevin Kelly, *One Singular Sensation: The Michael Bennett Story* (New York: Zebra, 1990), 234. The issue of manipulation was also brought up by the original cast during its appearance on the TV show *Donahue*, Multimedia Entertainment, 23 March 1990, transcript 2909, show 0323–90.

6. Nicholas Dante, "Back on the Line: *A Chorus Line*'s Nicholas Dante Recovers from an Overdose of Fame and Fortune," interview by Edward Guthmann, *Advocate*, 10 October 1989, 57.

7. James Kirkwood wrote an article about his participation in the musical; it is entitled "Not in My Wildest Dreams ... did I imagine Co-authoring B'way's Longest Running Show," *Playbill*, September 1983, 8–12. Obviously, there was no interest in inviting Dante to write his testimony.

8. Nicholas Dante, quoted in Kelly, *One Singular Sensation*, 196–97; emphasis in the original.

9. According to Nicholas Dante, "'Jimmy Kirkwood and I went to rehearsal one day and there were about eight new lines in the show that neither of us recognized. I always assumed that Michael had wrote them, because Michael could be very funny and often came up with wonderful lines. I didn't find out until about four years after the show opened that Neil Simon wrote them. I never knew.'" Dante, quoted in Denny Martin Flinn, *What They Did For Love: The Untold Story Behind the Making of A Chorus Line* (New York: Bantam, 1989), 127. See also Mandelbaum, *A Chorus Line*, 147. As for Simon's own account of his participation in the preliminary phase of the musical, see Gary Stevens and Alan George, "Doctoring the Book," in *The Longest Line: Broadway's Most Singular Sensation: A Chorus Line* (New York: Applause, 1995), XV–XVI.

10. Kevin Kelly clearly states how Bennett appropriated *A Chorus Line*: "Publicly as well as privately, Michael Bennett proclaimed *A Chorus Line* as basically his own. In a 1986 interview on National Public Radio he said, 'It's the longest-running show in history. And it's mine! It's amazing. And it's the story of my life on top of it's amazing." Bennett, quoted in Kelly, *One Singular Sensation*, 392–93.

11. Nicholas Dante, quoted in Kelly, *One Singular Sensation*, 85.

12. Nicholas Dante, quoted in Mandelbaum, *A Chorus Line*, 334.

13. Nicholas Dante, "Big Night for the Chorus Line," interview by Tom Buckley, *New York Times*, 23 May 1975, L 28.

14. "News & Notes: AIDS 1991," *Entertainment Weekly*, 29 November 1991, 11.

15. Emory Lewis, "'Chorus Line' Glitters," *Jersey Record*, 22 May 1975, B 1.

16. Paul's monologue is reproduced in Kelly, *One Singular Sensation*, 191–95. The monologue went into *A Chorus Line* almost exactly as Dante had narrated his life story in the first planning session for the musical. For details, see Mandelbaum, *A Chorus Line*, 109, 128, and 334. Mandelbaum states, "Prime considerations throughout were to avoid excessive melodrama and any mono-

logue that would detract from Paul's, the Nick Dante story, which was intended to stand alone as the evening's climax" (128).

17.   Charisse was in the films *Singin' in the Rain* (1952), *Brigadoon* (1954), and *Silk Stockings* (1957).

18.   Judith Butler, "Performative Acts and Gender Constitution: An Essay in Phenomenology and Feminist Theory," in *Performing Feminisms: Feminist Critical Theory and Theatre*, ed. Sue-Ellen Case (Baltimore: Johns Hopkins University Press, 1990), 278–79.

19.   Stuart Hall, "New Ethnicities," in *Critical Dialogues in Cultural Studies*, ed. David Morley and Kuan-Hsing Chen (New York: Routledge, 1996), 445–46.

20.   Marjorie Garber discusses "category crisis" as follows: "Since, as I will argue, one of the most consistent and effective functions of the transvestite in culture is to indicate the place of what I call 'category crisis,' disrupting and calling attention to cultural, social, or aesthetic dissonances, there has been no attempt here to produce a seamless historical narrative of the 'development' of the transvestite figure—indeed, as will quickly become clear, I regard the appropriation of the transvestite as a figure for development, progress, or a 'stage of life' as to a large extent a refusal to confront the extraordinary power of transvestism to disrupt, expose, and challenge, putting in question the very notion of the 'original' and of stable identity. . . ." Marjorie Garber, *Vested Interests: Cross-Dressing and Cultural Anxiety* (New York: Routledge, 1995), 16.

21.   Frank Rich, "Critic's Notebook: The Magic of 'Chorus Line' No. 3,389," *New York Times*, 1 October 1983, 13.

Chapter Four

1.   For example, Migdalia Cruz, Eduardo Machado, Liza Loomer, and Elaine Romero write in English; Pedro R. Monge Rafuls and Héctor Santiago write in Spanish; Alicia Mena and Dolores Prida write bilingual pieces; Teatro Campesino's *Actos* and Nuyorican theater are interlingual, and most of the works are bicultural.

2.   Eliana Rivero, "From Immigrants to Ethnics: Cuban Women Writers in the U.S.," in *Breaking Boundaries: Latina Writings and Critical Readings*, ed. Asunción Horno-Delgado et al., (Amherst: University of Massachusetts Press, 1989), 191.

3.   The seminal work on U.S. Latino theater is Nicholás Kanellos's *A History of Hispanic Theatre in the U.S.: Origins to 1940* (Austin: University of Texas, 1990). Kanellos traces the evolution of Latino theater as he recovers theatrical traditions grounded in Hispanic enclaves such as New York City, Los Angeles, San Antonio, and Tampa. These early manifestations were in Spanish and belonged to the theatrical traditions of *carpas* (circuses), vaudeville, religious ceremonies, *variedades* (variety shows), *zarzuelas* (musical comedies), *revistas* (revues), and comic sketches. Given that these theatrical productions mainly functioned as entertainment that served to revitalize and reassure ethnic pride and communal ties with Hispanic cultural roots and national origins, I differentiate them from the emergence of U.S. Latino theater in the 1960s, the latter

centering on the problems of hybrid identities and the concept of home. For a history of U.S. Latino theater see Beatriz Rizk's essays "El teatro latino de Estados Unidos," *Tramoya* 22 (1990): 5–20; "El teatro hispano de Nueva York," in *Centro de documentación teatral* vol. 2, ed. Moisés Pérez Coterillo (Madrid: Técnicas Gráficas FORMA, 1988), 307–23; "Haciendo historia: multiculturalismo y el teatro latino en los Estados Unidos," *Ollantay Theater Magazine* 1, no. 1 (1993): 9–18; "El teatro latino de los Estados Unidos como discurso de resistencia posmoderna," *Ollantay Theater Magazine* 2, no. 1 (1994): 114–24; and "El teatro latino en los Estados Unidos," *Brújula/Compass*, 11 (1991): 25–27.

4.   In 1971, the board of Los Teatros Nacionales de Aztlán (TENAZ) was formed to promote, preserve, and enhance Chicano/Latino performing arts. Theater festivals took place in order to establish alliances and update the political and theatrical expressions of *la raza* (the race, the people).

5.   Luis Valdez, *Early Works: Actos, Bernabé and Pensamiento Serpentino* (Houston: Arte Público Press, 1990), 12.

6.   Rosa Luisa Márquez, *The Puerto Rican Traveling Theatre Company: The First Ten Years*, (Ph.D. diss., Michigan State University, 1977), 56.

7.   Demographics in the U.S. are undergoing remarkable changes. The U.S. Bureau of the Census projects that the non-Hispanic white population will increase by approximately 6 percent between the years 2000 and 2025; in contrast, the Hispanic population is projected to increase by approximately 90 percent in that same time period. *Statistical Abstract of the United States 1996* (Springfield, Va.: U.S. Department of Commerce, October 1996), 26.

8.   William A. Henry III, "Visions From the Past," *Time* special issue, ¡*Magnifico! Hispanic Culture Breaks Out of the Barrio*, 11 July 1988, 83.

9.   José Rivera, "An Interview with José Rivera," by David Román, *Performing Arts* 31, no. 6 (1997): 6.

10.   Michel Foucault, *The Order of Things: An Archaelogy of the Human Sciences*, (New York: Vintage, 1973), 156.

11.   Ibid., 156–57.

12.   David Richards, "On Stage, Survival of the Fizziest," *New York Times*, 12 June 1994, sec. 2, p.1.

13.   Ibid.

14.   Ibid., p. 2.

15.   For a critical, historical, and cultural reading of Broadway and Times Square, see Steve Nelson, "Broadway and the Beast: Disney Comes to Times Square," *Drama Review* T146 (1995): 71–85. Disney's appropriation of Broadway represents an effort to attract tourists and to commercialize and sanitize the area. With productions of *Beauty and the Beast* and *The Lion King* (and others to come), the audiences are entertained with pure spectacle, special effects, machinery, and pyrotechnics.

16.   Richard Eder, "Theater: 'Zoot Suit,' Chicano Music-Drama," *New York Times*, 26 March 1979, C 13.

17.   Brendan Gill, "The Theatre: Borrowings," *New Yorker*, 2 April 1979, 94.

18.   Jack Kroll, "Heartbeats From the Barrio," *Newsweek*, 9 April 1979, 86; emphasis added.

19. "Zoot Suit," *Variety*, 28 March 1979, 78; emphasis added.

20. John Simon, "West Coast Story," *New York Times*, 9 April 1979, 93.

21. Gill, "Borrowings," 94.

22. Mel Gussow, "The Stage: 'Short Eyes,'" *New York Magazine*, 8 January 1974, 24.

23. John Simon, review of *Short Eyes*, *New York*, 10 June 1974, 76.

24. Brendan Gill refers to the processes of identification in relation to race and the stage: "On opening night it was interesting to observe the difference in response to the play made by whites and blacks in the audience. The whites seemed bludgeoned into silence by the misfortune of the characters on stage; the blacks, apparently taking the misfortune for granted, shouted with glee at every sign that an individual was fighting back, no matter on what side of the dispute." Gill, "De Profundis," *New Yorker*, 3 June 1974, 68. George Oppenheimer observed, "My only displeasure with 'Short Eyes' came with certain elements in the preview audience, black and white alike, who behaved as if they were at a prizefight, screaming, applauding in the wrong places, and drowning out the words. Any derogatory references to whitey were greeted with happy shouts of laughter." Oppenheimer, "A Prison Play that Breaks Free," *Newsday*, 7 April 1974, part 2, p. 9.

25. Rumors are that Teatro Campesino plans to move from San Juan Bautista to San Jose. Such a move signals a moment of social and cultural transition: the theater is leaving behind its rural beginnings for an urban site, as well as interacting and sharing common experiences with other Latinos/as.

26. Dolores Prida, "Interview with Dolores Prida," by Luz María Umpierre, *Latin American Theatre Review*, (1988), 84.

27. Dolores Prida, "The Show Does Go On," in Horno-Delgado, ed., *Breaking Boundaries*, 186.

28. Published anthologies of U.S. Latino theater are scarce and published mainly under ethnic rubrics; for example, Cuban: *Cuban Theatre in the United States: A Critical Anthology, Cuban American Theater, Teatro 5 Autores Cubanos*; Chicano: *Zoot Suit and Other Plays, Luis Valdez: Early Works, Necessary Theater: Six Plays About the Chicano Experience, El Teatro de la Esperanza: An Anthology of Chicano Drama, Contemporary Chicano Theatre*; Puerto Rican: *Nuestro New York* and *Recent Puerto Rican Theatre*. In the 1990s, anthologies of Latina theater are booming: *Shattering the Myth: Plays by Hispanic Women; Latinas on Stage: Criticism and Practice* (forthcoming); and *Puro Teatro: A Latina Anthology* (forthcoming). The works of gays and lesbians are starting to appear in national anthologies: Janis Astor del Valle in *Torch to the Heart: Anthology of Lesbian Art and Drama* and in *Intimate Acts: Eight Contemporary Lesbian Plays*; Astor del Valle and María Irene Fornes in *Amazon All Stars: Thirteen Lesbian Plays*; Guillermo Reyes in *Staging Gay Lives: An Anthology of Contemporary Gay Theater*; Rane Arroyo and Ana María Simo in *Tough Acts to Follow: One-Act Plays on the Gay/ Lesbian Experience*, Edwin Sánchez in *The Actor's Book of Gay and Lesbian Plays*. Like gays and lesbians, women of color are practicing a politics of affinity, and thus are included in their own anthologies. Only a few Latino/a playwrights have solo anthologies of their own solo collected works: Estela Portillo Tram-

bley, María Irene Fornes, Cherríe Moraga, Dolores Prida, Carlos Morton, Luis Valdez, Pedro Pietri, Iván Acosta, Edward Gallardo, Eduardo Machado, Miguel Piñero, Rick Najera, Lynne Alvarez, José Rivera, and Edwin Sánchez. To date, only two anthologies have been inclusive in terms of nationality and ethnicity: *Nuevos Pasos: Chicano and Puerto Rican Drama* and *On New Ground: Contemporary Hispanic-American Plays*. Despite the dearth of such published work, the comedy groups Latins Anonymous and Culture Clash have published anthologies of their work.

29. To define "diversity" I turn to Arturo Madrid, Chicano community activist and professor of literature: "Diversity, from the Latin *divertere*, meaning to turn aside, to go different ways, to differ, is the condition of being different or having differences, is an instance of being different. . . . Diversity is lack of standardization, of regularity, of orderliness, homogeneity, conformity, uniformity. Diversity introduces complications, is difficult to organize, is troublesome to manage, is problematical. Diversity is irregular, disorderly, uneven, rough. The way we use the word diversity gives us away. Something is too diverse, is extremely diverse. We want a little diversity. When we talk about diversity, we are talking about the *other*, whatever that other might be: someone of a different gender, race, class, national origin; somebody at a greater or lesser distance from the norm; someone outside the set; someone who possesses a different set of characteristics, features, or attributes; someone who does not fall within the taxonomies we use daily and with which we are comfortable; someone who does not fit into the mental configurations that give our lives order and meaning." Arturo Madrid, "Diversity and Its Discontents," *Academe*, November/December 1990, 18; emphasis in the original.

30. Eduardo Machado, "What's a Hispanic Play? That's a Tough Question," interview by John Glore, *American Theater* 3, no. 9 (1986): 39.

31. Nicolás Kanellos has clearly expressed the function of Latino theater in the U.S. since its beginnings: "The Hispanic tradition in the United States is not one that can be characterized exclusively by social dysfunction, poverty, crime, and illiteracy, as the media would often have us believe. Rather, if we focus on theatre, we can draw alternative characterizations: the ability to create art even under the most trying of circumstances, social and cultural cohesiveness and national pride in the face of racial and class pressures, cultural continuity and adaptability in a foreign land." Kanellos introduction to *A History of Hispanic Theatre*, xiv–xv.

32. Important factors contributing to the professionalization of Latino theater are playwrighting labs and workshops, for example the PRTT's Performing Lab, INTAR's Playwright's Unit, and the South Coast Repertory's Hispanic Playwright Project, under the direction of José Cruz González. María Irene Fornes has also been a role model, an inspiring teacher, and a mentor to a new generation.

33. Michael Alassa, quoted in Sam H. Shirakawa, "Beyond the Ghetto Mentality," *Theater Week*, 16–22 May 1988, 33–34. Such a desire to censor "kitchen sink dramas" is a political and economic move backing the interests mainly of middle-class Latino playwrights who do not indentify with Latino

working classes and "ghetto" realities. Such an attitude is also loaded with racist and classist prejudices.

34. Dolores Prida uses this phrase to describe "kitchen sink drama" in Prida, "Interview with Dolores Prida," 82.

35. Alvan Colón Lespier, "Teatro Pregones: Finding Language in Dialogue," in *Reimaging America: The Arts of Social Change*, ed. Mark O'Brien and Craig Little (Philadelphia: New Society, 1990), 254.

36. Ed Morales, quoted in Ana Paula Ferreira, "'Los críticos (no) hacen falta': el crítico o la crítica como productores de significado," *Ollantay Theater Magazine* 2, no. 1 (1994): 84. For an excellent article on the diversity of U.S. Latino theater, see Ed Morales, "Making Monsters," *American Theater* 11, no. 7 (1994): 26–27. The ninth Festival de Teatro Hispano, reviewed by Morales in this article, took place at Teatro Avante in Miami in June 1994.

Chapter Five

1. Richard Goldstein, "The Implicated and the Immune: Responses to AIDS in the Arts and Popular Culture," in *A Disease of Society: Cultural and Institutional Responses to AIDS*, ed. Dorothy Nelkin, David P. Willis, and Scott V. Parris (New York: Cambridge University Press, 1991), 20.

2. Michael Cunningham, "After AIDS, Gay Art Aims for a New Reality," *New York Times*, 26 April 1992, sec. 2, p. 1.

3. David Román, *Acts of Intervention: Performance, Gay Culture, and AIDS* (Bloomington: Indiana University Press, 1998), 48.

4. In *Acts of Intervention*, Román examines most of these mainstream plays. His critical reading centers on how AIDS has been represented in the dominant culture and how gay men have used theater and performance to intervene in the crisis of AIDS. Román's study is not limited to the mainstream; he covers community-based social performances such as fund-raisers, benefits, memorials, protest marches, and vigils. He also takes into consideration solo performances, African American and Latino theater performances, and even the representation of HIV-negative gay men in AIDS theater. In my collaboration with Román, "Caught in the Web: Latinidad, AIDS, and Allegory in *Kiss of the Spider Woman, The Musical*," *American Literature* 67, no. 3 (1995): 554–85, we, as spectators with a political consciousness of AIDS, read *Kiss Of The Spider Woman, The Musical* as an allegory of AIDS. The essay is a hybrid example of cultural criticism that combines testimonial discourse, semiotic analysis of the text, theorization on spectatorship, identificatory practices, and performance. This alternative reading aims to reveal how the text in its deep ideological structure is the discursive product/production of the AIDS epidemic, which has shaken the whole Broadway theatrical world. We do not only limit our analysis to the text, but theorize how dominant representations of Latinos/as shape our own "Latinidad." In our case, we center on how gay and lesbian Latino/a images are either misrepresented, stereotyped, or silenced in dominant theatrical productions. Our ultimate goal is to construct a politics of collaboration resulting from the difficulties of scholarship when a colleague is affected by AIDS. This

collaboration serves as a recovery process in which the person with AIDS can continue to be productive and intellectually active thanks to a collaborative effort and a politics of affinity.

Another Broadway musical that cannot be overlooked is the 1996 megahit *Rent*, written by Jonathan Larson. Two of its protagonists are Latinos with AIDS: Mimi, and Angel (the latter a drag queen). In both cases, AIDS and sexuality, rather than their ethnicity, determine their identities. This is similar to the character Paul's articulation of his gay identity in *A Chorus Line*.

5. Larry Kramer, *Reports from the Holocaust: The Making of an AIDS Activist* (New York: St. Martin's Press, 1989), 46, 233, 245.

6. Ibid., 263, 270.

7. *The Way We Live Now: American Plays and the AIDS Crisis*, ed. M. Elizabeth Osborn (New York: Theater Communications Group, 1990). Only two plays by women—both white—appear in this anthology: Paula Vogel's *The Baltimore Waltz* and Susan Sontag's *The Way We Live Now*. In a review of the anthology, Joseph Cady, in his review of this collection, has made some illuminating comments on white gay representation: "The gay community was hit first and hardest by AIDS in America . . . and because, as social outcasts even before AIDS, they had nothing left to lose in taking up the stigmatized subject, gay men have predominated in, and written, almost all our AIDS literature to date." On minority underrepresentation and silence, Cady states that the "complex reasons for this silence need exploring. One is surely the prior devastation of IV-drug users by poverty and racial prejudice; another is the ironic reluctance of heterosexuals to acknowledge AIDS because of their traditional status as social insiders (in contrast to the impetus that gay men's status as outsiders has given them to confront the disease)." Another important issue that Cady notes is the absence of any popular, group, or documentary theater in the volume. He closes his review with a brilliant remark: "Does this distribution simply represent the best work available, or does it, at least in part, express a cultural choice, an attempt to detoxify the stigmatized subject via association with famous writers?" Cady, "AIDS on the National Stage," review of *The Way We Live Now: American Plays and the AIDS Crisis*, *Medical Humanities Review* 6, no. 1 (1992): 24, 26. For the underrepresentation of women in mainstream AIDS theater, see Lizbeth Goodman, "AIDS and Live Art," in *Analysing Performance: A Critical Reader*, ed. Patrick Campbell (Manchester: Manchester University Press, 1996): 203–18.

8. Michael Feingold, introduction to Osborn, ed., *The Way We Live Now*, xv–xvi.

9. Therese Jones, ed., *Sharing the Delirium: Second Generation AIDS Plays and Performances* (Portsmouth, N.H.: Heinemann, 1994).

10. Jones, introduction to *Sharing the Delirium*, x–xi.

11. "Delirium," *The American Heritage Dictionary of the English Language*, 3rd ed., (Boston: Houghton Mifflin, 1992), 494.

12. Jones, introduction to *Sharing the Delirium*, ix.

13. Larry Kramer, *Reports*, 238.

14. There is also a performance group composed of gay African Ameri-

cans, Pomo Afro Homos, that stages the AIDS experiences in their communities through their shows *Fierce Love* and *Dark Fruit*. For a critical reading of their work, see chapter 5, "Pomo Afro Homos' *Fierce Love:* Intervening in the Cultural Politics of Race, Sexuality, and AIDS," in Román, *Acts of Intervention*.

15. Frank Rich, "A Black Family Confronts AIDS," *New York Times*, 11 March 1992, C 22.

16. George Whitmore, *Someone Was Here: Profiles in the AIDS Epidemic* (New York: New American Library, 1988), 24.

17. Jan Zita Grover, "The Convergence of Art and Crisis," *High Performance* 36 (1986): 31; emphasis in the original.

18. John Preston, "AIDS Writing: The Imperative to 'Get It All Down,'" *Outweek*, 13 March 1991, 61; emphasis in the original.

19. Paul Rudnick, "Laughing at AIDS," editorial, *New York Times*, 23 January 1993, 21.

20. *HIV/AIDS Surveillance Report* 9, no. 2 (Atlanta: U.S. Department of Health and Human Services/Public Health Service, 1997, 16; *Statistical Abstract 1997* (Springfield Va.: U.S. Department of Commerce, 1997), 19.

21. *HIV/AIDS Surveillance Report*, 16.

22. *HIV/AIDS Surveillance Report*, 8–9; *Statistical Abstract*, 45–47.

23. David Richards writes, about AIDS theater in general, "If you are looking for enduring art, most AIDS plays don't qualify, which doesn't mean they don't serve a purpose. They tell us what the temperature is right now and capture the current state of our fears and prejudices. That's useful information to have. As sociological documents, filed from the edge, they can still hit hard." Richards, "The Theater of AIDS: Attention Must Be Paid," *New York Times*, 5 January 1992, sec. 2, p. 5.

24. Max Navarre, "Art in the AIDies: An Act of Faith," *High Performance* 36 (1986): 32–36.

25. Román, *Acts of Intervention*, 201.

26. Ibid.

27. Jorge B. Merced, "Teatro y SIDA," *Ollantay Theater Magazine* 2, no. 2, special issue, *Latino Theater on AIDS* (1994): 26. Translation for this volume by Diana Taylor.

28. Luis Alfaro, Monica Palacios, and Alberto Antonio Araiza are Latino performers bringing AIDS to the stage through their solo performance monologues.

29. Rosa Luisa Márquez, "Creación colectiva: con y sin texto," *Ollantay Theater Magazine* 2, no. 2, special issue, *Latino Theater on AIDS* (1994): 16, 17. Translation for this volume by Diana Taylor.

30. Quotations from the play will hereafter be cited by page number parenthetically in the text.

It is interesting to observe that Cuban exiles are out of the closet more often than other Latinos/as. In their plays, the criticism of compulsory heterosexuality is overt and direct. The logic behind such a liberal position is that, for Cuban exiles, leaving Cuba meant total freedom. Consequently, in the U.S. democratic society, freedom of speech goes hand in hand with freedom of sexuality. The goal of Cuban exiles is to dismantle homophobia inherited from Cuba by U.S. Cuban communities.

There is also a questioning of gender roles at work, and the invention of new identities in exile, as well as second-generation identity formation. For these new identities, homosexuality is no joke, *la loca* (the effiminate faggot) is no laughing matter. On the other hand, traditional values are caricatured. The audience can laugh at old ways of seeing and doing by portraying how racist, homophobic, classist, and sexist Latino culture can be. I am grateful to Nancy Saporta Sternbach for helping me formulate this interpretation.

31.   Unlike many Latino AIDS plays, *Noche de ronda* shows the protagonist migrating to avoid the cultural stigmatism of his homosexuality. A large number of plays deal with AIDS when it hits home because many Latinos lack the financial independence to move away from their intolerant communities. There is no place like home to start dismantling oppression, machismo, and homophobia: these plays break the silence and deconstruct degrading depictions of Latinos; they attack gender binarism, affront machismo, and question Catholic oppression and homophobia. (It should not be forgotten that many Anglo-American men have migrated to the cities, leaving their families behind because of newfound economic independence.) For Latinos/as, the heart of the family is where acceptance and tolerance need to begin.

32.   "La hija de nadie" was a *ranchera* (a popular Mexican folkloric song) made popular by Yolanda del Río.

33.   The song "Noche de ronda" was composed by María Teresa Lara. It was introduced in Mexico by Agustín Lara. For a cultural analysis of Agustín Lara's boleros, see Carlos Monsiváis, *Amor perdido* (Mexico City: Biblioteca Eva, 1988), 61–86. Monsiváis places the bolero in its sociohistorical context in order to examine the representation of prostitution, marginality, and sexuality in urban Mexico in the 1930s and 1940s.

34.   Louis Delgado, Jr., *A Better Life, Ollantay Theater Magazine* 2, no. 2, special issue, *Latino Theater on AIDS* (1994): 140. Hereafter, quotations from the play will be cited parenthetically in the text.

35.   Stuart Hall, "New Ethnicities," in *Critical Dialogues in Cultural Studies,* ed. David Morley and Kuan-Hsing Chen (New York: Routledge, 1996), 443, 446.

36.   "We Gotta Get Out of This Place," music and words by Eric Burden, 1965.

37.   Ilka Tanya Payán, "Ilka Tanya Payán: An Interview by Carmen Navarro," *Body Positive,* April 1994, 12.

38.   Hank Tavera, "What is AIDS Theater?" manuscript, 1996.

Chapter Six

1.   I use Jill Dolan's definitions of "gender" and "sex": "Sex is biological, based in genital differences between males and females. Gender, on the other hand, is a fashioning of maleness and femaleness into the cultural categories of masculinity and femininity. These adjectives described cultural attributes that determine social roles. Sex is empirical, but gender is an interpretation

that can only take place within a cultural space." Dolan, *The Feminist Spectator as Critic* (Ann Arbor: University of Michigan Press, 1988), 6. For "patriarchy" I use the following definition: "An important term used in a variety of ways to characterize abstractly the structures and social arrangements within which women's oppression is elaborated. Means an ideology which arose out of men's power to exchange women between kinship groups; as the power of the father; to express men's control over women's sexuality and fertility; to describe the institutional structure of male domination." Sheila Rowbotham, "The Trouble with 'Patriarchy'," *New Statesman* 28 (1979): 72, cited in *A Feminist Dictionary,* ed. Cheris Kramarae and Paula A. Treichler (London: Pandora, 1985), 323.

2. I do not attempt in this essay to trace the genealogy of the beautiful señorita in mainstream discursive representations. Nevertheless, I would like to point out some specific historico-cultural constructions of the trope that I initiated in chapter 1 with a critical reading of Carmen Miranda. For example, Harry L. Foster's *A Gringo in Mañana-Land* (New York: Dodd, Mead, 1924) dedicates a chapter to "Those Dark-Eyed Señoritas!" The travelogue describes Mexican beautiful señoritas in detail, reinforcing stereotypes of femininity in Latin America. As seen in chapter 1, during the 1940s many songs on Broadway and Holywood portrayed Latin American women as beautiful señoritas. Among these incarnations, those of Chiquita Banana and Carmen Miranda are the most memorable. See John J. Johnson, *Latin America in Caricature,* for the representation of Latin America as a beautiful señorita in political cartoons from the nineteenth century to the present. In the 1990s, Carmen Miranda has even been appropriated by gay men in order to survive the AIDS epidemic; for example, see John Glines's excerpt of his play *The Demonstration,* in *Arts and Understanding,* 4, no. 1 (1995): 8–11. In this piece, instead of going to a political demonstration, a gay man dressed as Carmen Miranda decides to go to the hospital to visit a friend with AIDS and entertain him.

3. Laura Mulvey observes, about the male gaze as the pleasure in looking at women, "In their traditional exhibitionist role women are simultaneously looked at and displayed, with their appearance coded for strong visual and erotic impact so that they can be said to connote *to-be-looked-at-ness.*" Mulvey, *Visual and Other Pleasures* (Bloomington: Indiana University Press, 1989), 19; emphasis in the original. I go a step further by including ethnicity as one of the components of the visual pleasure of exoticizing, displaying the "other". Such is the case of Carmen Miranda.

4. Presently I am working on a two-book project in collaboration with Nancy Saporta Sternbach, forthcoming from the University of Arizona Press. Volume one will be titled *Puro Teatro: A Latina Anthology;* volume two will be a theoretical and critical reading of U.S. Latina playwriting and performance, titled *Stages of Life: Cultural Performance and Identity Formation in Latina Theatre.* For this reason, I do not analyze Chicana theater and performance in this chapter.

5. Dolores Prida wrote *Beautiful Señoritas* after attending a theater festival in Venezuela in 1976. The play was in response to the absence of plays centering on women's issues and representation. See also Dolores Prida, "The Show

Does Go On," 181–88, and Alberto Sandoval-Sánchez, "Dolores Prida's *Coser y Cantar:* Mapping the Dialectics of Ethnic Identity and Assimilation," 201–20, both in *Breaking Boundaries: Latina Writings and Critical Readings,* ed. Asunción Horno-Delgado et al. (Amherst: University of Massachusetts Press, 1989).

6.   Dolores Prida, "Interview with Dolores Prida," by Luz María Umpierre *Latin American Theatre Review,* Fall (1988), 82; emphasis in the original.

7.   For a definition of "compulsory heterosexuality" see the influential article by Adrienne Rich, "Compulsory Heterosexuality and Lesbian Existence," in *Blood, Bread, and Poetry* (New York: W. W. Norton, 1986), 23–75. Sue-Ellen Case, in *Feminism and Theatre,* has summarized Rich's argument, saying, "The critique of the patriarchal oppression of women by sexual means is sometimes extended to a critique of what Adrienne Rich has termed 'compulsory heterosexuality.' In what has become a central lesbian document within radical feminism, 'Compulsory Heterosexuality and Lesbian Existence,' Rich describes the 'institution of heterosexuality as a beach head of male dominance.' Rich identifies two ways in which heterosexuality is made compulsory: through 'the constraints and sanctions that, historically, have enforced or ensured the coupling of women with men' and, in a phrase she borrowed from Catherine MacKinnon, 'the eroticization of women's subordination.' The contradiction to compulsory heterosexuality is lesbian existence. Rich places lesbianism in the context of patriarchal oppression rather than in the bi-gender context of homosexuality. The lesbian, she suggests, performs an act of resistance to the patriarchal assumption that men have the right of access to women." Case, *Feminism and Theatre* (New York: Methuen, 1988), 75.

8.   Dolores Prida, *Beautiful Señoritas* (Houston: Arte Público Press, 1991), 20. Hereafter, quotations from the play will be cited parenthetically in the text.

9.   Jill Dolan has made this observation about the gaze of the male: "The woman's image is constructed so specifically to fulfill male desire that his gaze is implicit in her own. The projection of male desire she wears completely denies her own subjectivity." Dolan, *The Feminist Spectator,* 54.

10.   This line was eliminated in the published version of the play. It appeared in the manuscript (1980; 15) as one of the lines in the song "They Do It All For Me."

11.   Yvonne Yarbro-Bejarano, "The Female Subject in Chicano Theatre: Sexuality, 'Race,' and Class," in *Performing Feminisms: Feminist Critical Theory and Theatre,* ed. Sue-Ellen Case (Baltimore: Johns Hopkins University Press, 1990), 145.

12.   Teresa de Lauretis, "Sexual Indifference and Lesbian Representation," *Theatre Journal* 40, no. 2, special issue, *Feminist diVERSIONs* (1988): 158.

13.   Janis Astor del Valle, *Where the Señoritas Are,* unpublished manuscript, 1993, 1; emphasis in the original. Hereafter, quotations from the play will be cited parenthetically in the text. An excerpt of the play is published in *Torch to the Heart: Anthology of Lesbian Art and Drama,* ed. Sue McConnell-Celi (New Jersey: Lavender Press, 1994), 83–96. I would like to thank the playwright for providing me with a copy of the manuscript of the play.

14.   Jill Dolan has theorized, regarding lesbian representation, "A body dis-

played in representation that belongs to the female gender class is assumed to be heterosexual, since male desire organizes the representational system. Disrupting the assumption of heterosexuality, and replacing male desire with lesbian desire, for example, offers radical new readings of the meanings produced by representation." Dolan, *The Feminist Spectator,* 63.

15. For theorizations on butch-femme role playing, and lesbian spectorial desire and identification, see Sue-Ellen Case, "Toward A Butch-Femme Aesthetic," in *Making a Spectacle: Feminist Essays on Contemporary Women's Theatre,* ed. Lynda Hart (Ann Arbor: The University of Michigan Press, 1989), 282–99. Teresa de Lauretis, "Film and the Visible," in *How Do I Look?: Queer Film and Video,* ed. Bad Object-Choices (Seattle: Bay Press, 1991), 223–64.

16. Jill Dolan has suggested that "in gay male drag, women fare no better. Female impersonation here is usually filtered through the camp sensibility, which removes it from the realm of serious gender play and deconstruction. . . . women are non-existent in drag performance, but woman-as-myth, as a cultural, ideological object, is constructed in an agreed upon exchange between the male performer and the usually male spectator. Male drag mirrors women's socially constructed roles." Jill Dolan, "Gender Impersonation Onstage: Destroying or Maintaining the Mirror of Gender Roles," *Women and Performance* 2, no. 2 (1985), 8.

17. Judith Butler, *Gender Trouble: Feminism and the Subversion of Identity* (New York: Routledge, 1990), 137–38; emphasis in the original.

18. Teresa de Lauretis, "Film and the Visible," 250–51.

19. Luli's definition does not imply gender understood as a role; as Judith Butler has said, "gender cannot be understood as a role which either expresses or disguises an interior 'self,' whether that 'self' is conceived as sexed or not. As performance which is performative, gender is an 'act,' broadly construed, which constructs the social fiction of its own psychological interiority. Butler, "Performative Acts and Gender Constitution: An Essay in Phenomenology and Feminist Theory," in Case, ed., *Performing Feminisms,* 279; emphasis in the original.

20. Adrienne Rich, "Compulsory Heterosexuality," 51–52.

21. Gloria Anzaldúa, *Borderlands/La Frontera: the New Mestiza* (San Francisco: Spinsters/Aunt Lute, 1987), 79.

22. For a critical reading of Marga Gómez's works, see Alberto Sandoval-Sánchez and Nancy S. Sternbach, "Rehearsing In Front of the Mirror: Marga Gómez's Lesbian Subjectivity as a Work-in-Progress," *Women and Performance,* 8:2, no. 16, special issue, *Queer Acts* (1996): 205–24. For Carmelita Tropicana, see Lillian Manzor-Coats, "Too Spik or Too Dyke: Carmelita Tropicana," *Ollantay Theater Magazine* 2, no. 1 (1994): 39–55. I would like to add that Monica Palacios's performance piece "Greeting From a Queer Señorita" deconstructs the stereotype of the beautiful señorita from a Chicana lesbian perspective.

Chapter Seven

1. Richard Rodriguez, *Hunger of Memory: The Education of Richard Rodriguez* (Boston: David R. Godine, 1992), 3.

2. Ibid., 4, 5, 189; ellipses in the original.

3. Ibid., 195.

4. In my forthcoming book in collaboration with Nancy Saporta Sternbach—*Stages of Life: Cultural Performance and Identity Formation in Latina Theatre*—we dedicate one chapter, "Homing the Stage, Staging Home: New Directions in U.S. Latina Theatre," to Latina conceptualizations of home. Our critical reading centers on three categories: home as imprisonment, home as a site of difference actualized in the lesbian body, and home as a mythical and allegorical journey.

5. José Rivera, *The House of Ramon Iglesia*, 216. In *On New Ground: Contemporary Hispanic-American Plays*, ed. M. Elizabeth Osborn, (New York: Theatre Communications Group, 1987): 191–242. Hereafter, quotations from the play will be cited parenthetically in the text.

6. For a critical study of the crisis of patriarchy after migration in Puerto Rican and U.S. Puerto Rican theater, see my article "La puesta en escena de la familia inmigrante puertorriqueña," *Revista Iberoamericana*, 162/163, special issue, *Puerto Rican Literature*, ed. Eliseo Colón (1993): 345–59.

7. Debbora Battaglia, "On Practical Nostalgia: Self-Prospecting among Urban Trobrianders," in *Rhetorics of Self-Making*, ed. Debbora Battaglia (Berkeley and Los Angeles: University of California Press, 1995), 78.

8. The ending of the play is ambiguous. Consequently, spectators and critics have their own interpretation of the final scene. Although this is not a happy ending celebrating assimilation, social mobility, and success, a critic imposed just such a happy ending upon it, saying that "Javier sighs, smiles, flicks on a portable tape machine and allows himself to sway his hips to a salsa beat. He's cheerful. He really loves his family and his heritage. Why not? He's free at last." Douglas Watt, "Winning Puerto Rican Entry is a Loser," *New York Daily News*, 17 March 1983, 83. In this way, the critic's misreading actualizes the dominant cultural and social expectations of assimilation upon children of immigrants. On the other hand, Una Chaudhuri reads the ending as an expression of multiculturalism and the formation of a new subjectivity in American theater, saying that "Javier uncreates an anguished, alienated, and lonely self by allowing his family to depart. They depart as it were, *through* him, their project of homecoming moving across and beyond his sense of homelessness. The Javier who remains is not the consummation of a self-creating process but—rather because of his journey to another 'home'—the token of a potentially new, more *multiply situated* model of subjectivity." Una Chaudhuri, *Staging Place: The Geography of Modern Drama* (Ann Arbor: University of Michigan Press, 1995), 210; emphasis in the original.

9. For recent theoretical and interdisciplinary studies on Puerto Rican migration and colonialism, see Frances Negrón-Muntaner and Ramón Grosfo-

guel, eds., *Puerto Rican Jam: Essays on Culture and Politics* (Minneapolis: University of Minnesota Press, 1997); and Carlos Antonio Torre, et al., eds., *The Commuter Nation: Perspectives on Puerto Rican Migration* (Río Piedras, P.R.: Editorial de la Universidad de Puerto Rico, 1994).

10.   Rivera, *Ramon Iglesia*, 94.

11.   Frank Rich, "Stage: 'Ramon Iglesia,' Breaking Away to Stay," *New York Times*, 13 March 1983, C 3.

12.   José Rivera, *Marisol, Theatre Forum* no. 2 (1992): 26. Hereafter, quotations from the play will be cited parenthetically in the text.

13.   Karen Fricker, "Another Playwright Confronts an Angel and the Apocalypse," *New York Times*, 16 May 1993, H 7.

14.   Robert Viagas, "Heavenly Harbingers," *New Haven Register*, 21 February 1993, D 2.

15.   Fricker, "Another Playwright," H 7.

16.   Dolores Prida, *Botánica*, unpublished manuscript, 11. Hereafter, all quotations from the play will be cited parenthetically in the text.

17.   Notice how the grandmother transforms "mumbo jumbo" into "mambo jambo." This change registers cultural and linguistic differences between generations.

18.   Millie's account of her education is one of the most emotional and dramatic discourses in U.S. Latino theater. When produced at Teatro Repertorio Español, audiences identified completely with the protagonist and her confession. Yet in his review of the play in the *New York Times* Frank Rich did not connect at all with this dramatic momentum. "All of the action is predictable," he claimed, "Indeed, a few of the characters seem to be thrown in only to be the butt of jokes. And some of the incidents are merely distracting, including one emotionally powerful moment between Millie and her grandmother. Dramatic logic is not Ms. Prida's strength." Frank Rich, "Street Smarts Round Out An Ivy-League Education," *New York Times*, 5 March 1991, C 16.

19.   In this play, the third generation functions as a second generation.

20.   Roy Conboy, *When El Cucui Walks* (San Francisco: Z Plays, 1993), 4. Hereafter, quotations from the play will be cited parenthetically in the text.

21.   Salman Rushdie, *Imaginary Homelands: Essays and Criticism 1981–1991* (New York: Penguin, 1991), 17.

22.   This political and existential notion of home is the one that through the years I have embraced and experienced since I migrated to the U.S. in 1973. This notion of a hybrid identity and home is the one that I share with my U.S. Latina students, and all other students, at Mount Holyoke College as they struggle to belong, to find their own way home.

23.   bell hooks, *Yearning: Race, Gender, and Cultural Politics* (Boston: South End Press, 1990), 148.

Bibliography

Alexander, William. "Clearing Space: AIDS Theater in Atlanta." *Drama Review* 34, no. 3 (1990): 109–28.

Algarín, Miguel, and Miguel Piñero, eds. *Nuyorican Poetry: An Anthology of Puerto Rican Words and Feelings.* New York: William Morrow, 1975.

Almaguer, Tomás. "Chicano Men: A Cartography of Homosexual Identity and Behavior." *differences: A Journal of Feminist Cultural Studies,* special issue, *Queer Theory* 3, no. 2 (1991): 75–100.

Alonso, Ana María, and María Teresa Koreck. "Silences: 'Hispanics,' AIDS, and Sexual Practices." *differences: A Journal of Feminist Cultural Studies* 1, no. 1 (1989): 101–24.

Alpert, Hollis. *Broadway! 125 Years of Musical Theater.* New York: Arcade, 1991.

Altman, Rick. *The American Film Musical.* Bloomington: Indiana University Press, 1989.

American Film Institute Catalog of Motion Pictures Produced in the U.S., vol. 3. Berkeley and Los Angeles: University of California Press, 1993.

American Heritage Dictionary of the English Language, 3rd ed. Boston: Houghton Mifflin, 1992.

Anderson, Benedict. *Imagined Communities,* London: Verso, 1991.

Andrews, Bart. *The "I Love Lucy" Book.* New York: Doubleday, 1985.

Anzaldúa, Gloria. *Borderlands/La Frontera: The New Mestiza.* San Francisco: Spinsters/Aunt Lute, 1987.

Anzaldúa, Gloria, ed. *Making Face, Making Soul/Haciendo Caras: Creative and Critical Perspectives by Women of Color.* San Francisco: Aunt Lute, 1990.

Anzaldúa, Gloria, and Cherríe Moraga. *This Bridge Called My Back: Writings by Radical Women of Color.* New York: Kitchen Table, 1983.

Aparicio, Frances R., and Susana Chávez-Silverman, eds. *Tropicalizations: Transcultural Representations of Latinidad,* 1–17. Hanover, N.H.: Dartmouth College Press, 1997.

Arnaz, Desi. *A Book.* New York: William Morrow, 1976.

Arnaz, Desi, and Al Stump. "America Has Been Good To Me." *American Magazine,* February 1955, 22–87.

Arrizón, Alicia. "Chicanas en la escena: teatralidad y performance." *Ollantay Theater Magazine* 4, no. 1, special issue, *Chicano Theater* (1996): 21–32.

Ashcroft, Bill, Gareth Griffiths, and Hellen Tiffin. *The Post-Colonial Studies Reader.* New York: Routledge, 1995.

Bachelard, Gaston. *The Poetics of Space.* Boston: Beacon Press, 1969.

Ball, Lucille. *Love, Lucy.* New York: G. P. Putnam's Sons, 1996.

Bakhtin, M. M., and P. M. Medvedev. *The Formal Method in Literary Scholarship: A Critical Introduction to Sociological Poetics.* Trans. Albert J. Wehrle. Cambridge, Mass.: Harvard University Press, 1985.

Barradas, Efraín. *Partes de un todo: Ensayos y notas de literatura puertorriqueña en los Estados Unidos.* Río Piedras, P.R.: Editorial de la Universidad de Puerto Rico, 1998.

Barradas, Efraín, and Rafael Rodríguez, eds. *Herejes y mitificadores: Muestra de poesía puertorriqueña en los Estados Unidos.* Río Piedras, P. R.: Huracán, 1980.

Barthes, Roland. *S/Z.* Trans. Richard Miller. New York: Hill and Wang, 1974.

Barthes, Roland. *Mythologies.* Trans. Annette Lavers. New York: Hill and Wang, 1979.

Battaglia, Debbora. "On Practical Nostalgia: Self-Prospecting among Urban Trobrianders." In *Rhetorics of Self-Making,* ed. Debbora Battaglia, 77–96. Berkeley and Los Angeles: University of California Press, 1995.

Baucom, Ian. "Dreams of Home: Colonialism and Postmodernism." *Research in African Literatures* 22, no. 4 (1991): 5–27.

Belsey, Catherine. *Critical Practice.* London: Routledge, 1980.

Belsey, Catherine. "Disrupting Sexual Difference: Meaning and Gender in the Comedies." In *Alternative Shakespeares,* ed. John Drakakis, 166–90. London: Methuen, 1985.

Berger, John. *Ways Of Seeing.* New York: British Broadcasting Corporation/ Penguin, 1981.

Berger, Joseph. "Old Film Mirrors New Immigrant Life," *New York Times,* 18 September 1991, B 2.

Bergman, David. *Gaiety Transfigured: Gay Self-Representation in American Literature.* Wisconsin: University of Wisconsin Press, 1991.

Bhabha, Homi K. *The Location of Culture.* London: Routledge, 1994.

Black, George. *The Good Neighbor.* New York: Pantheon, 1988.

Blau, Eleanor. "Nicholas Dante, 49; Dancer and a Writer of 'A Chorus Line.'" *New York Times,* 22 May 1991, D 25.

Blaut, J. M. "The Ghetto as an Internal Neo-Colony." *Antipode* 6, no. 1 (1974): 37–41.

Blaut, J. M. "Assimilation Versus Ghettoization." *Antipode* 15, no. 1 (1983): 35–41.

Blonsky, Marshall, ed. *On Signs.* Baltimore: Johns Hopkins University Press, 1985.

Boffin, Tessa, and Sunil Gupta, eds. *Ecstatic Antibodies: Resisting the AIDS Mythology.* London: Rivers Oram Press, 1990.

Bolivar Arostegui, Natalia. *Los Orishas en Cuba.* Havana: Ediciones Unión, 1990.

Booth, John E. *The Critic, Power, and the Performing Arts.* New York: Columbia University Press, 1991.

Bordman, Gerald. *American Musical Theatre: A Chronicle.* New York: Oxford University Press, 1986.

Brady, Kathleen. *Lucille: The Life of Lucille Ball.* New York: Hyperion, 1994.

Broyles-González, Yolanda. "Women in El Teatro Campesino: '¿Apoco Estaba Molacha la Virgen de Guadalupe?'" In *Chicana Voices: Intersections of Class, Race, and Gender,* ed. Teresa Córdova, et al., 162–87. Austin; Tex.: CMAS Publications, 1986.

Broyles-González, Teresa. "Toward a Re-Vision of Chicano Theatre History: The Women of El Teatro Campesino." In *Making a Spectacle: Feminist Essays on Contemporary Women's Theatre,* ed. Lynda Hart, 209–38. Ann Arbor: University of Michigan Press, 1989.

Broyles-González, Teresa. "What Price 'Mainstream'?: Luis Valdez' *Corridos* on Stage and Film." *Cultural Studies,* special issue, *Chicana/o Cultural Representations* 4, no. 3 (1990): 281–301.

Broyles-González, Teresa. *El Teatro Campesino: Theater in the Chicano Movement.* Austin: University of Texas Press, 1994.

Burton, Julianne. "Don (Juanito) Duck and the Imperial-Patriarchal Unconscious: Disney Studios, the Good Neighbor Policy, and the Packaging of Latin America." In *Nationalisms and Sexualities,* ed. Andrew Parker, et al., 21–41. New York: Routledge, 1992.

Butler, Judith. *Gender Trouble: Feminism and the Subversion of Identity.* New York: Routledge, 1990.

Butler, Judith. "Performative Acts and Gender Constitution: An Essay in Phenomenology and Feminist Theory." In *Performing Feminisms: Feminist Critical Theory and Theatre,* ed. Sue-Ellen Case, 270–82. Baltimore: Johns Hopkins University Press, 1990.

Butler, Judith. *Bodies That Matter: On the Discursive Limits of "Sex".* New York: Routledge, 1993.

Cady, Joseph. "AIDS on the National Stage." Review of *The Way We Live Now: American Plays and the AIDS Crisis. Medical Humanities Review* 6, no. 1 (1992): 20–26.

Cady, Joseph, and Kathryn Montgomery Hunter. "Making Contact: The AIDS Plays." In *The Meaning of AIDS: Implications for Medical Science, Clinical Practice, and Public Health Policy,* ed. Eric T. Juengst and Barbara A. Koenig, 42–49. New York: Praeger, 1989.

Candelaria, Cordelia. "Film Portrayals of la Mujer Hispana." *Agenda* 11, no. 3 (1981): 32–36.

Cardenas, Don, and Suzanne Schneider, eds. *Chicano Images in Film.* Denver: Denver International Film Festival and Bilingual Communications Center, 1981.

Carlson, Marvin. *Performance: A Critical Introduction.* London: Routledge, 1996.

"Carmen Miranda Is Dead at 41: Movie Comedienne and Dancer." Obituary. *New York Times,* 6 August 1955, 15.

Carter, Erica, and Simon Watney, eds. *Taking Liberties: AIDS and Cultural Politics.* London: Serpent's Tail, 1989.

Case, Sue-Ellen. *Feminism and Theatre.* New York: Methuen, 1988.

Case, Sue-Ellen. "Toward a Butch-Femme Aesthetic." In *Making a Spectacle:*

Feminist Essays on Contemporary Women's Theatre, ed. Lynda Hart, 282–99. Ann Arbor: University of Michigan Press, 1989.

Case, Sue-Ellen, ed. *Performing Feminisms: Feminist Critical Theory and Theatre.* Baltimore: Johns Hopkins University Press, 1990.

Centro de Estudios Puertorriqueños Bulletin 2, no. 8, special issue, *Latinos and the Media* (1990).

Centro de Estudios Puertorriqueños Bulletin 3, no. 1, special issue, *Latinos and the Media* (1990–91).

Chaudhuri, Una. *Staging Place: The Geography of Modern Drama.* Ann Arbor: University of Michigan, 1995.

Choldin, J. Harvey M. "Statistics and Politics: The 'Hispanic' Issue in the 1980 Census." *Demography* 23, no. 3 (1986): 403–18.

Clum, John M. *Acting Gay: Male Homosexuality in Modern Drama.* New York: Columbia University Press, 1992.

Colón Lespier, Alvan. "Teatro Pregones: Finding Language in Dialogue." In *Reimaging America: The Arts of Social Change*, ed. Mark O'Brien and Craig Little, 251–54. Philadelphia: New Society, 1990.

Columbus, Christopher. "The Third Voyage of Columbus." In *The Four Voyages of Columbus*, vol. 2, Cecil Jane, New York: Dover, 1988.

Cortes, Carlos E. "Chicanas in Film: History of an Image." In *Chicano Cinema: Research, Reviews, and Resources*, ed. Gary D. Keller, 94–108. Binghamton, N.Y.: Bilingual Review Press, 1985.

Coward, Rosalind, and John Ellis. *Language and Materialism: Developments in Semiology and the Theory of the Subject.* Boston: Routledge, 1980.

Cresswell, Tim. *In Place/Out of Place: Geography, Ideology, and Transgression.* Minneapolis: University of Minnesota Press, 1996.

Crimp, Douglas, ed. *AIDS: Cultural Analysis/Cultural Activism.* Cambridge, Mass.: MIT Press, 1989.

Crimp, Douglas, and Adam Ralston. *AIDS Demo Graphics.* Seattle: Bay Press, 1990.

Cultural Relations Programs of the U.S. Department of State, Historical Studies 2. Washington, D.C.: U.S. Department of State, 1976.

Cunningham, Michael. "After AIDS, Gay Art Aims for a New Reality." *New York Times*, 26 April 1992, sec. 2, p. 1.

Dante, Nicholas. "Big Night for the *Chorus Line.*" Interview by Tom Buckley. *New York Times*, 23 May 1975, L 28.

Dante, Nicholas. "Interview: Nick Dante." By Gaby Rodgers. *Christopher Street*, July 1977, 37–40.

Dante, Nicholas. "Back on the Line: *A Chorus Line's* Nicholas Dante Recovers From an Overdose of Fame and Fortune." Interview by Edward Guthmann. *Advocate*, 10 October 1989, 57.

Davies, Carole Boyce. *Black Women Writing and Identity: Migrations of the Subject.* New York: Routledge, 1994.

Davis, R. G., and Betty Diamond. "'Zoot Suit': From the Barrio to Broadway." *Ideologies and Literature* 3 (1981): 124–33.

De Groot, Joanna. "'Sex and Race': The Construction of Language and Image in the Nineteenth Century." In *Sexuality and Subordination: Interdisciplinary Studies of Gender in the Nineteenth Century,* ed. Susan Mendus and Jane Rendall, 89–128. New York: Routledge, 1989.

de Jongh, Nicholas. *Not In Front Of The Audience: Homosexuality On Stage.* New York: Routledge, 1992.

De La Roche, Elisa. *¡Teatro Hispano! Three Major New York Companies.* New York: Garland, 1995.

Delano, Jack. *Puerto Rico Mío: Four Decades of Change.* Washington, D.C.: Smithsonian Institution Press, 1990.

de Lauretis, Teresa. *Alice Doesn't: Feminism, Semiotics, Cinema.* Bloomington: Indiana University Press, 1984.

de Lauretis, Teresa. *Technologies of Gender: Essays on Theory, Film, and Fiction.* Bloomington: Indiana University Press, 1987.

de Lauretis, Teresa. "Sexual Indifference and Lesbian Representation." *Theatre Journal* 40, no. 2, special issue, *Feminist diVERSIONs* (1988): 155–77.

de Lauretis, Teresa. "Film and the Visible." In *How Do I Look? Queer Film and Video,* ed. Bad Object-Choices, 223–76. Seattle: Bay Press, 1991.

de Lauretis, Teresa, ed. *Feminist Studies/ Critical Studies.* Bloomington: Indiana University Press, 1996.

deLeon, Dennis. "My Hopes, My Fears, My Disease." Editorial. *New York Times,* 15 May 1993, 19.

Delgado, Celeste Fraser and José Esteban Muñoz, eds. *Everynight Life: Culture and Dance in Latin/o America.* Durham, N.C.: Duke University Press, 1997.

Derrida, Jacques. *Of Grammatology.* Trans. Gayatri Chakravorty Spivak. Baltimore: Johns Hopkins University Press, 1976.

Disch, Thomas M. "The Death of Broadway." *Atlantic Monthly,* March 1991, 91–104.

Dolan, Jill. "Gender Impersonation Onstage: Destroying or Maintaining the Mirror of Gender Roles." *Women and Performance* 2, no. 2 (1985): 5–11.

Dolan, Jill. *The Feminist Spectator as Critic.* Ann Arbor: University of Michigan Research Press, 1988.

Dolan, Jill. "'Lesbian' Subjectivity in Realism: Dragging at the Margins of Structure and Ideology." In *Performing Feminisms: Feminist Critical Theory and Theatre,* ed. Sue-Ellen Case, 40–53. Baltimore: Johns Hopkins University Press, 1990.

Dolan, Jill. "Practicing Cultural Disruptions: Gay and Lesbian Representation and Sexuality. In *Critical Theory and Performance,* ed. Janelle G. Reinelt and Joseph R. Roach, 263–75. Ann Arbor: University of Michigan Press, 1992.

Dolan, Jill. *Presence & Desire: Essays on Gender, Sexuality, Performance.* Ann Arbor: University Press of Michigan, 1993.

Dorfman, Ariel and A. Mattelart. *Para leer al Pato Donald: Comunicación de masa y colonialismo.* Mexico City: Siglo Veintiuno, 1979.

Drake, Paul W. "From Good Men to Good Neighbors." In *Exporting Democracy: The United States and Latin America,* ed. Abraham F. Lowenthal, 3–40. Baltimore: Johns Hopkins University Press, 1991.

During, Simon, ed. *The Cultural Studies Reader.* New York: Routledge, 1993.

Dyer, Richard. *Only Entertainment*. New York: Routledge, 1992.

Eagleton, Terry. *Literary Theory: An Introduction*. Minneapolis: University of Minnesota Press, 1983.

Eco, Umberto. *The Theory of Semiotics*. Bloomington: Indiana University Press, 1979.

Eco, Umberto. *Semiotics and the Philosophy of Language*. Bloomington: Indiana University Press, 1984.

Ellis, Sure, and Paul Heritage. "AIDS and the Cultural Response: *The Normal Heart* and *We All Fall Down*." In *Coming on Strong: Gay Politics and Culture*, ed. Simon Sheperd and Mick Wallis, 39–53. London: Unwin Hyman, 1989.

Engel, Lehman. *American Musical Theater*. New York: Collier, 1975.

Engel, Lehman. *Words With Music: The Broadway Musical Libretto*. New York: Schirmer, 1981.

Enloe, Cynthia. *Making Feminist Sense of International Politics: Bananas, Beaches and Bases*. Berkeley and Los Angeles: University of California Press, 1990.

Epstein, Helen. *Joe Papp: An American Life*. Boston: Little, Brown, 1994.

Esteves, Sandra María. "Ambivalencia o activismo desde la perspectiva poética de los Nuyoricans." In *Imágenes e identidades: El puertorriqueño en la literatura*, ed. Asela Rodríguez de Laguna, 195–201. Río Piedras, P.R.: Huracán, 1985.

Ewen, David. *Complete Book of the American Musical Theater*. New York: Holt, Rhinehart and Winston, 1959.

Fanon, Frantz. *Black Skin, White Masks*. Trans. Charles Lam Markmann. New York: Grove Press, 1982.

Feingold, Michael. Introduction. In *The Way We Live Now: American Plays and the AIDS Crisis*, ed. M. Elizabeth Osborn, xi–xvii. New York: Theatre Communications Group, 1990.

Ferguson, Russell, et al., eds. *Out There: Marginalization and Contemporary Cultures*. Cambridge, Mass.: MIT Press, 1991.

Fernández, Enrique. "Spitfires, Latin Lovers, Mambo Kings." *New York Times*, 19 April 1992, sec. 2, pp. H 1, H 30.

Ferreira, Ana Paula. "Los críticos (no) hacen falta: el crítico o la crítica como productores de significado." *Ollantay Theater Magazine* 2, no. 1 (1994): 81–88.

Fetterley, Judith. *The Resisting Reader: A Feminist Approach to American Fiction*. Bloomington: Indiana University Press, 1981.

Fields, Sidney. "Only Human: Writers Joined Golden 'Line.'" *Daily News*, 29 April 1976, 102.

Figueroa, Pablo. *Teatro: Hispanic Theatre in New York City/1920–1976*. New York: El Museo del Barrio, 1971.

"Films' Latin-American Cycle Finds Congarhumba Displacing Swing Music." *Variety*, 6 November 1940, 1, 22.

Flinn, Denny Martin. *What They Did For Love: The Untold Story Behind the Making of A Chorus Line*. New York: Bantam, 1989.

Flinn, Denny Martin. *Musical! A Grand Tour*. New York: Schirmer Books, 1997.

Flores, Arturo C. *El teatro campesino de Luis Valdez*. Madrid: Editorial Pliegos, 1990.

Flores, Juan. *Divided Borders: Essays on Puerto Rican Identity.* Houston: Arte Público Press, 1993.

Flores, Juan. "The Latino Imaginary: Dimensions of Community and Identity." In *Tropicalizations: Transcultural Representations of Latinidad,* ed. Frances R. Aparicio and Susana Chávez-Silverman, 183–93. Hanover, N.H.: University Presses of New England, 1997.

Foster, Harry L. *A Gringo in Mañana-Land.* New York: Dodd, Mead, 1924.

Foucault, Michel. *The Archaeology of Knowledge and the Discourse on Language.* Trans. A. M. Sheridan Smith. New York: Pantheon, 1972.

Foucault, Michel. *The Order of Things: An Archaeology of the Human Sciences.* New York: Vintage, 1973.

Fragoso, Víctor. "Notas sobre la expresión teatral de la comunidad puertorriqueña de Nueva York." *Revista del I.C.P.,* January/March, 1976, 21–26.

Fregoso, Rosa Linda. *The Bronze Screen: Chicana and Chicano Film Culture.* Minneapolis: University of Minnesota Press, 1993.

Frew, Jim. *Lucy: A life in Pictures.* New York: MetroBooks, 1996.

Friedman, Lester D., ed. *Unspeakable Images: Ethnicity and the American Cinema.* Chicago: University of Illinois Press, 1991.

Fung, Richard. "Working Through Cultural Appropriation," *Fuse Magazine* 16, nos. 5/6 (1993): 16–24.

Fusco, Coco. *English Is Broken Here: Notes on Cultural Fusion in the Americas.* New York: New York Press, 1995.

Galeano, Eduardo. *Memory of Fire. Book 3, Century of the Wind.* Trans. Cedric Belfrage. New York: Pantheon, 1988.

Gänzl, Kurt. *Gänzl's Book of the Broadway Musical.* New York: Schirmer Books, 1995.

Gänzl, Kurt. *Song & Dance: The Complete Story of Stage Musicals.* London: Carlton, 1995.

Garber, Marjorie. *Vested Interests: Cross-Dressing and Cultural Anxiety.* New York: Routledge, 1992.

García Berumen, Frank Javier. *The Chicano/Hispanic Image in American Film.* New York: Vantage Press, 1995.

Garebian, Keith. *The Making of West Side Story.* Toronto: ECW Press, 1995.

Gates, Henry Louis, Jr., ed. *"Race," Writing, and Difference.* Chicago: University of Chicago Press, 1986.

Geertz, Clifford. *The Interpretation of Cultures.* New York: Basic, 1973.

Gil-Montero, Martha. *Brazilian Bombshell: The Biography of Carmen Miranda.* New York: Donald I. Fine, 1989.

Gimenez, Martha E. "'Latino'/'Hispanic'—Who Needs a Name?: The Case Against a Standardized Terminology." *International Journal of Health Services* 19, no. 3 (1989): 557–71.

Ginsberg, Elaine K. *Passing and the Fictions of Identity.* Durham, N.C.: Duke University Press, 1996.

Glines, John. *The Demonstration* (excerpt). *Arts and Understanding* 4, no. 1 (1995): 8–11.

Glore, John. "What's a Hispanic Play? That's a Tough Question." *American The-ater* 3, no. 9 (1986): 39–41.

Goldstein, Richard. "The Implicated and the Immune: Responses to AIDS in the Arts and Popular Culture." In *A Disease of Society: Cultural and Institutional Responses to AIDS,* ed. Dorothy Nelkin, David P. Willis, and Scott V. Parris, 17–42. New York: Cambridge University Press, 1991.

Gómez, Javier. "Actores latinos en Broadway," *Ollantay Theater Magazine* 5, no. 1 (1997): 52–60.

Goodman, Lizbeth. *Contemporary Feminist Theatres: To Each Her Own.* New York: Routledge, 1993.

Goodman, Lizbeth. "AIDS and Live Art." In *Analysing Performance: A Critical Reader,* ed. Patrick Campbell, 203–18. Manchester: Manchester University Press, 1996.

Gordon, Joanne. *Art Isn't Easy: The Theater of Stephen Sondheim.* New York: Da-Capo Press, 1992.

Gottfried, Martin. *Broadway Musicals.* New York: Abradale Press/Harry N. Abrams, 1979.

Gottfried, Martin. *More Broadway Musicals Since 1980.* New York: Harry N. Abrams, 1991.

Green, David. *The Containment of Latin America: A History of the Myths and Realities of the Good Neighbor Policy.* Chicago: Quadrangle Books, 1971.

Green, Stanley. *The Encyclopedia of the Musical Film.* New York: Oxford University Press, 1981.

Green, Stanley. *The World of Musical Comedy,* 4th ed. New York: DaCapo Press, 1984.

Green, Stanley. *Broadway Musicals: Show by Show,* 3rd ed. Milwaukee: Hal Leonard, 1987.

Green, Stanley. *Hollywood Musicals: Year by Year.* Milwaukee: Hal Leonard, 1990.

Greene, Gayle, and Coppelia Kahn, eds. *Making a Difference: Feminist Literary Criticism.* London: Methuen, 1985.

Grossberg, Lawrence, Cary Nelson, and Paula A. Treichler, eds. *Cultural Studies.* New York: Routledge,1992.

Grover, Jan Zita. "The Convergence of Art and Crisis." *High Performance* 36 (1986): 28–31.

Guernsey, Otis L., Jr., ed. *Broadway Song and Story.* New York: Dodd, Mead, 1985.

Habell-Pallán, Michelle. "Family and Sexuality in Recent Chicano Performance: Luis Alfaro's Memory Plays," *Ollantay Theater Magazine* 4, no. 1, special issue, *Chicano Theater,* 4, no. 1 (1996): 33–42.

Hadley-Garcia, George. *Hispanic Hollywood: The Latins in Motion Pictures.* New York: Citadel Press, 1990.

Hall, Stuart. "New Ethnicities." In *Critical Dialogues in Cultural Studies,* ed. David Morley and Kuan-Hsing Chen, 441–49. New York: Routledge, 1996.

Hart, Lynda, ed. *Making a Spectacle: Feminist Essays on Contemporary Women's Theatre.* Ann Arbor: University of Michigan Press, 1992.

Hart, Lynda, and Peggy Phelan, eds. *Acting Out: Feminist Performances.* Ann Arbor: University of Michigan Press, 1993.

Hawkins, Peter. "Naming Names: The Art of Memory and the Names Project AIDS Quilt." *Critical Inquiry* 19, no. 4 (1993): 752–79.

Hawthorn, Jeremy. *A Concise Glossary of Contemporary Literary Theory,* 2nd ed. London: Edward Arnold Press, 1994.

Hayes-Bautista, David E. "Identifying Hispanic Populations: The Influence of Research Methodology Upon Public Policy." *American Journal of Public Health* 70, no. 4 (1980): 353–56.

Hayes-Bautista, David E., and Jorge Chapa. "Latino Terminology: Conceptual Bases for Standardized Terminology." *American Journal of Public Health* 77, no. 1 (1987): 61–72.

Henderson, Brian. "A Musical Comedy of Empire." *Film Quaterly* 35 (1981–82): 2–16.

Henry, William A. III. "Visions From the Past (in Latino Theatre)." *Time,* special issue, *¡Magnífico! Hispanic Culture Breaks Out of El Barrio,* 11 July 1988, 82–83.

Hewitt, Charles E., Jr. "Welcome Paupers and Crime—Porto Rico's Shocking Gift to the United States." *Scribners Commentator,* March 1940, 11–17.

Hirsch, Foster. *Harold Prince and the American Musical Theatre.* Cambridge: Cambridge University Press, 1989.

HIV/Surveillance Report 9, no. 2 (1996). Atlanta: U.S. Dept. of Health and Human Services/Public Health Service.

Holden, Stephen. "Tragic Figure Beneath a Crown of Fruit." *New York Times,* 5 July 1995, C 11.

Holob, Robert C. *Reception Theory: A Critical Introduction.* London: Methuen, 1984.

hooks, bell. *Feminist Theory: From Margin to Center.* Boston: South End Press, 1984.

hooks, bell. *Yearning: Race, Gender, and Cultural Politics.* Boston: South End Press, 1990.

Horno-Delgado, Asunción, et al., eds. *Breaking Boundaries: Latina Writings and Critical Readings.* Amherst: University of Massachusetts Press, 1989.

Huerta, Jorge. "Where Are Our Chicano Playwrights?" *Revista Chicano/Riqueña* 3, no. 4 (1975): 32–42.

Huerta, Jorge. *Chicano Theater: Themes and Forms.* Ypsilanti, Mich.: Bilingual Press/Editorial Bilingüe, 1982.

Huerta, Jorge. "Moraga's *Heroes and Saints:* Chicano Theatre for the '90's." *TheatreForum* 1 (1992): 49–52.

Huerta, Jorge. "Looking for the Magic: Chicanos in the Mainstream." In *Negotiating Performance: Gender, Sexuality, and Theatricality in Latin/o America,* ed. Diana Taylor and Juan Villegas, 37–48. Durham, N.C.: Duke University Press, 1994.

Huerta, Jorge. "An Overview of Chicano Dramaturgy," *Ollantay Theater Magazine* 4, no. 1, special issue, *Chicano Theater* (1996): 91–102.

"Interview: Loisaida Players." *Centro de Estudios Puertorriqueños Bulletin,* special issue, *Youth Culture in the 1990s* 5, no. 1 (1993): 66–79.

Jameson, Frederic. *The Political Unconscious: Narrative as a Socially Symbolic Act.* Ithaca, N.Y.: Cornell University Press, 1981.

Jauss, Hans Robert. *Toward an Aesthetic of Reception.* Trans. Timothy Bahti. Minneapolis: University of Minnesota Press, 1982.

Johnson, John J. *Latin America in Caricature.* Austin: University of Texas Press, 1993.

Johnson, Randall, and Robert Stam. *Brazilian Cinema.* East Brunswick, N.J.: Associated University Presses, 1982.

Jones, David Richard, and Susan J. Jones. *Two Latina Playwrights: A Study Guide for* Café con leche *by Gloria González and* Botánica *by Dolores Prida.* New York: Spanish Theatre Repertory, 1991.

Jones, Gerald. *Honey, I'm Home! Sitcoms: Selling the American Dream.* New York: Grove Weidenfeld, 1992.

Jones, James W. "The Sick Homosexual: AIDS and Gays on the American Stage and Screen." In *Confronting AIDS Through Literature: The Responsibilities of Representation,* ed. Judith Laurence Pastore, 103–23. Urbana: University of Illinois Press, 1993.

Jones, Therese, ed. *Sharing the Delirium: Second Generation AIDS Plays and Performances.* Portsmouth, N.H.: Heinemann, 1994.

Kanellos, Nicolás, ed. *Mexican American Theatre: Then and Now.* Houston: Arte Público Press, 1983.

Kanellos, Nicolás. *Hispanic Theatre in the United States.* Houston: Arte Público Press, 1984.

Kanellos, Nicolás. *Mexican American Theater: Legacy and Reality.* Pittsburgh: Latin American Literary Review Press, 1987.

Kanellos, Nicolás. *A History of Hispanic Theatre in the United States: Origins to 1940.* Austin: University of Texas, 1990.

Kanellos, Nicolás. *The Hispanic Almanac: From Columbus to Corporate America.* Detroit: Visible Ink Press, 1994.

Kanellos, Nicolás, and Jorge A. Huerta, eds. *Nuevos Pasos: Chicano and Puerto Rican Drama.* Houston: Arte Público Press, 1989.

Keith, Michael, and Steve Pile, eds. *Place and the Politics of Identity.* New York: Routledge, 1993.

Keller, Gary D., ed. *Chicano Cinema: Research, Reviews and Resources.* Binghamton, N.Y.: Bilingual Review/Press, 1985.

Keller, Gary D. *Hispanics and United States Films.* Tempe, Ariz.: Bilingual Review/Press, 1994.

Kelly, Kevin. *One Singular Sensation: The Michael Bennett Story.* New York: Zebra Books, 1990.

King, John, Ana M. López, and Manuel Alvarado, eds. *Mediating Two Worlds: Cinematic Encounters in the Americas.* London: British Film Institute, 1993.

Kirkwood, James. "Not in My Wildest Dreams . . . Did I Imagine Co-authoring B'way's Longest Running Show." *Playbill,* September 1983, 8–12.

Kobal, John. *Gotta Sing Gotta Dance: A History of Movie Musicals.* New York: Simon and Schuster, 1983.

Kondo, Dorinne. *About Face: Performing Race in Fashion and Theater.* New York: Routledge, 1997.

Kramer, Larry. *Reports from the Holocaust: The Making of an AIDS Activist.* New York: St. Martin's Press, 1989.

Lambert, Bruce. "AIDS Travels New York-Puerto Rico 'Air Bridge.'" *New York Times,* 15 June 1990, B 1.

Lawson, D. S. "Rage and Remembrance: The AIDS Plays." In *AIDS: The Literary Response,* ed. Emmanuel S. Nelson, 140–54. New York: Twayne, 1992.

Lee, Josephine. *Performing Asian American: Race and Ethnicity on the Contemporary Stage.* Philadelphia: Temple University Press, 1997.

Lerner, Alan J. *The Musical Theater: A Celebration.* New York: DaCapo Press, 1989.

Lewis, Oscar. *La Vida: A Puerto Rican Family in the Culture of Poverty.* New York: Random House, 1965.

López, Ana M. "Are All Latins from Manhattan? Hollywood, Ethnography, and Cultural Colonialism." In *Unspeakable Images,* ed. Lester D. Friedman, 404–24. Urbana: University of Illinois Press, 1991.

Lott, Eric. "Love and Theft: The Racial Unconscious of Blackface Minstrelsy." *representations* 39 (1992): 23–50.

Macdonell, Diane. *Theories of Discourse: An Introduction.* New York: Basil Blackwell, 1986.

Macherey, Pierre. *A Theory of Literary Production.* Trans. Geoffrey Wall. London: Routledge, 1980.

Mack, Arien, ed. *Home: A Place in the World.* New York: New York University Press, 1993.

Madrid, Arturo. "Diversity and Its Discontents." *Academe,* November/December 1990, 15–19.

¡Magnífico!: Hispanic Culture Breaks Out of the Barrio. Time, special issue, 11 July 1981.

Mandelbaum, Ken. *A Chorus Line and the Musicals of Michael Bennett.* New York: St. Martin's Press, 1989.

Manzor-Coats, Lillian. "'Who Are You, Anyways?': Gender, Racial, and Linguistic Politics in U.S. Cuban Theater." *Gestos* 11 (1991): 163–74.

Manzor-Coats, Lillian. "Too Spik or Too Dyke: Carmelita Tropicana." *Ollantay Theater Magazine* 2, no. 1 (1994): 39–55.

Márquez, Rosa Luisa. *The Puerto Rican Traveling Theatre Company: The First Ten Years.* Ph.D. diss., Michigan State University, 1977.

Márquez, Rosa Luisa. "Modelo para armar: El sí-dá." In *Brincos y saltos: El juego como disciplina teatral,* 80–87. Puerto Rico: Ediciones Cuicaloca, 1992.

Márquez, Rosa Luisa. "Creación colectiva: con y sin texto." *Ollantay Theater Magazine* 2, no. 2, special issue, *Latino Theater on AIDS* (1994): 16–19.

Marrero, María Teresa. "Chicano/Latino Self-Representation in Theater and Performance Art." *Gestos* 6, no. 11, special issue, *Representations of Otherness in Latin American and Chicano Theater and Film,* ed. Juan Villegas and Diana Taylor (April 1991): 147–62.

Marrero, María Teresa. "Real Women Have Curves: The Articulation of Fat as a Cultural/Feminist Issue." *Ollantay Theater Magazine* 1, no. 1 (1993): 61–70.

Marrero, María Teresa. "The Insertion of Latina Theater Entrepreneurs, Playwrights and Directors into the Historical Record." *Ollantay Theater Magazine* 4, no. 1, special issue, *Chicano Theater* (1996): 74–90.

Marsolais, Ken, Roger McFarlane, and Tom Viola. *Broadway Day & Night: Backstage and Behind the Scenes.* New York: Pocket Books, 1992.

Martínez, Thomas, and José Peralez. "Chicanos and the Motion Picture." *La Raza* 1, no. 4 (1971): 32–35.

Martínez, Thomas, and José Peralez. "The Profit of Advertisement: Racism." *La Raza* 1, no. 4 (1971): 23–31.

Massey, Doreen. "A Global Sense of Place." *Marxism Today* 35 (1991): 24–29.

Mast, Gerald. *Can't Help Singin': The American Musical on Stage and Screen.* New York: Overlook Press, 1987.

McClay, Michael. *I Love Lucy: The Complete Picture History of the Most Popular TV Show Ever.* New York: Warner Books, 1995.

Merced, Jorge B. "Teatro y SIDA." *Ollantay Theater Magazine* 2, no. 2, special issue, *Latino Theater on AIDS* (1994): 20–26.

Mercer, Kobena. *Welcome to the Jungle: New Positions in Black Cultural Studies.* New York: Routledge, 1994.

Miller, John C. "Hispanic Theatre in New York, 1965–1977." *Revista Chicano/Riqueña* 7, no. 1 (1978): 40–59.

Modleski, Tania. "Femininity as Mas[s]querade: A Feminist Approach to Mass Culture." In *High Theory/Low Culture: Analyzing Popular Television and Film,* ed. Colin MacCabe, 37–52. New York: St. Martin's Press, 1986.

Modleski, Tania, ed. *Studies in Entertainment: Critical Approaches to Mass Culture.* Bloomington: Indiana University Press, 1986.

Mohanty, Chandra. "Under Western Eyes: Feminist Scholarship and Colonial Discourses." *Feminist Review* 30 (1988): 61–68.

Mohr, Nicholasa. "The Journey Toward a Common Ground: Struggle and Identity of Hispanics in the U.S." *Americas Review* 18, no. 1 (1990): 81–85.

Moi, Toril. *Sexual/Textual Politics: Feminist Literary Theory.* London: Methuen, 1985.

Molineu, Harold. *U.S. Policy Toward Latin America: From Regionalism to Globalism.* Boulder, Colo.: Westview Press, 1986.

Montrose, Louis. "The Work of Gender in the Discourse of the Discovery." *representations* 33 (1991): 1–41.

Monsiváis, Carlos. *Amor perdido.* Mexico City: Biblioteca Eva, 1988.

Morales, Ed. "Shadowing Valdez." *American Theatre* 9, no. 7 (1992): 14–19.

Morales, Ed. "Welcome to Aztlán." *American Theatre* 10, no. 3 (1993): 38–40.

Morales, Ed. "Making Monsters." *American Theatre* 11, no. 7 (1994): 26–27.

Morand, José. "The Rumba is Here to Stay." *Song Hits Magazine* 5, no. 7 (1941): 13, 34.

Morton, Carlos. "Nuyorican Theatre." *Drama Review* 20, no. 1 (1976): 43–49.

Morton, Carlos, ed. *Ollantay Theater Magazine* 4, no. 1, special issue, *Chicano Theater* (1996).

Mulvey, Laura. *Visual and Other Pleasures.* Bloomington: Indiana University Press, 1989.

Muñoz, José Esteban. "Famous and Dandy Like B. 'n' Andy: Race, Pop, and Basquiat." In *Pop Out: Queer Warhol,* ed. Jennifer Doyle, Jonathan Flatley, and José Esteban Muñoz, 144–79. Durham, N.C.: Duke University Press, 1996.

Murphy, Timothy F., and Suzanne Poirier, eds. *Writing AIDS: Gay Literature, Language, and Analysis.* New York: Columbia University Press, 1993.

Navarre, Max. "Art in the AIDies: An Act of Faith." *High Performance* 36 (1986): 32–36.

Navarro, Ray. "Eso, me está pasando." In *Chicanos and Film: Representation and Resistance,* ed. Chon A. Noriega, 312–15. Minneapolis: University of Minnesota Press, 1992.

Negrón-Muntaner, Frances, and Ramón Grosfoguel, eds. *Puerto Rican Jam: Essays on Culture and Politics.* Minneapolis: University of Minnesota Press, 1997.

Nelkin, Dorothy, David P. Willis, and Scott V. Parris, eds. *A Disease of Society: Cultural and Institutional Responses to AIDS.* New York: Cambridge University Press, 1991.

Nelson, Candace, and Marta Tienda. "The Structuring of Hispanic Ethnicity: Historical and Contemporary Perspectives." *Ethnic and Racial Studies* 8, no. 1 (1985): 49–74.

Nelson, Emmanuel S., ed. *AIDS: The Literary Response.* New York: Twayne, 1992.

Nelson, Steve. "Broadway and the Beast: Disney Comes to Times Square." *The Drama Review* T146 (1995): 71–85.

"News & Notes: AIDS 1991." *Entertainment Weekly,* 29 November 1991, 10–12.

Newton, Judith, and Deborah Rosenfelt, eds. *Feminist Criticism and Social Change: Sex, Class, and Race in Literature and Culture.* New York: Methuen, 1985.

Ngugi wa Thiong'o. *Decolonising the Mind: The Politics of Language in African Culture.* London: James Currey, 1987.

"Nicholas Dante." Profile. *Playbill,* September 1979, 43.

Norback, Peter, and Craig Norback, eds. *Great Songs of Madison Avenue.* New York: Quadrangle, 1976.

Noriega, Chon [A.]. "Godzilla and the Japanese Nightmare: When Them! is U.S." *Cinema Journal* 27, no. 1 (1987): 63–77.

Noriega, Chon A. "Chicano Cinema and the Horizon of Expectations: A Discursive Analysis of Film Reviews in the Mainstream, Alternative, and Hispanic Press, 1987–1988." *Aztlán* 19, no. 2 (1990): 1–32.

Noriega, Chon [A.]. "Citizen Chicano: The Trials and Titillations of Ethnicity in the American Cinema, 1935–1962." *Social Research* 58, no. 2 (1991): 413–38.

Noriega, Chon A. "El Hilo Latino: Representation, Identity, and National Culture." *Jump Cut* 38 (1993): 45–50.

Noriega, Chon A. "Internal Others: Hollywood Narratives about Mexican Americans." In *Mediating Two Worlds: Cinematic Encounters in the Americas,* ed. John King, Ana M. López, and Manuel Alvarado, 52–66. London: British Film Institute, 1993.

Noriega, Chon A., ed. *Chicanos and Film: Representation and Resistance.* Minneapolis: University of Minnesota Press, 1992.

Noriega, Chon [A.], and Ana M. López, eds. *The Ethnic Eye: Latino Media Arts*. Minneapolis: University of Minnesota Press, 1996.

Oboler, Suzanne. *Ethnic Labels, Latino Lives: Identity and the Politics of (Re)Presentation in the United States*. Minneapolis: University of Minnesota Press, 1995.

O'Connell, Shaun. "The Big One: Literature Discovers AIDS." *New England Journal of Public Policy* 4, no. 1 (1988): 485–506.

O'Connor, John J. "One Woman's Tragedy, Playing the Latin Clown." *New York Times*, 6 October 1995, D 18.

Oppenheimer, Jess. *The "I Love Lucy" Book*. New York: Doubleday, 1985.

Ortiz Cofer, Judith. *The Latin Deli*. Athens, Ga.: University of Georgia Press, 1993.

Osborn, M. Elizabeth, ed. *The Way We Live Now: American Plays and the AIDS Crisis*. New York: Theatre Communications Group, 1990.

Padilla, Felix M. "On the Nature of Latino Ethnicity." *Social Science Quarterly* 65, no. 2 (1984): 651–64.

Padilla, Felix M. "Latin America: The Historical Base of Latino Unity." *Latino Studies Journal* 1 (1990): 7–27.

Padilla, Ivelyse. "Cultural Gentrification: Latino Theater Groups in New York." *Ollantay Theater Magazine* 1, no. 2 (1993): 50–53.

Parish, James Robert. *The Fox Girls*. New Rochelle, N.Y.: Arlington House, 1971.

Pastore, Judith Laurence, ed. *Confronting AIDS Through Literature: The Responsibilities of Representation*. Urbana: University of Illinois Press, 1993.

Payán, Ilka Tanya. "Ilka Tanya Payán: An Interview by Carmen Navarro." *Body Positive*, April 1994, 10–13.

Pérez Firmat, Gustavo. *Life on the Hyphen: The Cuban-American Way*. Austin: University of Texas Press, 1994.

Pettit, Arthur G. *Images of the Mexican American in Fiction and Film*. College Station: Texas A & M University Press, 1980.

Peyser, Joan. *Bernstein: A Biography*. New York: Beech Tree Books/William Morrow, 1987.

Piedra, José. "Donald Duck Discovers America/O Pato Donald descubre las Américas." *Abject, America* 1, no. 4 (n.d. 199?): 119–29.

Piedra, José. "Pato Donald's Gender Ducking: *The Three Caballeros*." *Jump Cut* 39, pt. 2, special issue, *U.S. Latinos and the Media* (1994): 72–82, 112.

Pike, Fredrick B. *FDR's Good Neighbor Policy*. Austin: University of Texas Press, 1995.

Playbill: A Chorus Line. September 1979.

Playbill: A Chorus Line. June 1983.

Pottlitzer, Joanne. *Hispanic Theater in the United States and Puerto Rico*. New York: Ford Foundation, 1988.

Preston, John. "AIDS Writing: The Imperative to 'Get It All Down.'" *Outweek*, 13 March 1991, 60–61.

Prida, Dolores, "Interview with Dolores Prida." By Luz María Umpierre. *Latin American Theatre Review*, (1988), 81–85.

Prida, Dolores. "The Show Does Go On." In *Breaking Boundaries: Latina Writings and Critical Readings*, ed. Asunción Horno-Delgado, et al., 181–88. Amherst: University of Massachusetts Press, 1989.

Ramírez Berg, Charles. "Immigrants, Aliens, and Extraterrestrials." *Cineaction* 18 (1989): 3–17.

Ramírez Berg, Charles. "Stereotyping in Films in General and of the Hispanic in Particular." *Howard Journal of Communications* 2, no. 3 (1990): 286–300.

Reinelt, Janelle G., and Joseph R. Roach, eds. *Critical Theory and Performance.* Ann Arbor: University of Michigan Press, 1992.

Reyes, Luis, and Peter Rubie. *Hispanics in Hollywood: An Encyclopedia of Film and Television.* New York: Garland, 1994.

Rich, Adrienne. *On Lies, Secrets, and Silence: Selected Prose 1966–1978.* (New York: W. W. Norton, 1979).

Rich, Adrienne. "Compulsory Heterosexuality and Lesbian Existence." In *Blood, Bread and Poetry: Selected Prose 1979–85*, 23–75. New York: W. W. Norton, 1986.

Rich, Frank. "On Broadway The Lights Get Brighter." *New York Times*, 31 May 1982, sec. 2, pp. 1, 27.

Rich, Frank. "A New Generation on Old Broadway." *New York Times*, 6 June 1993, sec. 2, p. 31.

Richards, David. "On Stage, Survival of the Fizziest." *New York Times*, 12 June 1994, sec. 2, pp. 1, 32.

José Rivera. "An Interview with José Rivera." By David Román. *Performing Arts* 31, no. 6, Southern California edition (1997): P-6.

Rivero, Eliana. "From Immigrants to Ethnic: Cuban Women Writers in the U.S." In *Breaking Boundaries: Latina Writings and Critical Readings*, ed. Asunción Horno-Delgado, et al., 189–200. Amherst: University of Massachusetts Press, 1989.

Rizk, Beatriz J. "El teatro hispano de Nueva York." *Centro de documentación teatral* 2, Madrid: Técnicas Gráficas FORMA, 1988.

Rizk, Beatriz J. "El teatro latino de Estados Unidos." *Tramoya* 22 (1990): 5–20.

Rizk, Beatriz J. "El teatro latino en los Estados Unidos." *Brújula/Compass* 11 (1991) 25–27.

Rizk, Beatriz J. "Haciendo historia: multiculturalismo y el teatro latino en los Estados Unidos." *Ollantay Theater Magazine* 1, no. 1 (1993): 9–18.

Rizk, Beatriz J. "El teatro latino de los Estados Unidos como discurso de resistencia posmoderna," *Ollantay Theater Magazine* 2, no. 1 (1994): 114–24.

Roberts, John S. *The Latin Tinge.* New York: Oxford University Press, 1979.

Roberts, Shari. "'The Lady in the Tutti-Frutti Hat': Carmen Miranda, a Spectacle of Ethnicity." *Cinema Journal* 32, no. 3 (1993): 3–23.

Rockefeller, Nelson A. "Will We Remain Good Neighbors After the War?" *Saturday Evening Post*, 6 November 1943, 16.

Rockefeller, Nelson A. "The Fruits of the Good Neighbor Policy." *New York Times Magazine*, 14 May 1944, 15, 30, 31.

Rodriguez, Richard. *Hunger of Memory: The Education of Richard Rodriguez.* Boston: David R. Godine, 1982.

Rogin, Michael. *Blackface, White Noise: Jewish Immigrants in the Hollywood Melting Pot*. Berkeley: University of California Press, 1996.

Román, David. "Performing All Our Lives: AIDS, Performance, Community." In *Critical Theory and Performance*, ed. Janelle G. Reinelt and Joseph R. Roach, 208–21. Ann Arbor: University of Michigan Press, 1992.

Román, David. *Acts of Intervention: Performance, Gay Culture and AIDS*. Bloomington: Indiana University Press, 1998.

Román, David, and Alberto Sandoval-Sánchez. "Caught in the Web: Latinidad, AIDS, and Allegory in *Kiss of the Spider Woman, The Musical*." *American Literature* 67, no. 3 (1995): 554–85.

Roosevelt, Franklin D. "The Year of the Crisis: 1933." In *The Public Papers and Addresses of Franklin Delano Roosevelt*, vol. 2. Comp. and collated by Samuel I. Roseman. New York: Random House, 1958.

Rosenberg, Bernard, and Ernest Harburg. *The Broadway Musical: Collaboration in Commerce and Art*. New York: New York University Press, 1993.

Rosenberg, Lou. "The House of Difference: Gender, Culture, and the Subject-in-Process on the American Stage." In *Critical Essays: Gay and Lesbian Writers of Color*, ed. Emmanuel S. Nelson, 97–110. New York: Harrington Park Press, 1993.

Rouse, Roger. "Mexican Migration and the Social Space of Postmodernism." *Diaspora* 1, no. 1 (1991): 8–23.

Rowbatham, Sheila. "The Trouble with 'Patriarchy.'" In *A Feminist Dictionary*, ed. Cheris Kramarae and Paula A. Treichler, 323–24. London: Pandora, 1985.

Rudnick, Paul. "Laughing at AIDS." Editorial. *New York Times*, 23 January 1993, 21.

Rushdie, Salman. *Imaginary Homelands: Essays and Criticism 1981–1991*. New York: Penguin, 1991.

Rusk, Howard A., M. D. "The Facts Don't Rhyme: An Analysis of Irony in Lyrics Linking Puerto Rico's Breezes to Tropic Diseases." *New York Times*, 29 September 1957, L 83.

Saalfield, Catherine, and Ray Navarro. "Not Just Black and White: AIDS Media and People of Color." *Centro de Estudios Puertorriqueños Bulletin* 2, no. 8, special issue, *Latinos and the Media* (1990): 70–78.

Said, Edward. *Orientalism*. New York: Vintage Books, 1979.

Sandoval-Sánchez, Alberto. "Dolores Prida's *Coser y Cantar*: Mapping the Dialectics of Ethnic Identity and Assimilation." In *Breaking Boundaries: Latina Writings and Critical Readings*, ed. Asunción Horno-Delgado, et al., 201–20. Amherst: University of Massachusetts Press, 1989.

Sandoval-Sánchez, Alberto. "La identidad especular del allá y del acá: Nuestra propia imagen puertorriqueña en cuestión." *Centro de Estudios Puertorriqueños Bulletin* 4, no. 2 (1992): 28–43.

Sandoval-Sánchez, Alberto. "La puesta en escena de la familia inmigrante puertorriqueña." *Revista Iberoamericana*, nos. 162/163 (1993): 345–59.

Sandoval-Sánchez, Alberto. "Re-viewing Latino Theatre: Issues of Crossing-Over, Mainstreaming, and Canonization." In *New Voices in Latin American*

Literature, ed. Miguel Falquez-Certain, 157–172. New York: Ollantay Center for the Arts, 1993.

Sandoval-Sánchez, Alberto. "Puerto Rican Identity Up in the Air: Air Migration, Its Cultural Representations, and Me 'Cruzando el Charco.'" In *Puerto Rican Jam: Essays on Culture and Politics*, ed. Frances Negrón-Muntaner and Ramón Grosfoguel, 189–208. Minneapolis: University of Minnesota Press, 1997.

Sandoval-Sánchez, Alberto. "¡Mira, que vienen los Nuyoricans!: El temor de la otredad en la literatura nacionalista puertorriqueña." *Revista de Crítica Literaria Latinoamericana* 45 (1997): 307–25.

Sandoval-Sánchez, Alberto, ed. *Ollantay Theater Magazine*, special issue, *Latino Theater on AIDS*, no. 2 (1994).

Sandoval-Sánchez, Alberto, and Nancy Saporta Sternbach, eds. "Rehearsing in Front of the Mirror: Marga Gomez's Lesbian Subjectivity as a Work-in-Progress." *Women and Performance*, special issue, *Queer Acts* 8:2, no. 16 (1996): 205–24.

Sandoval-Sánchez, Alberto, and Nancy Saporta Sternbach, eds. *Puro Teatro: A Latina Anthology*. Forthcoming, University of Arizona Press.

Sandoval-Sánchez, Alberto, and Nancy Saporta Sternbach, eds. *Stages of Life: Cultural Performance and Identity Formation in Latina Theatre*. Forthcoming, University of Arizona Press.

Santiago, Soledad. "Notes on the Nuyoricans." *Village Voice*, 19 February 1979, 12–15.

Scarry, Elaine. *The Body in Pain: The Making and Unmaking of the World*. New York: Oxford University Press, 1985.

Schmidhuber, Guillermo. "El teatro chicano o la sabiduría de heredar el patrimonio hispano," *Ollantay Theater Magazine* 4, no. 1, special issue, *Chicano Theater* 4, (1996): 9–20.

Scott, Rebecca. "The Dark Continent: Africa as Female Body in Haggard's Adventure Fiction." *Feminist Review* 32 (1989): 69–80.

Shatzky, Joel. "AIDS Enters the American Theatre: *As Is* and *The Normal Heart*." In *AIDS: The Literary Response*, ed. Emmanuel S. Nelson, 131–39. New York: Twayne, 1992.

Sheldon, Caroline. "Lesbians and Film: Some Thoughts." In *Gays and Film*, ed. Richard Dyer, 5–26. New York: Zoetrope, 1984.

Shirakawa, Sam H. "Beyond the Ghetto Mentality." *Theater Week*, 16 May 1988, 33–34.

Shohat, Ella. "Gender and Culture of Empire: Toward a Feminist Ethnography of the Cinema." *Quarterly Review of Film and Video* 13, nos. 1–3 (1991): 45–84.

Shohat, Ella. "Imagining Terra Incognita: The Disciplinary Gaze of Empire." *Public Culture* 3, no. 2 (1991): 41–70.

Shohat, Ella, and Robert Stam, eds. *Unthinking Eurocentrism: Multiculturalism and the Media*. New York: Routledge, 1994.

Singer, Merrill et al., eds. "SIDA: The Economic, Social, and Cultural Contest of AIDS Among Latinos." *Medical Anthropology Quarterly* 4, no. 1 (1990): 72–114.

Silverman, Kaja. *The Subject of Semiotics.* New York: Oxford University Press, 1983.

Sixth Report of the U.S. Geographical Board: 1890–1932. Washington, D.C.: U.S. Government Printing Office, 1932.

Smith, Cecil, and Glenn Litton. *Musical Comedy in America.* New York: Theatre Arts Books, 1981.

Smith, Paul. *Discerning the Subject.* Minneapolis: University of Minnesota Press, 1988.

Sommers, Laurie Kay. "Symbol and Style in *Cinco de Mayo.*" *Journal of American Folklore* 98, no. 390 (1985): 476–82.

Sommers, Laurie Kay. "Inventing Latinismo: The Creation of 'Hispanic' Pan-ethnicity in the United States." *Journal of American Folklore* 104 (1991): 32–53.

Sommers, Laurie Kay. "Latinismo and Ethnic Nationalism in Cultural Performance." *Studies in Latin American Popular Culture* 10 (1991): 75–86.

Sopher, David E. "The Landscape of Home: Myth, Experience, Social Meaning." In *The Interpretation of Ordinary Landscapes: Geographic Essays,* ed. D. U. Meinig, 129–49. New York: Oxford University Press, 1979.

Spitta, Silvia. *Between Two Waters: Narratives of Transculturation.* Houston, Tex.: Rice University Press, 1995.

Spitta, Silvia. "Transculturation, the Caribbean, and the Cuban-American Imaginary." In *Tropicalizations: Transcultural Representations of Latinidad,* ed. Frances R. Aparicio and Susana Chávez-Silverman, 160–80. Hanover, N.H.: Dartmouth College Press, 1997.

Statistical Abstract of the United States 1997. Springfield, Va.: U.S. Department of Commerce, October 1997.

Stevens, Gary, and Alan George. *The Longest Line: Broadway's Most Singular Sensation: A Chorus Line.* New York: Applause Theatre Book Publishers, 1995.

Sturken, Marita. "Conversations With the Dead: Bearing Witness in the AIDS Memorial Quilt." *Socialist Review* 22, no. 2 (1992): 65–95.

Suntree, Susan. *Hispanics of Achievement: Rita Moreno.* New York: Chelsea House, 1993.

Taylor, Diana, and Juan Villegas, eds. *Negotiating Performance: Gender, Sexuality, and Theatricality in Latin/o America.* Durham, N.C.: Duke University Press, 1994.

Tienda, Marta, and Vilma Ortiz. "'Hispanicity' and the 1980 Census." *Social Science Quarterly* 67, no. 1 (1986): 3–20.

Toll, Robert C. "Show Biz in Blackface: The Evolution of the Minstrel Show as a Theatrical Form." In *American Popular Entertainment,* ed. Myron Matlaw, 21–32. Westport, Conn.: Greenwood, 1979.

Torre, Carlos Antonio, Hugo Rodríguez Vecchini, and William Burgos, eds. *The Commuter Nation: Perspectives on Puerto Rican Migration.* Río Piedras, P.R.: Editorial de la Universidad de Puerto Rico, 1994.

Treichler, Paula A. "AIDS, Homophobia and Biomedical Discourse: An Epidemic of Signification." *Cultural Studies* 1, no. 3 (1987): 263–305.

Treviño, Fernando M. "Standardized Terminology for Hispanic Populations." *American Journal of Public Health* 77, no. 1 (January 1987): 69–72.

Tumbusch, Tom. *The Theatre Student: Guide To Broadway Musical Theatre.* New York: Rosen, 1983.

"U.S. Film Stars the Best Good Will Ambassadors, Say Latin Americans." *Variety,* 19 February 1941, 1, 21.

Valdez, Luis. "Notes on Chicano Theater." *Latin American Theatre Review,* Spring, 1971, 52–55.

Vasey, Ruth. *The World According to Hollywood 1918–1939.* Madison: University of Wisconsin Press, 1997.

Viagas, Robert, Baayork Lee, and Thommie Walsh. *On the Line: The Creation of 'A Chorus Line.'* New York: William Morrow, 1990.

Watney, Simon. *Practices of Freedom: Selected Writings on HIV/AIDS.* Durham, N.C.: Duke University Press, 1994.

Weedon, Chris. *Feminist Practice and Poststructuralist Theory.* New York: Basil Blackwell, 1987.

Weiss, Judith A. "'Broadway es solo una calle': Dolores Prida y el teatro hispano de Nueva York." *Areito* 7, no. 28 (1981): 51–53.

Weiss, Judith A. *Street, Stage and School: Teatro Nuestro, GALA Hispanic Theatre and LatiNegro: Ten Years of Community Theatre in Washington D.C.* Washington, D.C.: Judith A. Weiss and Teatro Nuestro, 1989.

Weiss, Judith A. "Mainstreaming Traditional Culture: Luis Valdez's Television Adaptation of the Pastorela." *Ollantay Theater Magazine* 2, no. 1 (1994): 31–38.

Welch, Sara J. "The Mirandification of America." *Samba* 2, no. 19 (1995): 1, 4.

West, Joan M., and Dennis West. "Carmen Miranda: Bananas Is My Business." *Cineaste* 22, no. 1 (1996): 41–43.

Whitmore, George. *Someone Was Here: Profiles in the AIDS Epidemic.* New York: New American Library, 1988.

Williams, Raymond. *The Sociology of Culture.* New York: Schocken, 1982.

Williams, Raymond. *Keywords.* New York: Oxford University Press, 1985.

Williamson, Judith. "Woman Is an Island: Femininity and Colonization." In *Studies in Entertainment: Critical Approaches to Mass Culture,* ed. Tania Modleski, 99–118. Bloomington: Indiana University Press, 1986.

Woll, Allen L. *The Latin Image in American Film.* Los Angeles: University of California Latin American Center Publications, 1977.

Woll, Allen L. "Bandits and Lovers: Hispanic Images in American Film." In *The Kaleisdoscopic Lens: How Hollywood Views Ethnic Groups,* ed. Randall M. Miller, 54–72. Englewood, N.J.: Jerome S. Ozer, 1980.

Woll, Allen L. "How Hollywood Has Portrayed Hispanics." *New York Times,* 1 March 1981, D 17, D 22.

Wood, Daniel B. "AIDS Now Affecting Lives of Fictional Characters." *Boston Globe,* 23 June 1987, 67.

Worthen, W. B. "Staging América: The Subject of History in Chicano/a Theatre." *Theatre Journal* 49 (1997): 101–20.

Yankauer, Alfred. "Hispanic/Latino—What's in a Name?" *American Journal of Public Health* 77, no. 1 (1987): 15–17.

Yarbro-Bejarano, Yvonne. "Cherríe Moraga's *Giving Up the Ghost:* The Representation of Female Desire." *Third Woman* 3, no. 1 (1986): 113–20.

Yarbro-Bejarano, Yvonne. "Chicanas' Experience in Collective Theatre: Ideology and Form." *Women & Performance* 2, no. 2 (1985): 45–58.

Yarbro-Bejarano, Yvonne. "The Female Subject in Chicano Theatre: Sexuality, 'Race,' and Class." In *Performing Feminisms: Feminist Critical Theory and Theatre*, ed. Sue-Ellen Case, 131–49. Baltimore: Johns Hopkins University Press, 1990.

Yarbro-Bejarano, Yvonne. "The Image of the Chicana in Teatro." In *Gathering Ground: New Writing and Art by Northwest Women of Color*, ed. Jo Cochran et al., 90–96. Seattle: Seal Press, 1984.

Yarbro-Bejarano, Yvonne. "The Role of Women in Chicano Theater Organizations." *El Tecolote* 2, nos. 3/4 (1981): 7, 10.

Yarbro-Bejarano, Yvonne. "Teatropoesía by Chicanas in the Bay Area: *Tongues of Fire*." *Revista Chicano-Riqueña* 11 (1983): 78–94.

Yarbro-Bejarano, Yvonne, and Tomás Ybarra-Frausto. "Un análisis crítico de 'Zoot Suit.'" *Conjunto* 42 (1979): 80–88.

Zeitlin, Ida. "Sous American Sizzler." *Motion Picture*, September 1941, 19.

Zadan, Craig. *Sondheim & Co.*, 2nd ed. New York: Harper and Row, 1989.

U.S. Latino/a Plays Studied in This Book

Astor del Valle, Janis. *Where the Señoritas Are.* Unpublished manuscript, 1993.

Conboy, Roy. *When El Cucui Walks.* San Francisco: Z Plays, 1993.

Delgado, Louis, Jr. *A Better Life. Ollantay Theater Magazine* 2, no. 2, special issue, *Latino Theater on AIDS* (1994): 112–62.

Monge Rafuls, Pedro R. *Noche de ronda.* Unpublished manuscript, 1987.

Prida, Dolores. *Beautiful Señoritas.* Manuscript, 1980.

Prida, Dolores. *Beautiful Señoritas and Other Plays.* Houston: Arte Público Press, 1991.

Rivera, José. *The House of Ramon Iglesia.* In *On New Ground: Contemporary Hispanic-American Plays*, ed. M. Elizabeth Osborn, 191–242. New York: Theatre Communication Group, 1987.

Rivera, José. *Marisol. Theatre Forum* 2 (1992): 26–44.

U.S. Latino/a Theater Anthologies

Antush, John V., ed. *Recent Puerto Rican Theater: Five Plays from New York.* Houston: Arte Público Press, 1991.

Antush, John V., ed. *Nuestro New York: An Anthology of Puerto Rican Plays.* New York: Mentor, 1994.

Cortina, Rodolfo J. *Cuban American Theater.* Houston: Arte Público Press, 1991.

Feyder, Linda, ed. *Shattering the Myth: Plays by Hispanic Women.* Houston: Arte Público Press, 1992.

Garza, Roberto J., ed. *Contemporary Chicano Theatre.* Notre Dame, Ind.: University of Notre Dame Press, 1976.

González-Cruz, Luis F. and Francesca M. Colecchia, eds. *Cuban Theater in the*

United States: A Critical Anthology. Tempe, Ariz.: Bilingual Press/Editorial Bilingüe, 1992.

Huerta, Jorge, ed. *El Teatro de la Esperanza: An Anthology of Chicano Drama.* Goleta, Calif.: El Teatro de la Esperanza, 1973.

Huerta, Jorge, ed. *Necessary Theater: Six Plays About the Chicano Experience.* Houston: Arte Público Press, 1989.

Leal, Rine, ed. *Teatro: 5 Autores Cubanos.* New York: Ollantay Press, 1995.

Moraga, Cherríe. *Heroes and Saints and Other Plays.* Albuquerque, N.M.: West End Press, 1994.

Rosenberg, Joe, ed. *¡Aplauso! Hispanic Children's Theater.* Houston: Piña Books, 1995.

Valdez, Luis. *Luis Valdez—Early Works: Actos, Bernabé and Pensamiento Serpentino.* Houston: Arte Público Press, 1990.

Valdez, Luis. *Zoot Suit and Other Plays.* Houston: Arte Público Press, 1992.

Published U.S. Latino/a Theater on AIDS

Astor del Valle, Janis. *Fuchsia.* In *Intimate Acts: Eight Contemporary Lesbian Plays,* ed. Nancy Dean and M. G. Soares, 85–111. New York: Brito & Lair, 1997.

Delgado, Louis, Jr. *A Better Life. Ollantay Theater Magazine* 2, no. 2, special issue, *Latino Theater on AIDS* (1994): 112–62.

Moraga, Cherríe. *Heroes and Saints.* In *Heroes and Saints and Other Plays,* 85–149. Albuquerque, N.M.: West End Press, 1994.

Reyes, Guillermo. *Men on the Verge of a His-panic Breakdown.* In *Staging Gay Lives: An Anthology of Contemporary Gay Theater,* ed. John M. Clum, 401–24. Boulder, Colo.: Westview Press, 1996.

Sánchez, Edwin. *The Road. Ollantay Theater Magazine* 2, no. 2, special issue, *Latino Theater on AIDS* (1994): 83–111.

Shamsul Alám, Juan. *Zookeeper.* In *Nuestro New York: An Anthology of Puerto Rican Plays,* ed. John V. Antush, 421–42. New York: Mentor, 1994.

Unpublished U.S. Latino/a Theater on AIDS

Alfaro, Luis. *Downtown.*

Araiza, Alberto Antonio. *H.I.Vato.*

Araiza, Alberto Antonio, Paul Bonin-Rodríguez, and Michael Marínez, *Quinceañera.*

Arroyo, Rane. *Wet Dream With Cameo by Fidel Castro.*

Cruz, Migdalia. *So . . . , Mariluz and the Angels.*

Fernández, Daniel. *Fuerte como la muerte.*

Flores, Raymond J. *Puzzle Box.*

Fox, Ofelia and Rose Sánchez. *Siempre Intenté Decir Algo (S.I.D.A.)/I Always Meant to Tell You Something.*

Gallardo, Jaime, and Matías Alvarez. *Joaquin's Deadly Passion.*

Garces, Michael John. *Now and Then.*

Gomez, Chuck. *Deal.*

Landrón, Eric. *El amor en los tiempos del Sida* (poetry book theatrical adaptation).
López, Esteban. *Paisanos*.
Mar, María. *Temple of Desire*.
Monge Rafuls, Pedro R. *Noche de ronda*.
Morton, Carlos. *At Risk*.
Muñoz, Elías Miguel. *The Greatest Performance*.
Pereiras, Manuel. *All Hallow Even*.
Ramírez, Alfonso. *The Watermelon Factory*.
Reconco, Oscar. *Elegía para un travestí/Elegy for a Transvestite*.
Rivera, Carmen. *Delia's Race*.
Rivera, José. *A Tiger in Central Park*.
Santiago, Héctor. *Camino de angeles, Un dulce cafecito, Al final del arco iris, Toda la verdad acerca del tío Rachel, Guerreros antes del apocalípsis,* and *¿Qué le pasó a la Tongolele?*
Sandoval-Sánchez, Alberto. *Side Effects*.
Tirado, Cándido. *Like the Dream*.
Teatreros Ambulantes de Cayey, *El Sí-Dá*.
Teatro VIVA, *Deep in the Crotch of My Latino Psyche*.

Reviews
Reviews of *Streets of Paris*

Anderson, John. "'Streets of Paris' Opens as Summer Review." *New York Journal and American*, 20 June 1939, 10.
Atkinson, Brooks. "'The Streets of Paris' Moves to Broadway." *New York Times*, 20 June 1939, L 25.
Dana, Joyce. "Carmen, Rio Style: This One Has a Last Name (It's Miranda) And She's the Good Neighbor Policy Itself." Clipping from Carmen Miranda file, Lincoln Center Library for the Performing Arts, New York; no sources available.
Kihss, Peter. "Gestures Put It Over for Miranda." *New York World Telegram*, 8 July 1939, 6.
Lockridge, Richard. "'The Streets of Paris,' a Bright Revue, Opens at the Broadhurst." *New York Sun*, 20 June 1939, 13.
Mantle, Burns. "There's Hellzapoppin' in this 'Streets of Paris' Revue, Too." *New York Daily News*, 20 June 1939, 33.
"New Shows in Manhattan." *Time*, 3 July 1939, 42–43.
Pollock, Arthur. "Carmen Miranda Tops 'Streets of Paris.'" *Brooklyn Daily Eagle*, 20 June 1939, 7.
Sullivan, Robert. "Carmen Miranda Loaves America and Vice Versa." Clipping from Carmen Miranda file, Lincoln Center Library for the Performing Arts, New York; no sources available.
Waldorf, Wilella. "'The Streets of Paris' Opens at the Broadhurst Theatre." *New York Post*, 20 June 1939, 10.

Zeitlin, Ida. "Sous American Sizzler." Clipping from Carmen Miranda file, Lincoln Center Library for the Performing Arts, New York; no sources available.

Film Reviews of *Down Argentine Way*

"Celluloid Hemispheric Bid." *Newsweek*, 28 October 1940, 59.
Crowther, Bosley. "Down Argentine Way." *New York Times*, 28 October 1940, 25.
"Down Argentine Way." *Variety*, 9 October 1940, 16.
Hartung, Philip T. "The Stage and Screen." *Commonweal*, 8 November 1940, 81.

Film Reviews of *Too Many Girls*

Atkinson, Brooks. "'Too Many Girls' Opens with a Score by Rodgers and Hart Under George Abbott's Direction." *New York Times*, 18 September 1940, 19.
Crowther, Bosley. "The Screen in Review." *New York Times*, 21 November 1940, 43.
Review of *Too Many Girls*. *Time*, 11 November 1940, 76.

Reviews of *West Side Story*

Kauffmann, Stanley. "The Asphalt Romeo and Juliet." *New Republic*, 23 October 1961, 28.
Parrilla, Arturo. "'West Side Story' sigue triunfando en Broadway." *El Mundo*, 27 August 1960, 10.
Pener, Degen. "*Upper* West Side Story?" *New York Times*, 11 April 1993, sec. 9, p. 2.
Robertson, Nan. "Maria and Anita in *West Side Story*." *New York Times*, 22 February 1980, C 4.
Sánchez, Luis Rafael. "En busca del tiempo bailado." *El Nuevo Día*, 26 November 1989, 11.
Sánchez, Luis Rafael. "En busca del tiempo bailado." *Más*, 1 (1989): 86.
Sweeney, Louise. "West Side Story—The Second Time Around." *Christian Science Monitor*, 18 September 1985, 25.
Vientós Gastón, Nilita. *Apuntes Sobre Teatro: 1955–1961*. San Juan, P.R.: Instituto de Cultura Puertorriqueña, 1989.

Reviews of *A Chorus Line*

Haun, Harry. "A Chorus Line." *Playbill*, May 1988, 12–16.
Lewis, Emory. "'Chorus Line' Glitters." *Jersey Record*, 22 May 1975, B 1.
Rich, Frank. "Critic's Notebook: The Magic of 'Chorus Line' no. 3,389." *New York Times*, 1 October 1983, 13.

Reviews of *Zoot Suit*

Eder, Richard. "Theater: *Zoot Suit*, Chicano Music-Drama." *New York Times*, 26 March 1979, C 13.

Gill, Brendan. "The Theatre: Borrowings." *New Yorker*, 2 April 1979, 94.

Kroll, Jack. "Heartbeats From the Barrio." *Newsweek*, 9 April 1979, 86.

Simon, John. "West Coast Story." *New York Magazine*, 9 April 1979, 93.

"Zoot Suit." *Variety*, 28 March 1979, 78.

Reviews of *Short Eyes*

Gill, Brendan. "De Profundis." *New Yorker*, 3 June 1974, 68.

Gussow, Mel. "The Stage: 'Short Eyes.'" *New York Times*, 8 January 1974, 24.

Oppenheimer, George. "A Prison Play that Breaks Free." *Newsday*, 7 April 1974, part 2, p. 9.

Simon, John. Review of *Short Eyes*. *New York*, 10 June 1974, 76.

AIDS Theater Reviews

Morris, Rebecca. "A Better Life." Review of Louis Delgado, Jr.'s *A Better Life*. *Back Stage*, 20 August 1993, 40.

Minero, Alberto. "El teatro hispano pone su atención en el SIDA." Review of Pedro R. Monge Rafuls's *Noche de ronda*. *El Diario La Prensa*, 17 February 1991, 30.

Rich, Frank. "The Theatre of AIDS: Attention Must Be Paid." *New York Times*, 5 January 1992, sec. 2, pp. 1, 5.

Rich, Frank. "A Black Family Confronts AIDS." Review of Cheryl L. West's *Before It Hits Home*. *New York Times*, 11 March 1992, C 17, C 22.

Rich, Frank. "Discovering Family Values at 'Falsettos.'" Review of William Finn's *Falsettos*. *New York Times*, 12 July 1992, sec. 2, pp. 1, 18.

Rich, Frank. "Laughing at AIDS Is the First Line of Defense." Review of Paul Rudnick's *Jeffrey*. *New York Times*, 3 February 1993, C 15, C 18.

Van Gelder, Lawrence. "Two Aspects of the H.I.V. Experience." Review of Louis Delgado, Jr.'s *A Better Life*. *New York Times*, 17 August 1993, C 17.

Reviews of *The House of Ramon Iglesia*

Rich, Frank. "Stage: 'Ramon Iglesia,' Breaking Away to Stay." *New York Times*, 13 March 1983, C 3.

Watt, Douglas. "Winning Puerto Rican Entry Is a Loser." *New York Daily News*, 17 March 1983, 83.

Reviews of *Marisol*

Fricker, Karen. "Another Playwright Confronts an Angel and the Apocalypse." *New York Times*, 16 May 1993, H 7.

Viagas, Robert. "Heavenly Harbingers." *New Haven Register,* 21 February 1993, D 2.

Review of *Botánica*

Rich, Frank. "Street Smarts Round Out An Ivy-League Education." *New York Times,* 5 March 1991, C 16.

Audio Recordings

A Chorus Line, Original Cast Recording. Music by Marvin Hamlisch and lyrics by Edward Kleban. Columbia, CK33581.

Arnaz, Desi. *The Best of Desi Arnaz the Mambo King.* RCA/BMG 66031-2.

Babalu Music! I Love Lucy's Greatest Hits. Columbia, CK48507.

Bernstein, Leonard, dir. *Leonard Bernstein Conducts West Side Story,* Deutsche Grammophon audiocassette 415 253-4.

Miranda, Carmen. *Carmen Miranda by Popular Demand,* MCA, MCLD19263.

The Songs of West Side Story, RCA/BMG 09026-627-07-2.

Videocassettes and Television Transcripts

Ball, Lucille. *A Tribute to Lucy.* Produced by Film Shows, Inc., compiled by Eileen Ruffolo. 93 mins. Goodtimes Video, 1989. Videocassette.

Ball, Lucille. *The I Love Lucy Collection,* vol. 4, pt. 1, "Lucy Goes to the Hospital." Produced by CBS Entertainment, directed by William Asher. Approx. 25 min. CBS/Fox Video, 1989. Videocassette.

Bernstein, Leonard. *Bernstein Conducts West Side Story.* Produced by Humphrey Burton and Thomas P. Skinner, directed by Christopher Swann. BBC, Unitel/Munich, and V.M.P., 1985. Videocassette.

A Chorus Line, the Movie. Produced by Cy Feuer and Ernest H. Martin, directed by Richard Attenborough. 117 min. Embassy Home Entertainment, 1986. Videocassette.

Donahue, Phil. *Donahue,* show 0323-90. Multimedia Entertainment, 1990. Transcript 2909.

Down Argentine Way. Produced by Twentieth Century Fox, directed by Irving Cummings. 89 min. Key Video, 1989. Videocassette.

Miranda, Carmen. *Carmen Miranda: Bananas Is My Business.* Produced by David Meyer, directed by Helena Solberg. 91 min. Fox-Lorber Home Video, 1994. Videocassette.

Miranda, Carmen. *Biography: Carmen Miranda, The South American Way.* Produced by Kerry Jensen-Izsak, directed by Elizabeth Bronstein. Twentieth Century Fox, 1996. Videocassette.

Panama Hattie. Produced by Arthur Freed, Norman Z. McLeod, 79 min., MGM/UA Home Video, 1992. Videocassette.

The Three Caballeros. Produced by Walt Disney, directed by Norman Ferguson, 71 min., Walt Disney Home Video, n.d. (1944). Videocassette.

Too Many Girls. Produced by and directed by George Abbott. 85 min., Republic Pictures Home Video, 1988. Videocassette.

West Side Story. Produced by Robert Wise, directed by Robert Wise and Jerome Robbins. 152 min., CBS/FOX Video, 1984. Videocassette.

Published Broadway Musicals

Kirkwood, James and Nicholas Dante. *A Chorus Line.* New York: Applause, 1995.

Laurents, Arthur. *West Side Story.* In *Romeo and Juliet/West Side Story,* ed. Norris Houghton, 131–224. New York: Dell, 1965.

Index